3.50

W9-AFB-134

PROPHETS
TRUE AND FALSE

BY
OSWALD GARRISON VILLARD

JOHN BROWN
A Biography of Fifty Years After
1910

GERMANY EMBATTLED
1915

NEWSPAPERS AND NEWSPAPER MEN
1923, 1926

PROPHETS: TRUE AND FALSE
1928

OSWALD GARRISON VILLARD

EDITOR OF *THE NATION*

PROPHETS

TRUE AND FALSE

MCMXXVIII

NEW YORK & LONDON: ALFRED·A·KNOPF

TO

FANNY GARRISON VILLARD

IN GRATITUDE FOR HER

NOBLE AND NEVER-DAUNTED VISION

CONTENTS

1. ALFRED E. SMITH: *Governor Extraordinary*   3

2. HERBERT C. HOOVER: *Supersalesman*   19

3. CHARLES E. HUGHES: *Old and New*   37

4. WILLIAM E. BORAH: *The Idaho Lion*   51

5. CHARLES G. DAWES: *Vice-President*   64

6. FRANK O. LOWDEN: *Farmer and Candidate*   78

7. JAMES A. REED: *A Modern Andrew Jackson*   89

9. GEORGE W. NORRIS: *Noblest of the Romans*   100

8. ALBERT C. RITCHIE: *Gentleman Governor*   112

10. A. VICTOR DONAHEY: *Governor of Ohio*   125

11. THOMAS J. WALSH: *A Great Prosecutor*   139

12. CHARLES CURTIS: *Jockey and Senator*   150

13. WOODROW WILSON: *A Supreme Tragedy*   158

14. COLONEL E. M. HOUSE: *His Nakedness*
    Self-Revealed   169

15. ROBERT M. LA FOLLETTE:
    A Great American   187

16. WILLIAM J. BRYAN: *Cabinet Officer*   202

17. FRANKLIN K. LANE: *Public Servant*   215

18. ROBERT LANSING: *Secretary of State*   233

19. PHILANDER C. KNOX: *Dollar Diplomat* 247

20. HENRY CABOT LODGE: *A Scholar in Politics* 258

21. LEONARD WOOD: *Military Administrator* 267

22. HENRY FORD: *The Eccentricity of Genius* 284

23. WILLIAM R. HEARST: *Failure* 300

24. HENRY LEE HIGGINSON:
     Pillar of Massachusetts 321

25. ANNA HOWARD SHAW: *Apostle of Justice* 332

26. ABRAHAM JACOBI: *Last of the Forty-Eighters* 341

27. KARL BITTER: *An American Sculptor* 350

FOREWORD

Some of the sketches in this volume have appeared in THE NATION; *others have been enlarged from abbreviated comments therein; still others appear here for the first time. It is hoped that they may not only be of interest in themselves, but also because of the political philosophy, or, if that is too high-sounding a phrase, the political point of view herein developed. These studies in character are the fruits of thirty-one years of close journalistic observation of men and women in the political and social life of the United States.*

OSWALD GARRISON VILLARD

PROPHETS
TRUE AND FALSE

ALFRED E. SMITH

Governor Extraordinary

"WOULD you vote for a Tammany Hall roughneck like 'Al' Smith? Would you have 'Al' spitting tobacco juice about the White House as he does in the Governor's room at Albany? Do *you* believe in electing to the Presidency a man who drinks too much for his own good, and is politically a rampant Wet? Would *you* vote for a Catholic in the White House? Do *you* believe in having as President a man who boasts that he has never read a book? Would *you* place in his hands the critical foreign affairs of this country when he does not know the difference between Albania and Abyssinia, or Angora and Anatolia? Can't we find a single gentleman in all America to grace the White House?"

These are the questions one hears whenever Alfred Smith's candidacy for the Presidency is discussed among the privileged and the prosperous. You cannot listen to them without becoming convinced that Governor Smith, if nominated by the Democrats, will become the acid test of our democracy. To millions his religion will be a fatal bar; to millions more his opposition to prohibition will be unforgivable. To multitudes of others "Al" Smith is still a Tammany heeler wearing a brown derby on one ear with a cigar in one corner of his mouth, who by dint of the aid of Tammany Hall has succeeded in having himself elected

Governor of New York no less than four times; reluctantly only do they concede his ability, his industry, his extraordinary talent for administration. They are unmoved by the fact that "Al" Smith's appeal is to the common people of Abraham Lincoln; they want in the White House what is known as a gentleman, a Wilson, a Taft, a Roosevelt. They are not willing to grant that Alfred Smith is by every precedent and tradition as much entitled to the highest office in the land as was Andrew Jackson, the frontier bully, cock-fighter, and duelist; or Andrew Johnson, the trader who never learned to read or write until he was married; or James A. Garfield, who drove a mule-team and steered a canal boat on an Ohio canal. For generations we have boasted that any child born under the American flag could rise to the Presidency if he merited it. The equality of opportunity in America, the ability of the lowliest born to achieve fame and fortune have been our stock in trade; they are our most-often cited arguments against any change in the society or government which we have.

How many of us are ready for an unread and uncultured man in the White House? Well, let us not spend much time on the fact that "Al" Smith has come up from the sidewalks of New York. That story is, as has been said before, worn threadbare; he himself has doubtless had enough of it. The man is simple, boyish, straightforward, and fascinating. He has a keen mind and he has wit and humour; he often sparkles—when not speaking as an official. He has Lincoln's understanding of the plain people they both sprang from, and he, too, frequently makes a point by a story which brings a laugh and goes home. He can sing a popular song and dance a few steps with all the zest of life that marked him when he was still on the sidewalks and a "parlour entertainer." He has a rare genius for friendship. More than that, he has a native common sense to guide him where the sophisticated so often fail—it has not been educated out of him—and he has a heart besides. Why was it that a murderer condemned to death had his sentence commuted although not a soul appeared before the Governor to ask for his life? Because to the Governor that fact made it seem his especial duty to inquire into the case. If the man had no friends then the Governor must be his public defender, must be doubly certain that no error of justice could come to pass. So personally he inquired into the facts and personally he decided that the man should not die.

It is not difficult to appeal to his sympathies, and yet the man who sits behind the Governor's desk at Albany is no soft and malleable person. Like many another man in public life he has grown harder with each year, and is often irritable. He is developing the impatience of the man who is master of his job and finds it harder and harder to put up with the ineptitudes, the fumbling, and the dullness or selfishness of the stream of persons who come to him for every conceivable purpose. He can do and still often does an extremely kindly act—even for a man he dislikes. But his glance is more steely, his determination more fixed. He can still tell a funny story, but when he ends it and becomes the

Governor again he is the hard-bitten public official, with deep lines in his face and all the dignity and self-possession and self-confidence that anybody need have either in or out of the White House. He has his play hours, he can unbend, but the years of office-holding and of exercising great authority are leaving their marks. When he hits out now he hits straighter and harder than ever, as his political adversaries know well.

Never before has the business of the State of New York marched along as under Governor Smith. He has wreaked himself on it; it is the breath of his body; the life of his soul. It fascinates him beyond anything else. A public document is his novel; a complicated set of figures entertains him more than a theatre. An extraordinarily retentive memory makes it possible for him to get up on his feet and be cross-examined as to the business of the State for hours on end without ever making a slip or hesitating for a figure. He works early and he works late; he knows where to get his material and he knows just whom to turn to in order to have that material put into the best shape for his use. He knows how to listen, and he will adopt without hesitation, in their entirety, suggestions that come to him from men and women whom he completely trusts. Public life has been his high school, his college, his post-graduate course, and when a supreme test came to him in the Constitutional Convention in New York in 1915 he proved how well he had learned. There were great public men, distinguished lawyers, and scholars in that convention, but

"Al" Smith, the product of Tammany Hall, outshone them all. More than that, he has graduated from the sophistries and the bunk of the ordinary politician. He spoke with amazing frankness in that Constitutional Convention. He often deliberately pokes fun at men in public life, exposes their absurdities and hypocrisies with all that flair for acting which has been his since the days of early youth. His devotion to his task is beyond all question. He has been for years planning for the Presidency, but he has been shrewd enough to see that the best way to move in that direction was to be the best possible Governor of New York, and he has publicly scorned those of his predecessors who tried to be Governors of New York when they had their eyes riveted upon the White House. This is the man who has such a hold upon the voters of the State that he has only to express his opposition to a constitutional amendment to see it snowed under by more than a half million votes, who can be Governor of New York as long as he wishes. He has won the confidence of the great mass of Republicans and Democrats, and he has merited it. He has been the best Governor, all in all, that New York has ever had.

Let us go back to our questions. Does "Al" drink and does he drink too much? Well, I am reliably informed that he drinks every day, and the number of his cocktails and highballs is variously estimated at from four to eight and more. It is positively denied that he is ever intoxicated, much gossip to the contrary notwithstanding. But he is a Wet, and he lives up to it in practice, and for that consistency he is to be praised. Every journalist knows dozens of nauseating political hypocrites who will go before any W. C. T. U. meeting, eulogize the Eighteenth Amendment and the Volstead Act, and then go and get drunk a few doors away; every journalist knows Senators and Congressmen who "vote Dry and drink Wet" wherever they happen to be; who, like the eminent Warren G. Harding, will uphold the cause of temperance and indulge in hard liquor to the wee sma' hours. One may differ with "Al" Smith on his attitude toward prohibition, but no one can call him a hypocrite. One may regret with all one's heart, as does the writer of these lines, that, being in an exalted position, he cannot set an example of abstinence to the millions whose State he governs, but at least one knows where he stands. If there be any Progressive who puts the prohibition issue above all others he will, of course, vote against "Al" Smith, and by the same test he ought to vote against a large majority of our politicians— "Wet" and "Dry."

Could I vote for a Catholic for the Presidency? I certainly could and I certainly have voted for Catholics for lesser offices, and to the best of my ability I propose to repel, wherever I can, as utterly unworthy of America, the suggestion that a man's religion has anything whatsoever to do with his fitness for the Presidency or for any other office. If there are persons so small as to believe that a vote for Smith is a vote for the Pope when Smith's cabinet at Albany at this moment contains only one Catholic to thirteen Protestants and one Jew, they belong in the class with those who still believe that women are nationalized in Russia, and that the Jews are organized in a gigantic conspiracy to control the world and to commit ritual murders on the sly. One may search "Al" Smith's records at Albany from end to end only to find that if anything he has leaned backward so far as his co-religionists are concerned. The Republicans, having tried their utmost for years to find something damaging to Alfred Smith, have never yet dared to insinuate that in choosing men and women for office he has been influenced by the religion they profess.

The Catholic church blunders badly in our politics as does the more powerful Methodist church. It has cardinals and archbishops who are stupid enough to dabble in politics and so afford ammunition to those who are determined that no Catholic shall ever enter the White House. But the average plain American, if he believes in fair play and a square deal, will never be kept from voting for "Al" Smith because he grew up in the Catholic church. The final proof of this is that in a Presidential year, 1920, he won a million more votes in New York State than did the Protestant Democratic candidate for the Presidency.

Well, what are the policies for which Governor Smith has stood at Albany? They are unquestionably progressive ones. One often doubts when one reads his solemn, conventional strictures upon bolshevism and socialism, notably that at Cornell in 1919, whether he

really knows how far-reaching some of his own recommendations are, whether he has the faintest idea as to
what socialism really is. I have frequently quoted from
his annual message to the Legislature in January, 1920,
the following nine recommendations:

1. *A minimum wage.*
2. *The eight-hour day for all women workers.*
3. *Maternity insurance for expectant mothers.*
4. *The extension of workmen's compensation to cover
occupational illnesses and accidents.*
5. *The appointment of State physicians and nurses in
rural communities now destitute of medical aid, in co-
operation with those communities.*
6. *The ownership, development, and operation of all
water-powers in the State.*
7. *State-owned and operated grain elevators in three
cities, after the manner of the Nonpartisan League experiments in North Dakota.*
8. *Control and supervision of the entire milk supply
of the State of New York on the theory that every child is
as much entitled to pure milk as to pure air and pure
water.*
9. *The municipal operation of public utilities.*

This from a man who declares: "I am unalterably opposed to the fundamental principles of the Socialist
Party!" Of these nine proposals, four have actually
been accepted by the State.

Some of these recommendations go further than
those of any socialistic platform I can remember, especially his insistence that the State guarantee to the child
as pure milk as he is now—supposedly—guaranteed

pure water and fresh air. It is perfectly obvious that if a Eugene Debs or a Victor Berger had offered a platform like this, the great New York dailies would have rent him limb from limb for his dangerous radicalism. Think of that suggestion of "Al's" that the State begin the socialization of the medical and nursing professions by taking over the doctors and nurses to supply the communities that are without them! Isn't that dangerously socialistic? As for his recommendation of State grain elevators, that came when the New York *Times* and our other great journalistic saviours of society were denouncing the North Dakota Nonpartisan League for building warehouses and grain elevators and otherwise putting the government into private business; yet no one denounced Smith. Viewed from the standpoint of the days of Grover Cleveland, Alfred E. Smith *is* a dangerous radical.

Adequately to set forth the progressive measures he has sponsored in addition to those mentioned above, would take almost an entire issue of a weekly. He has from the beginning fought for better working conditions for men, women, and children. His greatest opportunity to improve working conditions came in consequence of the Triangle factory fire with its terrible sacrifice of 145 girls' lives. The Legislature constituted an investigating commission of which the present Senator Wagner and "Al" Smith were the chief and the most useful political members. In consequence the session of 1913 was marked by the passage of an unprecedented number of labour bills, epoch-making in their improvement of labour conditions in the Empire State. Smith not only sponsored these bills but fought them through the Legislature. As a result the State Federation of Labour declared: "We doubt if any State in the Union can now compare with our Empire State in its present code of labour laws." Read any one of his annual messages and it is amazing how many subjects he touches upon that relate to the social progress of the people of his State. Take that of January 6, 1926, for example. It records the fact that New York leads the country in human-welfare activities. It deals with education, public health, institutional care, conditions of employment, housing, recreation, child welfare, and the rehabilitation of the unfortunate. Through "Al" Smith's activities a hundred million dollars will have been spent upon the institutions of the State which had been gradually falling behind the needs of the people during the administrations of his predecessors. He has consistently built for the future, especially for the ever-growing army of insane, thanks in large part to the fifty-million bond issue which he obtained from the State. It is largely because he has had to build for the past and the future that he has had so heavily to increase the expenditures of the State and has been attacked by the Republicans for his "extravagance." Apropos of his financial policies the Governor annually issues a financial statement of the State's situation which is a model of clearness and compactness—comparable only to the best bank statements.

In the message of January, 1926, he also asked that the Legislature declare that labour is not a commodity

and demanded a revision of the use of the injunction in
labour disputes. He appealed once more for the forty-
eight-hour week for women and minors, and for a
minimum-wage board. He asked for an extension of the
emergency rent laws and set forth a plan for the solution
of the tenement problem in New York City which was in
large part adopted by the Legislature, with the exception of his plan for the creation of a State Housing
Bank similar to the Federal Land Bank, which proved
too socialistic for the Republican leaders. (It must be
admitted that the results are not what the Governor and
his advisers hoped.) To the question of the parks he has
given unending attention, and nothing is more to his
credit than his refusal to allow rich property owners of
tremendous political and social influence to divert him
from his plan to establish State parks on Long Island
—the owners of large estates did not want the "masses
from New York" pouring out in their direction. He did
sidestep the ratification of the child-labour amendment to
which he was pledged and he has blundered badly in
coming out for the dropping of the federal inheritance
tax on the obvious plea that this form of taxation should
be reserved to the States. Within limits he has been a
genuine social crusader, and there is no doubt that this
is largely due to his admirable group of advisers. It
must be admitted, however, that they could have done
nothing for him had he not had an open mind and a remarkably sympathetic understanding and appreciation
of the needs of the people of his State. You can talk
social reform to a hundred men; only those will react

whose hearts and minds are attuned to the gospel preached.

Even more to Governor Smith's credit is his keeping his head during and immediately after the war. He talked of course the usual lies about the war and its aims during that struggle, but with much less hate and bitterness than did most others, and he refused to see red when the war was over. He pardoned the Communist James Larkin and other political prisoners. He opposed the stupid and un-American ousting of the Socialists from the Assembly in 1920, promptly invited them to his home and called a special election at which all of the five Socialists were re-elected. He vetoed the bill permitting teachers to be questioned regarding their loyalty and political views, with a penalty of dismissal if their views were not entirely satisfactory to their examiners, and he also vetoed a bill requiring private schools to submit their courses of study to the State for approval. He vetoed a third bill under which the Attorney General could institute proceedings before the Appellate Division of the Supreme Court against any candidate whose views he considered radical. His are admirable veto messages; there is dispute as to who wrote them, but there can be none as to the name signed to them and as to Governor Smith's entire belief in them. As Mr. Henry F. Pringle has said of them, they are statesmanlike papers and they throw much light on a side of the Governor's character which has not been sufficiently emphasized. They prove, like his opposition to a censorship—though he did sign one very bad bill to padlock theatres producing improper plays—that he is opposed to abridgment of freedom of thought and utterance, and that he has sympathy and tolerance for views other than his own.

Finally, I must also mention his water-power policy upon which he has fought all the great power combinations within the State, to prevent the exploitation by private capitalistic interests of what is the heritage of all the people. Again, he has done everything possible to develop the State Barge Canal, except to furnish the traffic that it so sorely needs to justify itself, and he has advocated whole-heartedly its use by the federal government as a part of the proposed ship canal from the Great Lakes to the sea. In all of these matters his course has been truly progressive.

In conclusion, Governor Smith has still much to do and much to say before Progressives can give him their complete confidence. He is still a Tammany man; against its excesses and wrongdoing in New York he never protests publicly, although he has at times used his influence to procure better nominations or to compel the Hall to endorse a bi-partisan judiciary candidate. But about the corruption of the courts and the police and the elections he has nothing to say—Tammany still steals elections with utmost brazenness. It remains an organization for public plunder. It is outwardly whiter; it has better figureheads and has drawn some fine young men into its ranks who hold the futile old idea that an organization like this may be reformed from within. But the so-called new Tammany—really a myth—if it

exists does not by any means owe the change merely to
"Al" Smith or to any one person. It no longer waxes rich
out of petty pilfering from prostitutes and gamblers
and saloon-keepers and the criminals it licenses to prey
upon the community, but it makes its money much more
easily, on a much larger scale.

As for the prohibition issue, Governor Smith must
tell the public exactly where he will stand if elected,
whether he will continue to have his drinks in the White
House or not, and whether he will determinedly uphold the Eighteenth Amendment. In foreign affairs he
remains an unknown quantity. It is true that in 1926 he
personally insisted that the Democratic State platform
contain an endorsement of the World Court, and that in
1920 he made many speeches favouring Article X of the
Covenant of the League of Nations and defending every
part of the Wilson program, probably without much
real understanding of what it was all about. But the
public has a right to ask how he stands today. Will he
again seek to put this country into the League? And
how does he think as to the Caribbean? Does he believe
that the flag follows every American dollar across the
seas and the Rio Grande? It is much to his credit that
he has said apropos of Mexico: "My personal attitude
is that . . . no country has the right to interfere in the
internal affairs of any other country"—but that is precisely what Mr. Coolidge has said while intervening in
Nicaragua and threatening to intervene in Mexico. Will
Governor Smith clarify his position by adding to the
words quoted above "as has been done by our brutal

and bloody interventions in Haiti, Santo Domingo, and Nicaragua"? Will he, too, hold to the policy of a huge army and navy when the world is sick almost beyond hope of recovery from the use of force "without stint"? Does or does he not believe in tariff reform?

As an administrator Governor Smith has no equal in America, not even in Herbert Hoover. But it is honest, radical, popular leadership that the country needs infinitely more than a great administrator in Washington. Will he always be for the people, or will he stand in the last resort with those whom Woodrow Wilson called "the bosses and their masters, the great capitalists"? What guaranty is there that he whom the corporations have regarded so complacently in New York, whom Wall Street has never feared, will become the regulator of big business? He has never formulated any deep-lying political philosophy. Doubtless he will be taught much, particularly about foreign affairs, before the convention meets, but he cannot quickly acquire the background of experience and the personal knowledge of the national and international events of his lifetime which are so necessary to an intelligent conduct of the affairs of the Republic.

Of all the candidates, Governor Smith on his record gives the fairest promise of progressive leadership along social and humanitarian lines. It is today, however, but a promise. Great masses of Americans, many of whom now never go to the polls, long for the coming of one more brave outspoken man, long again to "see one straightforward conscience put in pawn to win a world."

These voters are to be had, but they must be convinced and won. From now on it is the Governor's opportunity to demonstrate that as he has been in New York so would he be in the nation. He in himself may be the acid test of America's democracy.

HERBERT C. HOOVER

Supersalesman

H ERBERT HOOVER is qualified to be a political President of the United States. I say this because thirty-one years of journalistic observation of men in political life has forced me to the conclusion that certain qualities are to be found in almost everyone who reaches our highest American office. The ability to play politics, to compromise, at times to deceive oneself and the general public; the ability to wear one aspect today and another tomorrow; the ability to be bravely humane and peace-loving one day, and to send American youths to their deaths in some foreign country the next; the power to talk incessant platitudes and ardently to defend the Golden Rule and the Commandments against all comers —as Calvin Coolidge has recently done for the five-hundredth time in Havana—and then to keep silent in the presence of national sin, and, above all, to be able to prevaricate when necessary—these are some of the attributes that carry men to final political success. They are the qualities which seem certain to develop if one stays long enough in politics and is sufficiently corroded by ambition and the deadly virus which so readily permeates the veins of men in high office.

Mr. Hoover has these attributes in such marked degree that he is surely completely qualified for the Presidency—I cannot see how he can be kept out of it, or how anyone can doubt that, barring a miracle and the open and avowed opposition of Calvin Coolidge, he will be the first Californian to occupy the White House.

This is my thesis; it is admittedly one side of the picture. A Lloyd George, or a Roosevelt, or a Bismarck can lie and steal (as Roosevelt "stole" the Panama Canal) and yet feel certain that he is serving humanity by doing so, and still have most engaging and admirable qualities. Indeed, men like these, or like a Woodrow Wilson, are capable of rousing such intense loyalty and enthusiasm that their most unethical acts take on a righteous aspect and are most hotly defended by men who would denounce similar misdeeds in a private individual. Herbert Hoover is capable of rising to great heights in his passion for righting a wrong; he is a rarely gifted administrator and executive; he has most admirable qualities, and he, too, has a following that in its adoration will not admit that he is capable of a single error. Any black act of his inevitably appears white to these devoted servitors. Yet he can face two ways, can compromise, and on occasion deceive, and play politics from morning till night while rendering great public service; he can, like Charles E. Hughes, be silent in the presence of the most scandalous criminality in the history of the Republic, although sitting beside it for years.

Consider the solemn assurance which Herbert Hoover, Charles E. Hughes, and twenty-nine other Republicans gave in 1920 to the Republicans who favoured our entrance into the League of Nations. Over their names they pledged their word that the best way to put the United States into the League was to vote for Harding. "I have to admit," says one of Mr. Hoover's former associates and present supporters, "that Hoover in signing that document was either a fool or a knave, and so were Hughes and the rest. There is no getting away from that, much as I like him." Now anyone may err in judgment, and Mr. Hoover may well have believed sincerely in the truth of that amazing statement; but when it was proved that he had been guilty of a monstrous deceit he continued to stay in Harding's Cabinet and never once apologized or referred to the matter in any way. Indeed, he stayed in the Cabinet— still without a word of regret or of shame—when President Harding again declared, in 1923, that he was absolutely opposed to the United States ever entering the League, and asserted that this country would never go to Geneva.

Like Mr. Hughes, Mr. Hoover sat in the Cabinet with Fall, Denby, and Daugherty throughout the period when they sold out the oil lands. If he did not know what was happening in the naval oil reserves, Senator La Follette did, and told the Senate so more than a year before any Senatorial action took place. Newspapermen in Washington knew about it. Did Mr. Hoover act? He did not. Did he resign? He did not, any more than he has protested against the wrongdoing of Colonel Forbes, Jess Smith, or the other members of the Harding entourage. His friends indignantly declare, as George Soule has pointed out in the *New Republic*, that Mr. Hoover is not the custodian of public morals, or of those of his associates; that he is Secretary of Commerce, not President, and that he cannot be resigning every day when something that he dislikes happens. Yes, but Mr. Hoover has stood before the public as something more than a mere politician; multitudes have felt that in Belgium he expressed a great moral indignation; that he then did combine conscience with administrative power. They looked to him to express these same things in the political life of America when he entered it. He even said himself (June 15, 1920) that "there has come to be a demand for a better justice and a higher standard of political conduct, and it would be well for the old-line politicians to pay heed to this." And then he went into the Cabinet of Harding, and allied himself not with a higher standard of political conduct, but with the lowest we have known. Even before that (March 10, 1920) he had declared: "I still object as much to the reactionary group as I do to the radical group in the Democratic Party." And then he was content to be a part of the two most reactionary administrations in our recent history. His fame and standing were loaned to give a cloak of respectability to men whose deeds have now found them out. He called himself once an "independent progressive" bitterly opposed to the "manufacture of officials by machine methods," and a year later took office under the President who had been manufactured solely by machine politics in an upper room of the Blackstone Hotel, with whose nomination the members of the Republican Party, and the convention itself, had no more to do than had the natives of the Hawaiian Islands. Promptly he found that the reactionary Harding platform was "constructive and progressive. Nothing prevents the compromise planks on labour, the League, etc., from being given a forward-looking interpretation." On March 4, 1921, having long been in doubt as to whether he was a Republican or a Democrat, he chose to be a Republican and entered the Cabinet.

When it comes to the ability to turn a complete somersault, Mr. Hoover obviously leads all candidates. He is now being supported by some of the most ardent opponents of the League of Nations, the World Court, and all the other post-war Wilsonian proposals which Mr. Hoover so eagerly espoused in 1919–1921. The explanation given is that Mr. Hoover has recanted every one of those heresies. He must now oppose the League of Nations and the World Court since his party is squarely committed to opposition. He has become the darling of such reactionary newspapers as the Cyrus K. Curtis properties, the Chicago *Tribune*, the Los Angeles *Times*, the New York *Herald Tribune*, the Boston *Transcript*, and the Kansas City *Star*, and there is nothing of the moral and the spiritual in their support of anybody. They are not only out for the maintenance of the existing social order, but of the political status of the moment. They are for the exaltation of business, as Mr. Coolidge has exalted it, and their taking up of

Mr. Hoover is indisputable proof that he has forgotten all that stuff he was talking, when he came back from Europe, about a new deal and a better political life in America, when he promised to be the alchemist who could turn the dross of the lost World War into the pure gold of spiritual values, and lead America out of its materialism into a union of political efficiency and idealism.

So it is a totally different Herbert Hoover with whom we have to deal today. He has become a skilful politician himself—the blundering ineptness of his pre-Harding years has disappeared. A splendid Hoover machine has been built up throughout the country, for the Department of Commerce touches our national life at innumerable points, and Mr. Hoover has never even been restricted to the confines of his department. He has extended its functions by having the Pensions Bureau and the Bureau of Mines transferred to it. Mr. S. Parker Gilbert, sarcastically called by the German Fascisti the "uncrowned Kaiser of Germany," once referred to Mr. Hoover as "Secretary of Commerce and Under-Secretary of all other departments." It was said admiringly, but it is a half-truth bitterly resented in the departments in question. He is hated in the State Department because he won the fight to keep control of the commercial attachés of our legations and embassies, because he has often thrown his weight with the President against the State Department, and in the matter of loans to foreign countries has flatly demanded that they be made for economic reasons alone. At times the Department of Agriculture, the Department of Labour, the Treasury Department, the Interstate Commerce Commission, the Shipping Board, the Federal Trade Commission, were reported to have protested against Mr. Hoover's playing the under-secretary in their shops. Their resentments have been carried to the President and constitute one reason, Washington believes, why President Coolidge publicly castigated Mr. Hoover in April, 1927, when the rumour again appeared that Secretary Kellogg was retiring and that Mr. Hoover would be his successor. With obviously intense feeling Mr. Coolidge assured the press correspondents that the Secretary of Commerce would never, never be Secretary of State. To some this may appear as evidence that Mr. Hoover has played his cards badly. Let us not be too sure of that.

As a matter of fact, Mr. Hoover has become a marvellous self-advertiser and publicity expert. His speeches are endless; his Department's press releases come like flakes of snow in a heavy storm, and they do not forget to mention Mr. Hoover. A small-town California editor declares he has received daily a piece of Hoover publicity, a picture, or a cut, for several years. Situations like the Mississippi flood have played into his hands precisely as did the Belgian relief, and justly so, for he deserved the credit, and being the head and forefront of the undertaking, he naturally took the spotlight. But even in periods when he was not doing one of his magnificent pieces of relief organization, Mr. Hoover won the first page of the newspapers so often that Mr. Cool-

idge was known to be distinctly nettled. Some men
would have resigned after such a rebuke as the President gave him, but when it comes to resigning Secretary
Hoover is not interested. This is the more curious because with regard to critical publicity he is the thinnest-
skinned man in Washington. After all these years of
public life, if an unfavourable article appears about
him Mr. Hoover winces like a tyro in politics. Emis-
saries soon call upon the offender to reason with him
and he may at times trace a desire to strike back. Mr.
Hoover is, like Woodrow Wilson, apt to be bitter and
intolerant toward all who take issue with him—a trait
that will be intensified if he enters the White House.

This sensitiveness is directly connected with Mr.
Hoover's emotionalism. For all his outward calmness
he is an extremely emotional man, capable of transmit-
ting that emotion to others, and of becoming almost
hysterical. Yet he can also be an admirable and an
evenly balanced adviser. When excited he exaggerates,
and uses very strong language. He can do so at all times
when a gentleman and an honest man ought to swear
at injustice or human weakness. But that tendency to
exaggerate has its dangers, for he can and does over-
state a situation as in Belgium, where he poured in much
too much food and money. There were measures which
he put through as Food Administrator during the war
that were rather bits of emotionalism than necessary
economic measures. Again, his attack on the British
rubber trust was unsound and emotionalized to such an
extent that some of his critics assert that it was de-

liberately conceived as a reply to the persistent charge that he is pro-British, that he once thought of becoming a British citizen and trying for a seat in Parliament. But, I repeat, it must be written in golden letters to his credit that his emotions are deeply moved, as one should expect a Quaker's to be, by suffering anywhere. I was with him at the Crillon in Paris on that day in March, 1919, when he got the French to agree with the English and Americans to permit the German fishing fleet to get fish for the starving German women and children. It was a joy to hear him tell of his final success after four months of unceasing and exhausting effort.

But Herbert Hoover will now make no frontal attack against heavy political entrenchments, nor batter himself against a stone wall, nor even stand up to a good public give and take. He likes best to be at his desk pulling the strings, a person of immense resources directing gigantic enterprises and getting all the credit for them; wielding enormous power like the Governor of the Bank of England, who has been able to affect the destinies of a people on the other side of the globe by a single word. Seated there he makes remarkably quick decisions, often involving millions upon millions of dollars. The great merits of Mr. Hoover's organizing have been admirably set forth by William Hard in his article on The New Hoover in the *Review of Reviews* for November, 1927, which everyone should read who desires a complete picture of it. It is not only that he picks able lieutenants and that he collects figures admirably and knows how to use them. When he moves in a matter like the Mississippi flood, or in feeding children in Russia or Austria, he puts the bulk of the work upon those who are involved—"for every American serving as assistant to Mr. Hoover in Vienna, there were literally more than one thousand Austrians so serving him." On the other hand, he seeks to concentrate all the relief work in his own hands—notably in the Russian famine aid—and throws his influence against any independent organization. When dealing with the problems affecting a given industry, he wisely gathers around him a group of its leaders. In this way he has initiated great reforms—he is said to have saved $200,000,000 for the consumer by changes in the lumber industry initiated by him, and it is asserted that he has won better wages for millions of Americans. As Mr. Hard puts it, Colonel Roosevelt got pure food by legislation; Mr. Hoover set about "giving us pure lumber without a law."

In other words his slogan is "self-government in industry." He prefers conferences and co-operation to legislative compulsion—the government, he thinks, too often becomes the "persecutor instead of regulator." Indeed, he declared on May 7, 1924, "it is vitally necessary that we stem this tide if we would preserve that initiative in men which builds up the character, intelligence, and progress of our people." Therefore, he seeks to change the attitude of the government toward business "from interference to co-operation," which he believes can be accomplished "if it is possible to devise, out of the conscience and organization of business itself, those restraints which will cure abuse." He sees in process a revolution in the whole organization of our economic life. "We are passing from a period of extremely individualistic action into a period of associational activities." He admits that there must be a "better division of the products of industry," but how to obtain it he does not suggest.

For Socialists and Bolsheviks he has only the bitterest scorn—that was an utterly false speech which he made on his return from Paris in 1919. Upon socialism he blamed the entire situation in Europe at that moment —just as if capitalism were innocent of the war and its horrors, and of the ruination of Russia. Socialism, he said, "has proved itself, with rivers of blood and suffering, to be an economic and spiritual fallacy." Fundamental intellectual honesty would have compelled Herbert Hoover at that moment to recognize the fact that socialism took hold of a dozen countries when they were utterly wrecked, and no one else was there to take charge. I hold no brief whatever for European socialism, but as an observer in Europe, at that time and later, I thought that the Socialists from the Rhine to Moscow did a marvellous job in just holding Europe together. But that is characteristic of Herbert Hoover. In all business transactions honesty personified, he does not hesitate to misrepresent his opponent if it suits his propaganda.

Hoover an economist? No, indeed. Even the New York *Times*, in justly praising his power of analysis, his marvellous grasp of facts, his untiring industry, and his efficiency, admits that some of his official acts or decisions "seem to be a bit hasty." He is a mining engineer in politics—not an economist, or a financier, or a currency expert. The farmers are right in holding him guilty of the sudden deflation in wheat prices after the war, although his friends have tried to shield him by unloading upon a committee the responsibility for that colossal economic blunder—committees, his critics say, are often his convenient smoke screens. So in the matter of the hog-raising farmers and the meat packers, there is no doubt that Mr. Hoover was partly responsible for the outcome that the farmers did not get the prices they understood were promised to them while the packers were protected.

In the matter of the unemployment problem, for which he called a conference in the fall of 1921, there has been no following up of the matter, and no results beyond the acquiring of useful data. He has never been really against the Power Trust though he has breached his own rule against the government's going into business by urging that it should build and equip and operate the Boulder Dam and its power plant. As to the coal situation, there, too, he has held a most useful conference with producers, distributors, and consumers of bituminous coal to eliminate waste, but the industry remains in chaos. It is well to tackle waste, but to grapple with the fundamental questions bravely and demand consolidation and complete reorganization, that Mr. Hoover cannot do, perhaps because it might lead to a logical demand for government ownership.

I suppose that Mr. Hoover must have called or instigated by this time some two hundred and fifty industrial conferences. Among them was one to consider
his proposal to link the hydro-plants and steam-electric
plants in eleven northeastern States; committees are still
at work studying the plans, but nothing is to date accomplished. He has, it is true, reduced the number of
different types of grinding wheels in use from 715,200
to 255,800, and has done much for American fish and
fishing. He is sincerely bent on raising the American
standards of living and eliminating waste, and he has
helped to raise a $20,000,000 national research en-
dowment to further laboratory progress in pure science
in the interest of discovering things to benefit the individual American, precisely as he headed the commission to save Americans from being killed by automobiles. None the less, for all these excellent moves, Mr.
Hoover will never reorganize our industry, although he
has the courage to dwell upon its faults and the wrongdoings of its managers, and to counsel them to reform
themselves from within.

Light on Mr. Hoover's economic vision is further
shown by his attitude toward Soviet Russia. He has repeatedly been of the opinion that the Bolshevik régime
would collapse. On January 17, 1920, for instance, he
spoke of the "total industrial demoralization and bankruptcy in production which will continue as long as
Socialism and Bolshevist rule lasts. . . . No one is
going to give them credit." Since that time the Soviet
has been more and more firmly established, has cele-

brated its tenth anniversary, and has just arranged to
have further credits in America. The removal of the
blockade in 1920 he favoured so that the "real truth of
the horror of Bolshevist rule" might come out of Russia; it would take, he said, "from under them one of
their greatest props." Yet large delegations of Americans are constantly going to Russia, and our trade with
Russia steadily increases. His mental attitude toward
ideas which he does not like is further shown by his
statement on the same day that "our frontier and port
officers must redouble their vigour against the export to
us of Bolshevist agents, propaganda, and money for
subsidizing criminals to create revolution." As if sub-
sidized criminals or anybody else could start a revolution in our happy and prosperous America!

For labour Mr. Hoover has never shown any special
understanding or feeling. He has given the impression
that he was opposed to child labour and then has refused
to come out against it. Labour feels uncomfortable, too,
about his record on the Lever food-control law. He positively assured the representatives of labour that it did
not forbid non-political strikes. Yet in 1919 a federal
judge enjoined a national coal strike and based his action on the Lever law. If Mr. Hoover was shocked by
this, as his intimates assert, he never betrayed this fact
publicly.

But that again is one of his marked traits; Mr.
Hoover keeps silent when he wishes to do so. He is, by
the way, a total failure as a platform speaker, having a
poor presence and no voice. Here are some of the im-

portant matters about which he has not spoken out—
there are many others:

*1. He has never said a word against the protective
tariff or shown that he in any way comprehends its vital
bearing on the foreign debts owed us, the plight of the
farmer, or our export trade, or on the whole question of
our international relations.*

*2. In the post-war period of hysteria and the red raids
of Mitchell Palmer, he never said one word for sanity
and the American policy of free speech and free assembly. Nor has he ever gone on record against the
countless violations of our civil liberties.*

*3. He has never once denounced the oil-grafters or
expressed any regret for the vast robbing of the public
during the Harding regime.*

*4. In the face of the Illinois and Pennsylvania elec-
tion scandals he is as silent as an oyster.*

*5. While he has protested by inference against the use
of American loans to buy arms and ammunition for
Central-American governments we are upholding, he has
never voiced one sentiment which would give ground for
the belief that he in any way disapproves our policy toward Mexico, or our killing of 3,500 Haitians by American marines (as attested by Major General Barnett of the
marines), or our present bombing of Nicaraguan men,
and probably women and children, on the ground that we
are destroying "bandits."*

*6. During the Mississippi flood disaster Mr. Hoover
directed the rescue operations, but he has committed himself to no one of the relief plans before Congress. Similarly no one knows how he stands as to Muscle Shoals, the
oil chaos, and other economic issues. And his reply to
Senator Borah on prohibition is a masterly bit of evasion
of the vital questions at issue.*

He has, however, declared that if elected he will "carry forward the great objectives of President Coolidge's policies"—which means that he wishes to be an abler, a glorified Coolidge. Heaven forbid!

Super-decisiveness, super-industriousness, super-business power—these are the qualities generally and rightly attributed to Mr. Hoover. To my mind they combine, with others, to make him a glorified engineer and a superb supersalesman to the American people. Those who wish a man of this type in the White House will need no urging to vote for Mr. Hoover. He will fulfil their highest expectations. There will be no drones in the White House or in the departments if he is President. He will be Chief Executive in deed as well as in name, in complete control of his subordinates, and carrying on a uniform policy, to which he will brook no opposition.

But those who look for something else, for an idealist who holds to his ideals at all times, for a President who will again give to America the moral leadership of the world and the friendship of the nations where we have today their contempt or fear or hatred —such as these need not turn to Mr. Hoover. In foreign affairs there will be no appreciable change if he enters the White House. There is no reason to think that he will alter our policy on the war debts owed to us, or that he will do anything to rewin the lost Latin-American belief in us and in the honesty of our intentions. On the contrary, the fact that he is our greatest efficiency engineer may well cause those smaller American nations to tremble whose industrial and social development has not reached our plane. As for those to whom the question of peace is supreme, who deny that there is anything on earth worse than war, let them not look to Mr. Hoover for support. The backsliding Quaker is one of the men most to be feared—witness A. Mitchell Palmer of Mr. Wilson's Cabinet. Mr. Hoover still goes on Sundays to the Friends' Meeting House in Washington; in their tolerance and sweetness of spirit they admit to their communion one who favoured war and helped bring it on; who quivered with just rage at German wrongdoings in Belgium, but despite his Quaker upbringing, abandoned the doctrines of love and forgiveness and could see no other way out except more killing and destroying.

I spent the first day of January, 1919, visiting in Pentonville jail some of the true Quakers, the true descendants of Fox and Joan Fry and all the long line of Quaker martyrs, and observed the wonderful spirit in which they took their imprisonment because they placed the teachings of their faith above any worldly might. To Quakers like these one could safely turn over the management of any section of human affairs—to Herbert Hoover *never*, that is, if one believes that a glorious faith like theirs cannot be forsworn and then picked up and put on again, like an old glove. Mr. Hoover, in my judgment, would have no scruple whatever about going to war for rubber, for iron, or for hemp, or "to save the world" again from bolshevism. And he would do so with passion and emotion, self-convinced that it was another war-ending crusade for humanity. He is a militant business imperialist of the precise British type.

Herbert Hoover is qualified to be a *political* and supersalesman President of the United States. Those liberals and progressives who seek something more will continue to scan the political horizon.

CHARLES E. HUGHES

Old and New

"Do you recognize anything about this man Hughes as pertaining to the Hughes that you and I supported more enthusiastically and loyally than any Republican editors when he was Governor?" asked Frank I. Cobb of me the last time I met the lamented editor of the *World*. I replied that I could not recognize anything about him as belonging to the Hughes of the insurance investigation and the governorship. "Nor can I," said Mr. Cobb. So it is with two Hugheses that one has to deal today. That is not unusual in politicians; there were two Woodrow Wilsons and two or more Theodore Roosevelts. In this case, however, the two Hugheses are not coterminous. The one existed, withered, and died before the Secretary of State was born. It was during his service on the Supreme Court, apparently, that this metamorphosis took place. Must that august body shoulder the responsibility for it?

It is easy to recall the thrill that came to New York when Mr. Hughes was chosen to conduct the insurance investigation and speedily made it clear that he cared not at all where the chips might fly. He displayed at once courage, resourcefulness, mental quickness, the ability to meet any situation as it arose, and a genuine sense of dramatic values. At last, it appeared, New York had found a fearless man of extraordinary ability, the kind of uncompromising reformer for whom city and State had been longing. But not big-business circles. They were all but speechless with indignation. He was laying ruthless hands upon an old-established private business, interfering with customs of long standing, with the right of the heads of the insurance companies to line their pockets and to provide sinecures for all their relatives at the expense of the policy-holders. When he attacked men like the McCalls and McCurdys, pillars of the business world and of the Chamber of Commerce, he was striking at the very foundations of society. More than that, he stood early for greater interference of the State with private business—one of the deadliest sins. If the term Bolshevik had been invented then the business community would have applied it to Charles E. Hughes.

As it was he was declared to be a notoriety-seeker, ruled by political ambition, grossly unfair and unjust in his cross-examinations, which were, it was said, deliberately spectacular and sensational, without giving the other side a chance to get its case before the public with similar space and a similar newspaper "spread." If he was not accused of advocating free love, it was merely an oversight. The other side went so far as to send out bogus news of the inquiry, for printing which a number of our press champions of honesty in public life received a dollar a line. It was typical of the man that when he heard about it, he put some of those high-minded publishers on the stand, including those of the

Boston *Herald* and St. Paul *Pioneer Press,* and proved
the whole conspiracy. That was the way he fought, the
way he inspired terror among his adversaries—and victims; and the way he fairly earned the governorship.
The rotten Republican machine which, about as much
as Tammany Hall, lived on the contributions of corporation magnates, traction-company highbinders, and business seekers after special favours, did not want him any
more than they had wanted Theodore Roosevelt to be
Governor in 1898. Public opinion made the Old Guard
bosses swing to him; they saw he was a winning card,
and he won.

He made an excellent Governor, clean-cut and challenging, and earned early the cordial dislike of the
machine. Throughout his nearly four years he had to
fight his own party associates in order to achieve the reforms he desired. The insurance bills were easily put
through; the public-service commissions, which confirmed Wall Street's dislike of him, since they inter-
fered with the exploiting of the city by the transportation companies, not so easily; the direct primary with
still greater difficulty. It is an interesting fact that the
public-service commissions have long since disappeared
and that the direct primary has proved anything but the
protection to the people it was hoped. Other Hughes reforms have proved to have been built on sand. But the
hour seemed to call for them and they in turn gave every
promise of achieving the desired reforms. Behind them

he put resistless energy and determination, tireless industry, direct, forceful, and most effective public presentation of his views, the years being marked by a growing self-confidence and personal power. Between Grover Cleveland and "Al" Smith no other Governor stands out as does Mr. Hughes. While far inferior to "Al" in his mastery of the public business—quite naturally, since he had had no such apprenticeship in Albany as the pride of Tammany Hall—he nevertheless wreaked himself upon it, and he received all the abuse which comes to a reformer who, among other things, stopped race-track gambling. He was holier-than-thou; he was "Charles the Baptist"; he was the "animated feather-duster"; he was a Pecksniff; he was that awful thing, a reformer with morals and principles.

Perhaps the greatest of his public services was his defeat, after his renomination, of William R. Hearst, then at the height of his noxious career. If Hearst had not been stopped then he would unquestionably have been a serious candidate for the Democratic Presidential nomination—indeed he had been in 1908. Mr. Hughes handled his adversary admirably, sparing his private life, while the Hearst newspapers piled one bit of abuse after another upon the Governor. Fortunately, their ridicule and their bitterness did not avail. But one thing Mr. Hughes did dwell upon—the shameful way in which Hearst sought to avoid responsibility for reckless reporting and bold-faced libelling, by organizing one company within another for the purpose of dodging judgments. Thus a litigant might sue for several years only to find out that the company he was suing was really not the owner of the particular Hearst paper in question at all. Mr. Hughes promised during the campaign to rectify that, and he did so; it is to him that we owe the law requiring newspapers to publish the names of their responsible owners and editors.

Re-elected, Mr. Hughes went at his task with renewed vigour, with a ripening understanding of where the real enemy lay within his own party's ranks, and by 1910 he was well on his way to a position of complete dominance and control. To this it was my good fortune to make a contribution, in that I was able to publish the charges of bribe-taking against Senator Jotham P. Allds, then Acting Lieutenant Governor, which resulted in Allds's resigning just in time to avoid being expelled from the Senate. That session of the legislature was entirely absorbed by the Allds trial, save for the necessary passing of the supply bills. It is just to add that it was in part due to Governor Hughes's counsel and aid —still in some respects unexplained even to me—that Allds's misconduct was brought into the open in what was probably the most sensational publication ever made in the old *Evening Post*. The Legislature adjourned, leaving Mr. Hughes with heightened prestige and power. It seemed as if he had at last arrived at the point where the Republican machine could be cleaned up once and for all. Suddenly, without the slightest warning, like a bolt from the blue, the Governor was laid by the heels and the whole structure built up during three and one-half laborious years collapsed; the old order came back.

The man who did this to Charles Evans Hughes and the State of New York and for all time ended Mr. Hughes's career as a militant reformer was the President of the United States, William H. Taft. He offered Mr. Hughes a seat upon the Supreme Court of the United States, and Mr. Hughes accepted. Mr. Hughes's Puritan conscience would not permit him to ask Mr. Taft to let his acceptance of the office remain a secret until he was ready to take office in October or December. The announcement was made in May, 1910, and at once Mr. Hughes's power left him as Samson was shorn of his by Delilah. The Legislature had adjourned; the Old Guard knew now that Hughes was done and that they had only a few months to wait before he got out. From that moment not a politician cared what the Governor did. It is a fact that Mr. Hughes was tired and worn after three and a half years of steady battling; that he was unduly depressed; that he had made up his mind not to run again for the governorship. I have before me as I write a long letter in which he set forth the reasons, convincing to him, why he felt that he must accept. After seventeen years I am still unconvinced, and my position is confirmed by the fact that so much of the Governor's achievements went for naught. It is, in consequence, just about the same old Republican elephant we have to deal with, just about as spotted, but a little more respectable, a little less corrupt, and infinitely stupider, as witness its campaigns against "Al" Smith.

The years that passed while Mr. Hughes was on the Supreme Court profoundly affected him in more ways than one, but did not still his ambition. It was early made clear that Mr. Hughes would not say no to an attempt to call him back to political life from the highest bench in the land. Other jurists and lawyers in plenty might feel that it was a mistake to establish a precedent that politicians might go to the Supreme Court and lure therefrom a justice to stand in the public forum and bid for the favour of the populace. Mr. Hughes felt differently, and his nomination filled with high hopes many who had fought under his banner in his active years. But it soon appeared that this was not the same man at all, that it was a changeling who wore the name. His campaign lacked inspiration, issues, and fire; it lacked conviction. It in no wise conformed to what he at first said privately that it was going to be. There was nothing whatever of the militant reformer about him, and his tactlessness in California, as everyone knows, cost him his election. He seemed to have grown colder, more austere, and suspicious. Wall Street after a brief period rallied to him; with its extraordinary intuition it sensed the change long before others did and realized that it had nothing further to fear from the man who had once defied the most powerful forces in American business life, and that at a time when the muck-raker was still abroad in the land. The editors of the *Evening Post* hoped until the last that one single word, one bit of righteous flaming indignation, one far-reaching and constructive appeal, one hopeful stimulating word about the horrible plight in which the world found itself might emerge from those once frank and outspoken lips. None came; at the last moment, disillusioned and disappointed, they reluctantly turned again to support the candidacy of Woodrow Wilson. The independent vote, which had been Governor Hughes's chief support and greatest power, was his no longer. True, he carried New York, but not the Union, and the bitterest disappointment that could come to an American citizen—to believe himself elected to the Presidency and find that this was not the case—was his.

The old fighting Hughes would have taken that dreadful disappointment like a man. But it was days, in 1916, before Mr. Hughes could bring himself to congratulate Woodrow Wilson, and then he did so with a lack of grace, of cordiality, and of sportsmanship that told its own tale of the inner change. Now the darling of the corporation gods, he went back to the practice of the law, and earned yearly what would be a fortune, indeed, to the bulk of the people of the United States. They know how to draw a reformer's teeth in Wall Street; they know how to make him the bulwark of all the things that be, the defender of family life, of the sacred right of private property, of the sanctity of great wealth. And there Mr. Hughes remained, admittedly the head of the American Bar since the death of Joseph H. Choate until he, "Charles the Baptist," the flaming apostle of personal righteousness in public life, accepted the invitation of President Harding to enter the crookedest Cabinet that has ever disgraced the United States of America. There he sat, the brilliant and able associate of, to put it mildly, the weakest and most vulgar of Presidents, of Daugherty, of Fall, and of the Denby whom the former associates of Mr. Hughes on the Supreme Court branded as recreant to his trust. What an irony of fate!

Of course, he kept himself intact. He was not one to join the Cabinet poker parties with the Ohio gang; he shared their drinks no more than their cards. But few can measure adequately the blow that it must have been to the pride of this extremely proud man to know the true character of the Cabinet at the head of which he sat on the right hand of the President. Never once has he, however, referred to it. Nor, as far as I can recall, has he ever scored faithless public servants in the abstract. Not as president of the New York Bar Association has he lifted his voice to denounce public corruption; thus reformers' lips are sealed. The technique of his own job as Secretary of State he mastered quickly and in conventional style. Every one of the outworn shibboleths of the statesmanship which went on the rocks in 1914, he made his own. With him the flag everywhere followed the dollar. Under him the powerful cliques in the State Department became more powerful, dollar diplomacy more firmly established, the aggressive imperialism of the country more marked, the dislike of the rest of the world for us stronger and stronger. Under him we finally broke with our traditional policy of granting the right of political asylum; it was he who gagged Count Karolyi when he visited the shores which once welcomed Louis Kossuth and gloried in his revolutionary activities. It was he who carried on our new policy of excluding anyone whose views or activities the State Department did not like. Able, wrapped in self-righteousness, absolutely satisfied that neither he nor his country could do the slightest wrong; not open to argument; unyielding in the face of all protests; as ready to doubt the Deity Himself as his own wisdom— this was Secretary Hughes.

There is something profoundly alarming in this type of mind when it reaches high office deeply inoculated with the virus of office-holding and of political ambition. That very self-righteousness makes for a ruthlessness that thinks nothing of sacrificing thousands upon thousands of lives of the youth of one's country to achieve one's ends—you invariably under these circumstances identify yourself with your country. "I and the country," "I and God," as the Kaiser put it, become the same thing. You meet any protestant with pity that he knows so little, that his arguments are so weak, that they make not a dent upon the armour of your right-thinking. You ponder with pity, as did Woodrow Wilson, that there are only three or four other minds comparable to your own. You are the court of final resort, and you pass upon all problems with the same competence, the same confidence, the same directness, and the same power dispensed by the Supreme Bench of the land. You have only pity for the reformer or idealist, who in his ignorance of official dispatches from official representatives upon the ground, dares to preach to you forbearance, patience, good-will on earth. It is for you, in your wisdom, to say what is right and to outline your policy, knowing that you have the force to make might right.

A brilliant Secretary? Yes. That was a brilliant performance, indeed, when Mr. Hughes opened the Washington Conference for the Limitation of Armaments, and stunned the Conference and thrilled the country with the concrete, business-like proposals for the reduction of armaments—proposals which went through, saved the taxpayers millions upon millions of dollars, and added enormously to the prestige of the United States. Few men are capable of a stroke like that —witness the disaster of a second-rate man and a half-hearted admiral at the abortive Coolidge conference in Geneva. Both President Harding and Mr. Hughes looked and acted their parts admirably on that memorable day in Washington. The former Secretary of State wears well the frock-coat of statesmanship, and uses ably the "right hand of oratory." The Washington newspaper correspondents testified to his accessibility, to the extraordinary lucidity and ability with which he expounded his ideas—and the skill with which he overwhelmed those who dared to doubt the completeness and the correctness of his creed that the sacred right of pri-

vate property is the foundation of the family and the
family the cornerstone of the state. The United States,
he maintained, had always stood for this principle; how
could we recognize Mexico or the Soviet Republic—
that profane, wicked institution that had laid bloody
hands upon private property? Against that profound
conviction nothing whatever could make headway. You
might, if you dared, and if you were not overwhelmed
by the torrent of words with which the Secretary of
State always defended his position, point out that the
United States itself never made compensation for the
property stolen by the revolutionists of 1776 from those
who remained loyal to King George; that it never com-
pensated the foreign owners of slaves for their slave
property of which Emancipation robbed them; that it
offered no redress to the foreign stockholders in distil-
leries and breweries and wine-making companies whose
private property was destroyed when prohibition came;
that the story of the United States Government's relations with the American Indian is a tale of incredible
theft of private property, violation of a sovereign's
word, the breaking of close to a hundred treaties that
should have been as sacred to us as her treaty with Belgium to Germany. Against Mr. Hughes's armour of self-
righteousness facts like these struck as uselessly as the
arrows of old against the armour of the Crusaders. Others might fail; others near him might steal and take
$100,000 bribes in black bags, and still others prove rec-
reant to the trust placed in them by 115,000,000 people,
but Charles E. Hughes stood up straight and strong and

adamant, and just, and good—so good one longed for one little touch of human frailty, one little tiny proof —never afforded—that underneath his polished and suave exterior, within that intellectual machine, directed with completest self-control, there is an organ known as a heart. One wonders whether what is needed here is not the lubricity of a few simple sins. Certainly something of the warm sympathy, the rich understanding of plain human beings, which was the one noble quality of Warren Harding, is lacking; something that Harding gained out of sordid experiences in the backrooms of Ohio saloons and of Ohio newspaper offices, out of his knowledge of the men with their wives and their mistresses who ran the machine that elevated Mr. Harding to the point where the Old Guard and Wall Street decided that he was to be the first citizen of the Republic.

Mr. Hughes in the White House? It's hard to vision it and to believe that it would mean anything to the plain people of America but a rigid, able, supremely self-righteous government imposed from above by one who must admire with all his unusual intellect the blood and iron of Otto von Bismarck. It would not mean one genuine reform, see not one of those radical progressive proposals enacted into law for which Roosevelt and Wilson contended in 1912. There would be the same old imperialistic dollar-diplomacy, no such foolishness as a direct Presidential primary, or the establishment of a referendum; no raising of the issue as to whether the courts or the people rule this country, no plan whatever to interfere with the big business overlordship of America, but the steady upbuilding of the might of the state and the executive power as against the people, and the crushing of all opposition—opposition would quickly be *lèse majesté* as it was to Woodrow Wilson. Certainly it is to the old world of what passed for statesmanship and power and righteousness, and narrow conventional religion—to be worn as a cloak but not applied—that Mr. Hughes belongs. And the new world? It may lag far around the corner, and yet it can be achieved, and some day it will be achieved by some young man using his God-given talents to tear the veils from people's eyes, to place something human and divine far above the worship of private property and riches and power and, yes, big business, as we know it in America, the "land of the free." Just as once a young lawyer in New York went forth to defy the concentrated power of wealth and business and of wealth-controlled politics, to rescue the invested insurance savings of multitudes, savings that meant to hundreds of thousands the entire product of their lives of toil.

WILLIAM E. BORAH

The Idaho Lion

IF any man in public life has been more often pictured and dissected and journalistically psycho-analysed than Senator Borah of Idaho it would be interesting to know who he is. Mr. Coolidge, perhaps, but that is only because he happens to be in the White House. Senator Borah is a puzzle, an enigma, who daily challenges the newspapermen to explain him and his motives and the fact that he is not the very greatest figure in Washington, which they think he ought to be. His early history has been rehearsed so often as to be known by all interested. His fearless prosecution as district attorney of Moyer, Pettibone, and Haywood, leaders of the Western Federation of Miners in the Idaho mining troubles in 1904 when even the Governor of Idaho was killed, drew attention to him as a man of extraordinary tenacity, resource, courage, and relentless determination. The tale has often been told of the train which, with blinds drawn, Mr. Borah successfully used at a grave crisis as a bluff, pretending that it contained troops. But this was only one dramatic moment in a tragic episode which shook his State to its foundations, launched Mr. Borah upon his national career, and brought him in 1907 to the Senate to make him often the despair of his associates and of the press. The large city dailies, particularly the writers on finance, have railed at him as if he were the devil's image, yet there have been periods when these same men applauded him with fervour for standing firm against some dangerous fad or radicalism. He is often the *bête noire* of those conservatives who think he ought to be "good" and pray that he soon will be, while liberals and radicals have for years seen their hopes rise and fall that here was the predestined one who was to lead the country out of the wilderness of special privilege, corruption, and black reaction back to progress and our abandoned personal liberties. Each group in our public life has turned to him only to be repelled and disillusioned. Yet there he stands, a great figure, a demonstration of how a single powerful personality can achieve a position of great influence without that passionate following which, in this country, helps one so effectively to climb to the highest political peak. Mr. Borah remains a lone fighter and not the leader of an army.

He is admittedly the greatest constitutional authority in Congress and probably its ablest debater— certainly he is one of the few in the Senate who measure up to the pre-Civil War giants. Other men are "dinner bells" who empty seats whenever they arise. When it is known that Borah is going to speak the cloakrooms begin to empty and the Senate Chamber and galleries to fill. He does not waste himself by speaking often, which is frequently a vexation to friends who wish him to declare himself on the particular question which is exciting them, especially when they know him to be in sympathy with their views. When he does take a position he prepares for it weeks in advance and goes into action so heavily laden with ammunition that it is extremely dangerous to engage him at close range.

A man of most determined and most impressive exterior, William E. Borah looks like a leader of men and of ideas, and a born fighter. His Western habit of wearing his thick, dark hair long does not produce the impression of eccentricity, but rather adds to the leonine aspect of his face, which bears every appearance of courage and of ability, yet is free from the deep lines one might expect to find in one who has long been in public life. He is cast in so large a physical mould that one has a right to expect big things of him, and he keeps himself in such excellent physical condition that one senses at once his ability to undertake any kind of a parliamentary struggle. More than that, his industry is tireless, his life remarkably regulated. His daily horseback ride in Rock Creek Park is as much an institution in the Capital as the Washington Monument itself. Few other men in the Senate have as good a record for attendance and for roll-call. Sought as a speaker all over the United States, he speaks outside the Senate only on rare occasions, and wins the first pages of the newspapers when he does so. He has the rare ability to make converts as he stands and speaks, and that is an achievement when one addresses men who usually have made up their minds, or have had them made up for them, long before the debate begins. He towers in debate above most of his contemporaries like a battleship in a fleet of light cruisers.

And still Mr. Borah does not fill the place to which his powers entitle him. There can be no doubt whatever that, if the Republican Party should choose the intellectually ablest among its Presidential candidates, it would have to select William E. Borah. There is only the remotest chance that this will happen in 1928 or in the future. That revolves about the possibility of Mr. Borah's coming to the front in a deadlock and making a sudden tremendous impression on, let us say, the subject of prohibition and the enforcement of the Constitution, a sort of prohibition cross-of-gold and crown-of-thorns speech, to sweep the delegates from their seats. His old and extremely rotten party will unfortunately decline to bestow its highest honour upon its ablest Senator, who would seem to have earned it by years of arduous labour.

What is the explanation? Is it that he merits the designation of the Lone Wolf who usually leaves the pack to hunt by himself? Is it true that his hand is against all men? That he is so individualistic that he will never pull in the traces? That he is erratic, peculiar, unstable, incapable of sustained loyalty? That he is without a carefully thought-out program? That he is thinking constantly of Mr. Borah? That he has lost his power to fight any fight to the end? That he can no longer see a thing through without counting the cost to himself? In all friendliness the truth must be written—it is not easy to pen when one so likes and admires a man and is proud to call him friend—that it is William E. Borah who is himself his worst enemy. He alone presents the great and as yet impassable obstacle which has prevented him from either leading his party in unquestioned primacy, or from being the great champion of those masses who, thoroughly disillusioned and discontented, will have nothing to do with either party.

These dissenters long for nothing so much as for a brave, outspoken leader willing to cast his all into the scales, caring not what happens to him or to his own reputation. This the five-million vote for Mr. La Follette showed. What could not Mr. Borah do today if he were to say "a plague o' both your houses" and decide to head a new party as Mr. La Follette did in 1924? Borah voted for the war; he did not bolt in 1912 when Roosevelt split his party and declared it to be utterly bankrupt in character and morals. He did not vote or speak for Robert La Follette in 1924, though he asked and received a letter of endorsement from that great American to use in his own campaign for re-election. He has been entirely regular whenever it has come to a crisis.

Yet the threat of revolt is always there, and reliable reports have it that before the death of President Harding Mr. Borah was ready to do precisely what Senator La Follette did—if only the sinews of war were forthcoming. At about that time, that is, in July, 1923, Senator Borah made a speech attacking vigorously both of the old parties, a speech that met with an amazing response from press and public at the time. But Harding died; the scene changed. The obscure, unpopular, and distrusted Vice-President became President and subsequently succeeded himself.

It may have been the absence of large means which kept Mr. Borah from crossing the Rubicon—though this is hardly likely, for there is one Senator who for several years, until quite recently in fact, was ready to invest millions and do his utmost to place Mr. Borah in the Presidency. It may have been the extraordinarily sudden change in the White House and Mr. Borah's own rise to the headship of the Foreign Relations Committee, with the veto power this gives him over the President's foreign policies, which brought about a different attitude. The fact is that, whereas in 1923 he was ready to go it alone, he now appears to have lost his zeal. A writer in the *Independent* declares that the Senator's stock as a possible Presidential candidate has never been so low. I do not think this is true, and I insist that Mr. Borah himself could change this overnight if he would only cut loose and talk the real truth as he knows it with such sincerity and vigour as, for example, mark Senator James A. Reed. It would need only a declaration on Borah's part that he proposed to tell the whole truth and nothing but the truth to start things. If he were then to say only what he as an honest man, and one of brains, must think of the Coolidge Administration, it would electrify the country. Should he then speak out about the Republican Party, as did Theodore Roosevelt in 1912, he would make his nomination on a third ticket inevitable. I am not saying that such a course would land Senator Borah in the White House, but I do maintain that it would give him the moral political leadership of the country. Yet, as in 1923, he lets I dare not wait upon I would.

Obviously this man is not wholly a Lone Wolf, for he has returned to the pack at crucial times. He has pulled in the traces on innumerable occasions—as during the war days. He is not incapable of loyalty because he is still loyal to some brands of Republicanism which his party today stands for. He has also been loyal to the timid little Mr. Coolidge in the White House. He is certainly not thinking all the time of William E. Borah, for in that case he would not have fought for numerous unpopular causes such as the recognition of Russia, the return of German enemy property, the restoration of civil liberties, the overhauling of the Alien Property Custodian's office, the recodification of international law, and numerous other things, to say nothing of his constant antagonizing of the powers that be in Wall Street. Mr. Borah still does battle against injustice without counting the cost to himself. His mind, when determinedly set to a course, holds to it as truly as a Sperry automatic electric helmsman steers a transatlantic liner. But the courses upon which he sets it are fewer, lead through smoother waters, and are less dramatic. When it appears to him that there is, after all, not as much at stake as he thought, the course may be abandoned, or the ship allowed to zigzag or turn about for another port. Take this very question of the Alien Property Custodian. Mr. Borah himself pushed through the Senate the resolution appointing a committee, of which he became the chairman, to overhaul the records of that office, which is a mass of graft and favouritism. Something changed the situation in his opinion; with the weapon given to his hand, he has never used it. Similarly, he has acquiesced in the situation in Nicaragua when he should be tearing it open and revealing the relationship of our governmental policy to certain financial enterprises there—and the folly of it all.

When Jane Addams and others appealed to him for his aid in the Sacco-Vanzetti case, and referred to the extraordinary outburst of opinion the world over against the execution of these men, Senator Borah replied most mistakenly that "It would be a national humiliation, a shameless, cowardly compromise of national courage to pay the slightest attention to foreign protests, or mob protests at home." Foreign interference he declared "to be an impudent and wilful challenge to our sense of decency and dignity and ought to be dealt with accordingly." Two days later he swung around to the other side, and, when it was too late, offered his services freely to the Sacco-Vanzetti Defense Committee to aid in getting things done. Curiously enough, there is not another man in the Senate who has so often touched England and Europe on the raw by expressing his opinions as to what they should do to set their own houses in order and how they should behave in international affairs—foreign interference, Europeans have called it.

Speaking of foreign affairs, Mr. Borah declared in 1914 with much truth that America's unpopularity among the nations is caused by her "incapacity" for minding her own affairs, but he later joined those who wished the United States to enter the war—the frontiersman's readiness to resort to violence coming to the front. He declared that it was "the crucial hour for American liberty"; that the war was "for American honour and American lives." He went with the mob at first only to wake up quickly to a realization of the fearful consequences to the United States of allowing Mr. Wilson to subordinate all constitutional safeguards to the waging of war; and he has done penance ever since. He now realizes the incredible folly of trying to right any human wrong by the crime of using force, and he states this in these words:

> *I am opposed to the recognition of the right to employ force against a sovereign nation in any contemplated plan of peace. After 2,000 years of this worship of force, after 2,000 years of this teaching what are the results; what are the fruits? If anyone is familiar with the vernacular of Hell, let him undertake to paint the picture. Human tongue is inadequate to the task.*

Which is precisely, of course, what those who opposed the United States going into the war said at the time when Senator Borah was being swept off his feet by his belief that American honour demanded our plunging into hell—a belief unworthy of one of his mentality.

The enemies of the people, namely, the business powers that control our government through the medium of the Republican Party which they own, are too often right in saying that Senator Borah can be counted on to draw back just before the irrevocable step. The Washington correspondents have in their files the records of many causes which Mr. Borah once embarked upon and did not carry through. Yet there is no man in Washington whom they go to more quickly and eagerly when he has a statement to give out; none whom they more gladly quote on any vital question concerning events and policies at home or abroad. Whatever people think of him in Europe—they are especially hurt that he never comes over to study European conditions for himself —anything that he says is immediately cabled abroad.

Let us, however, not forget. However much he may vacillate now and then, however often he starts something and fails to see it through, William E. Borah has done more than enough to win him the lasting gratitude of the American people. He has determinedly opposed monopoly. He has opposed our Caribbean imperialism, especially our treatment of Nicaragua, and though at one time in 1916 he favoured using the armed force of the United States to protect our people in Mexico, precisely as he was in favour of going to war with Germany, he has in these latter years followed a much wiser and more humane course. Speaking at New Haven, Connecticut, on March 20, 1927, he rightly declared that "there is a higher and better, and more peaceful and lawful method by which to protect our interests. God has made us neighbours—let justice make us friends." Those were thrilling and unanswerable speeches he made against the vicious peace treaty and its injustices.

It was he who later pointed out the indefensible character of the Shantung awards and rammed home the fact that nearly one-third of the population of the world protested against the territorial maladjustments of the peace treaty. In fact, his fight against ratification and against the League of Nations give a full measure of his farsighted statesmanship—it is inconceivable that if he had been in Wilson's place at Paris any such abortion, such a mass of disgraceful compromises, could have come into existence and been offered to the American people as the fruit of their victory. He is often too much of an isolationist for me. But I recall his persistent statement that while opposed, in the spirit of George Washington, to any entangling alliances, he favours anything "that will bring nations closer together, promote friendliness, and remove causes of friction." It must also not be forgotten that it was Senator Borah who originally proposed the Conference for the Limitation of Armaments which took place in Washington.

Everyone owes him gratitude for his straightforward decency to our late enemies in all matters since the war, and for his advocacy of peace, notably his championship of the outlawry of war. Not the least of his services is his attitude toward Soviet Russia, his demand that we recognize one of the stablest governments in Europe, and that we refuse to allow ourselves to be blinded in our relations with that great country because we do not like the form of its government or its social ideals.

As for his attitude on domestic issues, he remains

blind like so many of the other progressive Senators to the evils of the protective tariff and fails to realize its direct connection with the wholesale corruption which has so often disgraced the Republican Party. So far as our race problem is concerned, while he has pleased the South by declaring that the Fourteenth and Fifteenth Amendments cannot be enforced because of inherent defects in those amendments, I am sure that our coloured citizens will never forget that while still an attorney in Idaho he was ready to risk his life to rescue a Negro whom a mob was preparing to lynch; that he sent a ringing notice in 1921 to certain North Carolina Republicans who were trying to drive the Negroes out of the Republican Party in that State, that he would rather leave it himself than lift one finger to aid them in so un-democratic and un-American a purpose. He was early for amnesty for political prisoners. It was the same Senator Borah of Idaho who sought to place upon the statute books a law making automatic the dismissal of any official who violated the right of public assembly, or contravened the personal rights of any individual as guaranteed by the Constitution of the United States. "The most vital provision of the Constitution of the United States is the First Amendment." This is his deliberate opinion in an article which he contributed to *The Nation*, and he added: "There is no subject of deeper concern in these days than that of preserving the civil rights of the citizen. . . . We cannot afford to barter these rights or sacrifice them for any purpose or under any circumstances."

So there we have William E. Borah, leader of the Senate, still somewhat youthful in effect as he takes the floor, quiet, poised, speaking frankly and directly, with clear enunciation and a musical voice. A tremendous believer in oratory, he is none the less free from the mannerisms of the ordinary spellbinder. He is never theatrical and rarely stops for an effect or tries for applause. If the Drys should decide to bolt both parties, here is their natural leader, their chief. None could be so effective as Borah if he should burn his bridges behind him and throw his fortunes into the scale. But if this does not come to pass, we should continue to see him a great, baffling personality; in the Senate he often seems a lion fighting as if at bay, baulked by his own faults, but justifying, as has been said, his every act and every position by Constitutional precedents, and continuing to worship at the shrine of the Founders of the Republic. Behind his slightly smiling lips, his kindly, searching, amused eyes, his keenness of mien, will continue to be the threat of a sudden powerful response overwhelming his adversaries whom he often goads into fury, trapping them by seemingly innocent and simple questions. Men will continue to admire the powers in him. Reformers will still feel that he is one of the few men in public life who can be stirred by a principle to battle fiercely for that principle. The public will, somehow, sense his greatness. But the marvel will remain that he whom nature plainly destined for a foremost place in our political life is by himself kept from occupying it.

CHARLES G. DAWES

Vice-President

IN the Vice-President of the United States we have in-
carnate the greatest mass of contradictions to be
found in the make-up of any public man today. For
here is one who is well bred and yet a vulgarian; who
has hosts of adoring friends and yet repels multitudes;
who is a darling of big business and the financial world,
and at the same time of great groups of farmers who
ought by every precedent to hate him and all his Wall
and State Street friends. This man can, moreover,
be at times fascinating, at times so surly and rude as
to anger those near him. He is a lover of the classics
and of art and is a fine amateur violinist—like Nicholas Longworth—with one popular composition to his
credit, and yet you could be with him for hours and
not dream that there was a fine side to him. He is skilled
in publicity, in swearing in public at just the right time,
in smoking his pipe upside down, and yet he lets great
opportunities slip by him or makes egregious tactical
blunders.

As a campaigner he is incredibly bad, and yet men
politically hostile to him who have travelled in his footsteps report that he makes a most favourable personal
impression. Essentially a man's man, he is extraordinarily popular with men—in Washington and in the
Senate and despite a well-founded belief that he plays

favourites in recognizing the Senators to whom he grants the floor. To many he appears a dangerously erratic, irresponsible, and ill-balanced man, who in the Presidency would constitute a grave danger to the country; to others he is an able banker, a great patriot, a genuine leader, a remarkable politician, a sheet-anchor to windward in the fight against "parlour-pinks," bolshevists, and all the others who wish to put a crimp in the easy ways of making money in which Dawes and his business friends rejoice. Finally, there is Clinton Gilbert who calls him "the one real personality in a timid conventional Washington, a great man or more nearly a great man . . . than any one else we have in Washington"; a "person, vital, various, striking, amazing, confounding, alive in every respect, admirable. . . ." In the face of all this where and who is the real Charles Dawes?

There is truth on both sides. It is to his credit that so many men like him; that he has won over a hostile Senate. But it is also true that he has most unpleasant traits and that he can behave like a boor. I do not doubt that some of this is studied, for he is distinctly a poseur, or, if you please, an actor, and often a poor one at that. There are those who think that he deliberately takes a leaf out of President Roosevelt's book, even to imitating his falsetto. As to that I do not know. But it is a fact that his friends adore him and assure you that he has one of the kindest of hearts. They tell you that he suffers from his impulses—they deny that the impulses are rehearsed in advance—and say it is because

he is so impulsive that he often gives such great offence. Accepting all this as correct, it still appears to
me that there are other "real personalities" in Washington besides General Dawes. Nor is it possible to ac-
quit him of being really erratic whether that be studied
or not. But it is true that he was a great success as
Chairman of the General Purchasing Board of the
American Expeditionary Force in France—a key position; that he did a fine job as Director of the Budget,
and at least he gave his name and prestige to the Dawes
Plan in Germany. He stands high in the world of banking and finance. It cannot, therefore, be asserted that
he is merely a colourful eccentric, especially as he was
an excellent Comptroller of the Currency as far back
as 1897. He is obviously a man of force and executive
ability.

But as a speaker on a public platform this General
is the world's worst, with the exception of Herbert Hoover. Mr. Hoover cannot be heard twelve feet away. He
has neither voice nor presence, and though elocution
can do marvels for some aspirants for the stage, Mr.
Hoover cannot, or will not, try to learn. To his aid has
come the radio and to it he cheerfully flees, and over it
he will campaign hereafter. Charles Dawes, per contra,
has all the brass in the world. Poor speaker that he is,
he will face any audience and his strident, unpleasant
voice, and his jack-in-the-box gestures worry him not
at all. I have two of his speeches especially in memory.
One of them was at a great dinner in Paris for a dele-

gation from the Cleveland Chamber of Commerce during the fateful treaty days in March, 1919. There were many distinguished Frenchmen there. General Dawes's speech was of the type to slap them in the face. It reeked with American self-satisfaction, assumption of superiority, and condescension—enough to make every Frenchman hate us. Of course, we had won the war and, of course, it was a grand thing to have American business men come over and show France how to reorganize and get ahead. That was the mortifying substance, the bad taste of it, fortunately immediately covered by a most graceful and tactful speech by General Dawes's warm friend and commander, General John J. Pershing.

The other speech Charles Dawes gave in Omaha during the La Follette campaign. Here are my notes made at the time:

I reached Omaha last night in time to hear Mr. Dawes. The streets around his hall were shut off by the police in expectation of a huge crowd, and loud speakers were attached to the walls for the waiting multitudes. But only twenty persons were listening outside, and they could easily have gone in. Mr. Dawes has unfortunate mannerisms of speech which, despite the amplifiers, made it impossible for more than one-half of his audience to hear him. He stamped, gesticulated, barked, and roared for twenty-two minutes. I have never heard a first-rate public man get as little applause as he did when he finished. It lasted by my watch exactly twenty seconds. The comments of the crowd were unflattering. Their amazement that the meeting was over in forty minutes was openly voiced. Dawes had nothing but his set speech—that the reds

> *menace our government and that La Follette will pull*
> *down the Supreme Court by order of the Socialists were*
> *his sole themes, save a long definition of the difference*
> *between a statesman and a demagogue, and a long quota-*
> *tion from Le Bon on the psychology of the crowd, to show*
> *that if you give the mob complete control of a government*
> *terrible things happen; witness the French and Russian*
> *revolutions. That went over the heads of his audience—a*
> *large and fine one, with many working people in it. Only*
> *his final appeal to save the American home and hearth-*
> *stone from the red flag of socialism stirred the audience*
> *at all.*

That was restrained and generous treatment of Mr. Dawes, for that speech lingers in my mind as one of the falsest and one of the most intellectually dishonest I have ever heard. There was not a constructive thought in it—nothing that would really give the hearer an idea of what Mr. Dawes stands for or his opponents either.

What does he stand for? Let us accept for the moment the most favourable estimates of Mr. Gilbert and the others who believe Mr. Dawes to be the greatest figure in Washington, and then see just what his social and political ideals are. It has long been rumoured that he was once a dues-paying member of the Socialist Party. He has even been portrayed on occasions as a liberal. Thus it is an amusing fact that when he spoke in Casper, Wyoming, during the 1924 campaign, a two-page advertisement heralded him as a progressive, "nominated at the Cleveland convention through the counsel of progressives," and gave these facts about his early political attitudes on the authority of a citizen of

Casper who, it was explained, had lived and worked with him in Nebraska:

> *Charles Gates Dawes moved to Lincoln from Ohio in 1887. He took a position as book-keeper in a paper mill. Later he branched out into the law business. He was intensely interested in the anti-monopoly fight, became a live foe of the railroads and a recognized leader of the farmer movement for lower freight rates. . . . He was always a friend of the under-dog.*

If these things were once true of Mr. Dawes he has long since reacted to quite the other extreme. He is to-day the most determined anti-union-labour man and general reactionary in political life. It was he who organized in Chicago the Minute Men of the Constitution, but the name was only a subterfuge. The organization was not established so much for protecting the Constitution as to attack the unions under the pretence of upholding our national charter and law-enforcement generally. He is particularly devoted to the use of injunctions in labour disputes, and he even goes so far as to declare that this has been made mandatory by the Constitution! That document, he has insisted, makes it the duty of judges to issue injunctions against all workers, whenever they strike or threaten to strike. Apparently he believes that men never have the right to lay down their tools. He was one of those who in September, 1922, acclaimed Attorney General Daugherty when he obtained a sweeping injunction against the striking railway shop-men. These were General Dawes's words:

The Daugherty injunction in my judgment future generations will regard as the beginning of a new era of law and order in this country, because our government, through it, announces that the right of a man to work is as sacred as the right of a man to stop work.

He was of those who helped directly or indirectly to smash the Chicago building unions, and he has repeatedly declared that labour opposes the use of injunctions only because it wishes to take its employers by the throat whenever it pleases. Here are some of his own words on the subject:

What is this claptrap about injunctions? Is there a man here . . . whether he belongs to a union organization or not, that does not know what the claptrap is about? Is it feared on the part of Sam Gompers, John H. Walker, and Victor Olander that it is encroachment upon the liberties of the American people by injunctions? What they are afraid of is not encroachments on the liberties of American citizens; they fear the encroachment of their privilege to assault American citizens and kill American citizens when they go peacefully to work.

So he doubtless upholds those recent injunctions which have made it impossible for three men to gather together for private conversation on the streets of certain Pennsylvania mining towns without laying themselves open to arrest, and impossible for others to meet in a church to sing hymns without courting prosecution for violating an injunction of a judge who is apparently the ally of the corporations that control the situation. No, it is still true that there are criminal labour leaders who believe that they can obtain their ends best by violence and murder, but they are little worse, from the point of view of ethical standards, than men like Mr. Dawes who propose to misuse the powers of the courts and of the government to break the labour organizations that they dislike. But this is only one phase of the man who in his person surely typifies everything to which American liberals are opposed. His is the philosophy of our masterful business men, raised to the nth degree. Indeed, he combines in himself some of their worst qualities—arrogance, a determination to rule at any cost, brutality in expression and in policy, and vindictiveness. I do not believe that there are any other business men in the world who have such a vindictive attitude toward those who oppose them or disagree with them.

So Mr. Dawes wants no interference with things as they are, with the control of big business over the economic life and the government of the United States. If he really has humane sentiments about uplifting the masses of the American people, he keeps them well concealed. He is a natural champion of the groups that propose to run this country for the purpose of lining their pockets at everybody else's expense, and he has always done his best to see that they had every chance to do it. He has passionate beliefs, passionately held, and the courage to announce and defend them, but if he has the slightest sympathy with the progressive platforms advocated by Wilson and Roosevelt in 1912, he has never given any evidence of it since he became

prominent. He is capable of bursting out with indignant utterance, but never on behalf of reform. I cannot recall that he has ever made a speech denouncing
the oil scandals. Mr. Dawes's most sympathetic companions, politically speaking, are the open-shoppers, the
financial friends of men of the type of Sinclair, Doheny, and Fall. His brother is president of the Pure Oil
Company; in the stock of this company Mr. Harding
and some of his associates, so it is reported, lost much
money when they tried to speculate in it on a tip from
friends. He and his associates did their best in 1924
to commit the Republican Party to a national campaign
upon the issue of the open shop.

Among the discredited men with whom Charles
G. Dawes has worked in the past is ex-Senator William
Lorimer, who was turned out of the Senate on account
of the bribery of the Legislature which had sent him to
Washington. This leads us directly to the most famous
incident in Mr. Dawes's banking career and the most
disputed. According to the critics, the facts are these:
Lorimer controlled a moribund national bank in Chicago and, when it was about to be closed by the Comptroller of the Currency, decided hastily to make it over
into a State bank. In order to do this he had to prove
to the satisfaction of the State Auditor of Public Ac-
counts that the bank had on hand $1,250,000 "actually
paid in in cash," and that such cash "is now in the hands
of the proper officers of the said association . . . and
is to be used by them solely in the legitimate business"
of the bank. Lorimer did not have that money. His friend

Charley Dawes, then head of the successful Central Trust Company, without asking permission of his directors or informing them, went beyond his authority and loaned the $1,250,000 to Lorimer with which he successfully deceived the State Auditor when that official came to make his inspection. The Auditor certified that Lorimer had complied with the law and gave him permission to operate as a State bank. Lorimer returned the $1,250,-000 to Dawes and went ahead, with the result that the bank collapsed and thousands of depositors lost their savings. When the matter was aired in the courts Charles G. Dawes, upholder of the sacred Constitution and the laws of the land, was soundly rebuked by the Supreme Court of his State for his part in the fraud.

To this story his friends reply that Dawes only followed a usual custom; that he and his Central Trust Company acted innocently in the matter; that they were merely helping out a friend who deceived them; that they received neither remuneration nor profit for their aid; that they believed the process to be lawful— though Dawes had himself been Comptroller of the Currency. They quote the opinion of one judge of the Illinois Appellate Court to this effect, but fail to add that this same judge held Mr. Dawes's bank liable for $978,029 because of its share in the transaction. Other judges held it liable for $1,250,000. The Supreme Court scored the transaction as wrongful taking of moneys but finally fixed the figure at only $110,457.51. Even that was a pretty price for the stockholders of Mr. Dawes's bank to pay for his ignorance plus his desire to help out a friend. The incident remains highly discreditable to the Vice-President, though doubtless his act was merely one of many similar laxities in the banking world.

When Mr. Dawes arrived in Washington for his inaugural he planned a sensation and he achieved one. Usually no one pays the slightest attention to what a just inaugurated Vice-President has to say, and no one loses thereby, for the Vice-President generally recites the dreariest of commonplaces. Not so Mr. Dawes. His becoming the presiding officer was too great an event to go unnoted, and so he hit upon the bright idea of berating his new associates and assuring them that their methods of conducting business were all wrong; that they had better be good boys and obey him promptly and change their rules. Naturally he appeared the next day on the first pages of all the dailies. Naturally the public snickered, and naturally the Senators, with the exception of a very few, were furiously indignant over his impudence and his proposals, which they promptly rejected. And not only they. The best of the Washington correspondents who have long observed both Senate and House were opposed to him. They pointed out, usually in private, that the Senate is the only worth-while debating body left in the United States; that the House of Representatives has been so submerged by the rules limiting debate that correspondents rarely go over there to report anything, and that the same fate would surely overtake the Senate if it were to respond to Mr. Dawes's wishes. Moreover, all observers agreed that if the Dawes change went through both House and Senate could be entirely controlled by a small clique of the majority party, whether Democratic or Republican.

In consequence Mr. Dawes got much less public support than had been expected. That did not discourage him nor did the good- or ill-natured tolerance of the bulk of the Senators depress him. He made a number of "snappy" speeches in various places during his first year in the Senate, always reiterating his denunciation of the Senate rules, and insisting, with utmost brag-gadocio, that he was bound to win, that he was going to bridle the only important debating body in the world that did not regularly use cloture of debate. Now, in his fourth year as Vice-President, one hears nothing more about the Senate's wicked rules. Whether General Dawes thereby confesses defeat or whether because of the mention of his name for the Presidency he thinks it well to postpone further campaigning on this issue, is not clear. It is worth noting, however, that even the enthusiastic Clinton Gilbert declares that that inaugural address was in bad taste; that it was thoroughly bad acting for so astute a public performer; that it utterly failed to achieve his purpose and to put Mr. Dawes on the map as a great national figure, as he consciously in-tended it to do. Thus this brooding Napoleon from Evanston, Illinois, lost his first battle. A few days later, this monitor of the Senate made possible the defeat of Charles B. Warren of Michigan for the position of At-torney General in Mr. Coolidge's Cabinet because he, Charles G. Dawes, was taking a nap at his hotel and

could not be awakened in time to cast his deciding vote
in Mr. Warren's favour. Naturally, he became the butt of
much thoroughly deserved ridicule. The preacher had
failed to practice the efficiency that he preached. That
he has, none the less, won the friendship of the Senators
speaks well for his personal traits, but it does not mean
that he has in the slightest degree changed their opinion
of his proposals.

Similarly he has failed either to be a warm friend
to Mr. Coolidge or an avowed critic. It is an open secret
in Washington that the two men do not love each other.
Dawes undoubtedly does not suffer from the inferiority
complex, which many of his friends attribute to him,
when with Mr. Coolidge. On frequent occasions the
Vice-President has differed from the President, and no
one need believe that Mr. Coolidge has ever forgiven
his understudy for that fateful nap which not only deprived him of the Attorney General he ardently desired,
but led to his public humiliation by the Senate's vote
that he had chosen an unfit man for his Cabinet. Mr.
Coolidge can cherish hatreds as well as Dawes. If the
latter is really a candidate, this must be discouraging
to his supporters, for at this writing the President can
still make or unmake any candidate by the aid of the
Presidential patronage and the prestige of Secretary
Mellon. But Mr. Dawes insists that he is not and cannot
be a candidate; that he and Mr. Lowden are bosom
friends and that as long as the former Governor of
Illinois is in the ring he cannot be. In this he appears to
be entirely sincere, for they have been devoted chums

for many years. Both tried to enter political life together in 1904 and both were defeated—Dawes for the
senatorship, Lowden for the governorship. Gossip has it
that they then clasped hands and swore that they were
for ever through with political life—amusing evidence
of the way the disease of political ambition recurs after
the poison has once been injected. But the truth is that
Dawes will be a candidate the instant that Lowden is
beaten or withdraws, and that the best possible policy
for the Vice-President to pursue in the event that Lowden and Hoover fail is to lie just as low as possible until the convention. Friendship and policy here go hand
in hand.

Neat, dapper, sociable, modest, musical, æsthetic,
efficient, industrious, domestic, and charming—these are
some of the adjectives that William Hard applies to the
Vice-President, to which must be added that the latter
is generous and charitably inclined. But a man may be
all these things and yet a demagogue, and that is precisely what Mr. Dawes is—a demagogue in the conservative camp, as much of a class agitator as any bolshevik.
None of his amiable qualities will conceal this fact. No
amount of charm or power to arouse intense and passionate personal loyalties can obscure the convincing
evidence that if he enters the White House it means the
enthronement of class hatred, of arrogance, of superla-
tive disregard for social progress, and the driving of
additional wedges between the haves and the have-nots.

FRANK O. LOWDEN

Farmer and Candidate

FRANK O. LOWDEN should be as easily pinned to a page and classified as one pins, mounts, and catalogs a familiar butterfly. He is rich, both by marriage and by his own efforts; he is allied to some of the greatest capitalistic enterprises in the country; he is a gentleman farmer on a huge scale; he is essentially a distinguished figure among the wealthy and privileged who control the destinies of the United States. Yet he cannot be dismissed as the rich man in politics taking the conservative or reactionary point of view on all issues, or be described as merely another man of the group to which Senator DuPont belongs, those powerful plutocratic defenders of the existing social and economic status. That is because once in a while Mr. Lowden amazes his supporters and critics alike by cutting loose and doing the unexpected. He shocked his rich friends and business associates by favouring the income tax when it was anathema to do so. Worse, he demanded enforced publicity for big business—he is himself a leading figure in the National Biscuit Company and the American Radiator Company. As Governor of Illinois, though a representative of the unsavoury Lorimer faction in the Republican Party of that State, he made a record which delighted, if it surprised, the liberals and the Progressives and won their support.

Mr. Lowden has again invited the wrath of his business associates by espousing the McNary-Haugen bill so bitterly denounced by the bankers, most economists, and Mr. Coolidge himself. It is a thoroughly unsound measure. It has been easy to say that he did this in order to win the farmer vote, but that is not fair. No man knows the farming situation better than he. He is himself a farmer's son, and he worked on the family farm until he was nearly of age. Today he is the owner of a 5,000-acre farm scientifically managed at Oregon, Illinois, and he owns and operates extensive cotton plantations in Arkansas and Texas. Few individuals have a greater personal stake in a wise solution of the agricultural problem. It is, therefore, hard to believe that he would deliberately favour what he considered an impractical or unnecessary or dangerous proposal in the hope of winning the Presidential nomination through the friendship of an economic group which has never yet dictated the nomination of a Republican candidate. If he were subordinating everything to political ambition he would be courting not the farmers, but their "enemies," the bankers and manufacturers.

Is this independence of action the reason for the failure of the Republican leaders to pick Mr. Lowden for the Presidency? He would seem to have exactly the record that Republican politicians like their candidates to possess, and every quality to stamp him as a darling of the Republican gods. He has character and ability, besides wealth. Like many another aspirant for the White House he largely educated himself, taught school to earn the money to go to college (the University of Iowa), was graduated at the head of his class, and then graduated with similar rank from a minor law college. At the bar his career was rapidly successful, and during it, for six years, he was an instructor in federal jurisprudence in the law school of Northwestern University. He very soon became counsel for great corporations.

But this did not satisfy his thirst for constructive enterprise. He sought other worlds to conquer; hence his return to farming, his affiliations with the management of some large companies, and his plunge into politics. Here he flew high at once, for, without a previous candidacy or any other office-holding, he tried, in 1904, for the governorship, only to be beaten by Charles S. Deneen. His career in politics temporarily seemed nipped in the bud. But two years later he decided to try for a lesser office and spent two terms in the House of Representatives—a Congressman colourless enough to make him available for any other office without fear of his having alienated anybody because of courage or independence. Next he turned, in 1916, to the governorship once more; this time he was victorious. Despite his occasional straying from the fold, he still has many warm friends in the sacred precincts of Wall Street and State Street. He is personally clean and incorruptible. He has a fine presence, is earnest, impressive, and dignified in public. Clarence Darrow, who greatly admires him, but belongs to an entirely different political school, has written of him in *Scribner's:*

> *As a campaigner Mr. Lowden has few equals. He is a*
> *scholar and has spent much of his life in court. Likewise,*
> *he has had a long experience on the stump. He is an easy*
> *and fluent speaker, has a fine personality, and is a good*
> *mixer. He has every quality needful for getting votes.*
> *In political considerations his strength as a candidate*
> *should not be overlooked.*

Finally, he comes from a large and important State. Why is he not, in view of all this, precisely the man for the Republicans to pick for the Presidency, especially when there is a serious farmer revolt under way; when he has the devotion of six or eight Middle-Western farming States?

In reply, the politicians give several reasons. Mr. Lowden is too old—he is in his sixty-eighth year—and he got into trouble in the pre-nomination campaign of 1920. Also he may not have the delegation of his State solidly behind him. These are excellent excuses, but one wonders if they tell the whole story. It is quite possible that he is not pliable enough; that the politicians still recall that he declined to become Secretary of the Navy in 1921, and that he refused the Vice-Presidency when Mr. Coolidge offered it to him in 1924. He then promptly answered the President in these words: "I can be of more service to the country through the activities in which I am now engaged than I could be as Vice-President"—meaning thereby his farming and his farm leadership. It is true that there has been no case where

a man in his sixty-ninth year has been sworn in as
President. But Mr. Lowden takes excellent care of himself now—there were traces of dissipation when he
was in Congress twenty years ago—and he is in fine
physical condition. The accepted age limit for candidates ought to be raised now that Dr. Osler is no longer
here to warn, and the tenure of life has been so mark-
edly increased for everybody. In England they have
never felt that a man of sixty-eight was too old to become Prime Minister; Gladstone was eighty-three when
last he took office. But at this writing there appears as-
tonishingly little prospect that Mr. Lowden will be
nominated. The oil scandals have undoubtedly had their
effect in making the Republican bosses extremely wary
of giving the Democrats any opportunity to talk about
other bribery and corruption in 1920.

As for that bribery, let the case be stated here.
Governor Lowden made the grave mistake of intrust-
ing his campaign to Louis Lincoln Emmerson (now Republican candidate for Governor of Illinois). Mr. Emmerson was not only open to criticism in the use of the
$413,000 he raised, but he was a failure as a strategist.
It finally came out that Governor Lowden's Missouri
managers had paid $2,500 apiece to two Missouri dele-
gates to the National Convention for which money no
services were asked or given. In all $32,303 was spent
in that State to influence delegates. When this came
out the Lowden campaign collapsed. Of course, $413,-
000 seems today a trifling sum compared to the million
and a quarter raised for Leonard Wood in 1920, and

the great sums spent in the Senatorial campaigns of
Messrs. Frank L. Smith of Illinois, and Vare and Pep-
per of Pennsylvania. As soon as Mr. Lowden heard of
the bribery he issued an excellent statement in which
he declared that his "injunctions to Mr. Emmerson were
to use no money except for legitimate purposes of the
campaign and to make no expenditure that could not be
made public." It was a doubly unfortunate happening
for the Republican Party, for it opened the way to the
nomination of Warren G. Harding by the oil corruption-
ists and the party bosses, with the resulting disgraceful
betrayal of the country.

Here it is a pleasure to record that Chicago liberals
are one in their belief that Mr. Lowden told the truth
and that he had no idea what use was being made of
his money. To quote Clarence Darrow again, "the country is now fully convinced, as was Illinois at the time,
that whether Lowden would make a good President or
not, his life and public record had placed him far above
the suspicion of corruption." He believes that if Mr.
Lowden is nominated in 1928 "no political enemy will
dare to raise the issue that probably caused his defeat
in 1920."

Let us turn back to his record as Governor for an
indication of how Mr. Lowden behaves in an executive
office. His political affiliations prior to his election were
with William Lorimer and his shady cohorts, the same
Lorimer who was and is the friend of Charles G. Dawes,
in turn one of Frank Lowden's dearest friends and intimates. But when Mr. Lowden took office in 1917 there

was no feeling against him on the score that he was
an ally of Lorimer. It soon appeared that the Governor
was his own master; that he had no intention of building up a political machine; that he had grown greatly
in stature and power and purpose since those disap-
pointing years in Congress. It also became clear that,
whether the politicians liked it or not, he proposed to
reorganize the government, cut off a lot of useless offices and sinecures, and reduce taxation. He actually
achieved a remarkable reorganization of the entire
State government; in place of no less than 128 boards
and commissions, many of them overlapping in their
functions, there were created nine major business departments for the State. Taxes came down $7,000,000
a year, and there was introduced a budget system which
put the State's finances on a business-like basis, and
could make waste impossible if it were properly used.
His appointments to office were political, but they were
beyond criticism as to the character of the appointees
and their efficiency. He stuck to his job and his desk with
fidelity, and ended his service without a scandal of any
kind. When it was over the Progressives agreed that he
had made a deep and lasting impression upon his
State.

There was, however, one grave blot upon Governor
Lowden's regime. Taking office in 1917 he was hardly
in the saddle before the United States entered the World
War, and he became an easy victim of the war hysteria.
At once he appointed a State Council of Defence and
in considerable measure turned over the Government to

big-business men like Samuel Insull, who became chairman of the Council, and politicians of the type of Roger Sullivan. Other and far better appointments to the Council he made—like those of Mrs. Joseph T. Bowen and Victor Olander; but the Insull group dominated. It is hard to see why these councils of defence were ever needed. In the main they all behaved alike, illegally receiving or usurping some or all the powers of the Executive. They usually instituted a reign of terrorism, a dragooning of all who did not approve of the war, together with wholesale suppressions of personal liberty and of the historic American right to dissent. They compelled men to contribute to war funds under threat of ruin; they made ..rrests right and left. Particularly obnoxious was Governor Lowden's attitude toward the People's Council, a group of pacifists which sought to meet in Chicago. Indeed, it was out of this intolerance on the part of Governor Lowden that there arose the trouble between him and Mayor William Hale Thompson, which has crystallized into a bitter and lasting feud.

It is, of course, open to question whether Mayor Thompson ever takes a position without an eye to the main chance. In that case, whether for political or other reasons, he was right, and was upholding historic American traditions. His political power of today is in considerable measure due to the gratitude of foreign-born groups who remember that in the war days he stood between them and intolerance and outrage when everybody else seemed hostile; that he respected minority opinion and was willing that it should make itself heard.

When the story of the ill-treatment of the foreign-born minorities during the war is written—even those which were not descendants of Germans or Austrians—one of the darkest chapters will deal with Illinois under Lowden.

Mr. Lowden can keep his own counsel and he has done so to a considerable degree as to his attitude on foreign affairs. He, too, seems to feel that silence on some vital issues is the surest way to success. He is on record, however, as opposing vigorously America's entry into the League of Nations. What is more important is the statement that he is an old-fashioned anti-imperialist, for it would be of enormous importance if one of the Republican leaders should come out flatly against our wicked and bloody policies in the Caribbean. Beyond this nothing is known of his views on foreign affairs, whether he is today a big-navy man, whether he favours insisting upon the payment of the foreign debts owed to the United States, or whether he would aid in their further reduction. On these and several other questions, notably the tariff, a man with so excellent a record as Mr. Lowden's ought to make himself unequivocally clear. As a farmer he must be opposed to tariff discrimination. Would he favour a general revision downward? So far he has been a high-tariff man. The public is entitled to further information as to his attitude on pressing social and economic questions. It is not in his favour that he has long been prominent in the Pullman Company and yet has done nothing to make it cease exploiting its coloured porters whose wages are in large part paid by the tips of the public. If Mr. Lowden has never been as outspoken against union labour as his friend, General Dawes, he does not stand out pre-eminently among its supporters.

There are other marked differences between Dawes and Lowden. In the latter the aggressive bitterness, the vindictiveness toward his political opponents, is fortunately absent, as well as that iron determination to impose his will on others. The Fascist qualities of Dawes, Mr. Lowden seems to be without. One can think of situations in which Dawes, the adorer of Napoleon, might well become dictatorial. Mr. Lowden would always be a somewhat old-fashioned American public man, conservative but not reactionary, faithful and reliable. Were he to be chosen President, he would not set the country on fire; he would probably not initiate new policies despite his constructive trend, but he would be an excellent administrator. He would make no impassioned plea for any far-reaching reform. Business would go on as usual and the hold of the great corporations upon the Government would be little relaxed. Mr. Darrow, who speaks with the background of many years of personal friendship, prophesies that if Frank Lowden wins "the newspapers will not criticize him. The public will not abuse him; he will not create a stir." And he gives the comforting assurance that "he will not seek foreign conquest. He will not embroil his country in war. He will try his best to help the United States to live at peace at home and abroad"—an encouraging prospect when one thinks of our escapades in Haiti and Nicaragua, to say nothing of China. Best of all Mr. Lowden has a heart, that organ which is lacking in so many politicians. In other words, Mr. Lowden would give us an old-type, honest, careful, and dignified administration in keeping with the best traditions of the White House. There would be no Jess Smiths or Albert Falls or Harry Daughertys about him; on the contrary we should see the rugged honesty and determination of Grover Cleveland. Free from any temptation to try for a second term because of his age, Mr. Lowden would surely strive to make a record for himself in the Presidency. If the country must have a conservative Republican in the White House during the four years to come, Frank Lowden appears the best of the 1928 pre-convention candidates of this type.

JAMES A. REED

A Modern Andrew Jackson

JAMES A. REED is the *enfant terrible* of the Senate.
Also he is its roughest and hardest hitter. No other
public man has such a mastery of bitter sarcasm, or is
a better hater. He carries his argument *ad hominem* in
that he attacks directly and, if need be viciously, the
man or men he sets out to attack. No pussyfooting here!
Has he not indicted Calvin Coolidge himself of "mis-
feasance in office" and this before a great California
audience which was at first awe-struck that anyone
should dare to criticize his tin majesty in the White
House, only to surge around the attacker when he finished, carried away by his fine presence, his glorious
speaking voice, his manifest sincerity, his obvious
desire to tell the truth without regard to persons or
authority or power? At this writing he is rendering a
profound public service by stumping the country recit-
ing the facts about the rottenness and corruption of the
Republican Party and the lawlessness of its leaders.

But let no one believe that he has the courage to
attack only his political opponents. There is no more
thrilling story in our recent history than Senator Reed's
defiance of his own party and its President, Woodrow
Wilson, when that gentleman was asserting despotic
rights over the consciences and the bodies of Americans
and trying by the power of all his great office to compel

a uniform subserviency of opinion to his views of what should be the policy and the aims of this country. "Jim" Reed, as the Senate calls him, fought a losing fight against the manœuvres which eventually led the United States into the war. Although he did not vote against the declaration of war, his opposition to some of Woodrow Wilson's policies won him the enmity of the President. He went back to his State to find himself an object of bitter insult and contumely, to learn that he was being burned in effigy. When he came up for re-election five years later, Woodrow Wilson bitterly denounced him and demanded his defeat in language that plainly revealed both Mr. Wilson's intolerance and the depth to which he had been hurt by Mr. Reed's opposition. Three times during this campaign Mr. Wilson wrote letters demanding that the Senator be defeated. In one he said that Mr. Reed had "shown himself as incapable of sustained allegiance to any person or any cause. He has repeatedly forfeited any claim to my confidence that he may ever have been supposed to have, and I shall not willingly consent to any further association with him." He called upon the voters to defeat the "marplot" Reed, and to "substitute a man of the true breed of Democratic principle." Finally, two weeks before the election he wrote that if Reed were returned to the Senate "he will, of course, be there a man without a party." Mr. Wilson went further; he accused Senator Reed of lying in saying that Mr. Wilson had given him a letter certifying to the correctness

of his conduct in the fight over the establishment of
the Federal Reserve System. It was one of the many
times that Mr. Wilson's love of truth, or his memory,
failed him. Senator Reed immediately produced a fac-
simile of a letter in which Mr. Wilson had written on
October 23, 1913: "I have felt all along the sincere
honesty and independence of judgment you were exercising in this whole matter, and you may be sure that
there has never been in my mind any criticism except
an occasional difference of judgment."

Never did a man have a harder fight to retain his
seat in the Senate than did Mr. Reed then. Incited by
Mr. Wilson, leaders of his own party openly warred
upon him, and so did the national and State organizations—they had prevented his participation in the
national convention of his party in 1920: Everywhere
Democrats fought under the slogan "Rid us of Reed."
An elaborate mock funeral was held in St. Louis at-
tended by many "mourners." The Democratic women
of Missouri organized to defeat him. The entire press
of the State spewed hate and malignity upon him, and
refused to admit that he had a chance of success. Yet
in the face of these tremendous odds, at times even in
danger of personal violence, he battled on to find himself returned to Washington by a majority of 43,000,
18,000 more votes than he had received when he ran
for the Senate seven years earlier. That was a magnificent triumph, as it was fresh proof of the ability of
the electorate to think and judge for itself even in the

face of every sort of misrepresentation and abuse of a candidate. Mr. Reed even carried the city of St. Louis, which for decades had been safely Republican; this was the answer of its voters to the mock funeral. Only a man of extraordinary ability, tenacity, honesty, and courage could have entered upon such a titanic struggle and won. It is evidence of the magnanimity of the man that he refrained in the hour of victory from sending a telegram to Woodrow Wilson informing him of the re- action of the voters of Missouri to Mr. Wilson's advice as to how they should cast their votes, as is also the fact that he sprang to the rescue of Woodrow Wilson when, during the war, it was urged that a committee·of Congress supervise and control the President's acts.

Surely Mr. Reed himself has admirably character- ized his own experience during the war, and the heroism that it called for, in his tribute to Senator Medill Mc- Cormick of Illinois, with whom he fought against the League of Nations. It was at a memorial service for Senator McCormick that Mr. Reed spoke these words:

> *But is there not a valour rarer than that which nerves the soldier's arm and turns his heart to steel and makes him with unwavering eye look in the face of death? Is not the moral courage to endure dishonour for the tongue- less, voiceless, impalpable thing we call principle, su- preme, incomparable, and rarest valour? To all the living Death must sometime come. Even at our birth his shaft is poised, and though the fight be long, it soon or late infallibly will strike the mark. The hero well may find contentment in the thought that he advances but by a*

little while the inevitable stroke. And so, with honour's
voice for his meed in life and requiem in death, he dares
to meet his fate. To stand before your people and endure
while the name "traitor" may be hissed into your ear,
to stand and know that friends are leaving you, that
doubt of your fidelity and manhood has been raised, and
yet to stand—that is the sublimest attribute of which the
human soul is capable.

Now this same James A. Reed is actually seeking
the Democratic nomination for the Presidency, he who
in 1917 had as little prospect of announcing himself as
a Presidential candidate as had Ramsay MacDonald at
the same time of becoming Premier of Great Britain—
he too had actively opposed his country's going to war.
Here in the lists Mr. Reed stands—a cigar-chewing,
tobacco-spitting Middle Westerner, American to his
finger-tips. Tall, lithe, and straight as an Indian, his
head is crowned by white hair over a ruddy countenance. His grey-blue eyes contain a direct and searching
challenge. He is a modern Lincoln in the effectiveness
of his stories, and in his extraordinary ability to turn
instantly from grave to gay, from the measured polished
diction of the statesman to the homely language of the
plain American. Like Lincoln he is not without coarse-
ness in private conversation, in which his references to
comrades or enemies are wittily unbridled. Yet as
William Hard has written, Mr. Reed may suddenly drop
the colloquial when he is speaking in order to rise "to
heights of sublimity which it is difficult to believe have
ever been surpassed in parliamentary history." Mr.

Hard adds that like Webster it is impossible for Mr. Reed "to be as great as he looks and sounds."

It is undeniable that this man, who asks that he be made the national leader of his party, is out of joint with the times. He sighs for a return of the government of Franklin Pierce which went its way unaware of the existence of the citizen, except so far as it called upon him to go to war or to pay taxes. That is, he would revert to the days of unlimited individualism; to the time when there was no legal interference with the working hours of women and children; when there was no woman suffrage; when a man could raise a thirst East and West of the Missouri and slake it publicly. He would even abolish the Civil Service Commission and again turn the offices over to party henchmen. As for government control of industry, the very thought is anathema to him. From that point of view he would be a profoundly acceptable candidate for Wall Street which is aware that he is identified with no far-reaching economic or social reforms. But not in other ways. He has fought against monopoly; he has magnificently assailed the protective tariff, and particularly the flexible tariff humbug, the failure of which, under the control of President Coolidge, has justified every word he uttered in opposition to the plan, and he has always appealed for lower taxes.

He does not hesitate to criticize some of Wall Street's most cherished plans and policies. He helped to defeat the nomination of Charles B. Warren for Attorney General on account of his connection with the sugar companies. He has repeatedly charged, with complete truth, that the financial interests rule and control Mr. Coolidge and his Administration, and he has shocked the financiers by his utter lack of respect and reverence for Secretary Mellon. Indeed, he laughs at Mellon and mocks him. For Herbert Hoover Senator Reed has a bitter antipathy; he always speaks of him as "Sir Herbert Hoover" or "that great British statesman, Hoover." He refuses even to bend the knee before Charles G. Dawes. He vigorously fought the Vice-President's plans to limit debating in the Senate, and he has repeatedly refused to listen to the warnings of Mr. Dawes that he must look toward the Vice-President when he talks on the floor—it will take more than a Vice-President to make Mr. Reed conform to anything against which he has taken a position. Only on the question of prohibition has he suddenly appeared to compromise. An avowed and defiant Wet, now that he is a candidate he has discovered that prohibition is a moral not a political question.

His opposition to every entangling foreign alliance is well known—he even opposed the Four-Power Treaty in the Pacific, which was one of the fruits of the Washington Conference for the Limitation of Armaments. Against the World Court he worked himself up into a perfect fury. He has condemned every one of the foreign-debt settlements. The only thing that would make him accept the French and British settlements would be if England and France should consent to sell us the West Indian islands which belong to them. The Italian debt settlement gave him the opportunity to contrast the interest which Italy is to pay to the United States government with the 9 per cent interest which he claims it is paying to private Wall Street bankers for loans made by them (they deny this). As for the League of Nations, the mere mention of it sets every drop of his blood to tingling with anger. He still stands where he stood on September 22, 1919, when he said:

> *I decline to help set up any government greater than that established by the fathers, greater than that baptized in the blood of patriots from the lanes of Lexington to the forests of the Argonne, greater than that sanctified by the tears of all the mothers whose heroic sons have gone down to death to sustain its glory and its independence. I decline to set up any government greater than the government of the United States of America!*

This passionate rage against any relationship with other nations was partly responsible for his putting through the resolution for the recall of our troops from garrison duty on German soil, which led to the return of our army much earlier than was satisfactory to the Allies.

It is undoubtedly due to this prejudice against foreigners that Senator Reed still believes in arming this country for defence. Unlike Calvin Coolidge in his saner moments, Mr. Reed still thinks, despite the lessons of the World War, that armies and navies protect nations from attack and insure victory when attacked. So fearful is he of any association with the rest of the world that he wishes America literally to lie on its arms by night and by day, and to squander more millions than the cost of a Panama Canal every year, because of his dread of a possible attack. This is the more interesting because of his demand for freer immigration, at least so far as skilled labourers are concerned, and because of his far-sighted opposition to the protective tariff. If that should be reduced it would, of course, mean ever closer social and trade relations with the rest of the world.

As to other domestic issues, Senator Reed has made one of his bravest fights against the Ku Klux Klan. He was a leader in the defeat of the ship-subsidy proposal, and some of his best work of late has been in connection with his chairmanship of the Senate committee to investigate campaign expenditures. Thanks to his vigorous leadership in this matter we have had a pretty complete picture of the huge expenditures in the last Senatorial elections in Illinois and Pennsylvania which resulted in the denial of their seats to Messrs. Smith and Vare. But this was not something new for Senator Reed; he played an equally striking part in the refusal to seat Senator Newberry. He is sincerely and deeply shocked by any evidence of corruption in public office, and so he was among the first to speak out about the Harding Administration, and he did not qualify his language when a mistaken jury in the District of Columbia acquitted Messrs. Fall and Doheny in the first of the criminal cases growing out of the theft of the naval-oil reserves. He would be just as ready to speak out against Democratic corruption; thus he was quick to denounce

William G. McAdoo for what Mr. Reed considered a violation of law when Mr. McAdoo acted as counsel for the Republic Steel and Iron Company in pressing a claim for a tax refund from the government within two years after Mr. McAdoo left the Cabinet of the United States.

Like Borah, this Democratic survivor from the days of Grover Cleveland lives and breathes by the Constitution. He will fight for it by the hour, the day, the month, the year, protesting that it is not his fault that he fights, but entirely the fault of those who insist on trying to lay hands upon our sacred fundamental law. Curiously enough, this great fighter insists that he is no fighter at all. With a straight face—it is a bit forbidding and rigid in repose—he insists that he really hates to fight. The truth is that there never was a fighter who could go down to defeat more often and yet bob up the next day ready for another dozen rounds and still more punishment. Certainly never was there a fighter favoured by Providence with a better temperamental or oratorical equipment to be a surpassing public prosecutor, a flagellator of faithless public servants, than this American who, typically, lived by hard work in the fields until he was twenty-one years old, and then achieved the legal education which made him prosecuting attorney in Kansas City, and twice mayor of that progressive trading-post on the Missouri. Inevitably Mr. Reed's resemblance to Andrew Jackson suggests itself. It is easy to visualize him as he would have looked in Jackson's time—the latter also a bold, handsome, swashbuckling, hard-drinking, roistering, dueling leader of men, of much the same political viewpoint.

It hardly seems within the range of possibility that James A. Reed will be nominated and elected. But if he should sleep in the same bed that Woodrow Wilson occupied in the White House, as the legitimate Democratic successor to that high-strung President, it would be one of the most ironic and colossal jokes of history, worthy of the pens of the greatest of the classic dramatists. Certainly nothing else could as quickly make Woodrow Wilson turn in his grave. Of one thing we could be certain. However reactionary his administration might be, and however slow to strike hands with other nations for a solution of the problems of the harassed world, if Jim Reed should become President we should again have in the White House a genuine personality, a leader of force, vigour, and effectiveness; a man who would speak out in the presence of wrong-doing, in the place of one who never knows his own mind until compelled to take a position, whose tongue fails him when it is a question of denouncing the high crimes of his Republican friends, associates, and benefactors.

GEORGE W. NORRIS

Noblest of the Romans

To George W. Norris, United States Senator,
    Greeting:
        For twenty years you have sat in the seats of the pow-
erful in Washington and served your country faithfully
and well. During all that time, unlike many of your legislative associates, your soul has been your own, your vote
the vote of conscience. Wherever you have gone men have
respected you, political opponents have envied and feared
you. They saw you enter the Senate a reformer, a progressive; some among them laughed cynically and, pointing to
many an example in the Senate Chamber, declared: "The
system will overcome him." The system found itself baf-
fled by a brave and honest man. The years passed; you
were progressive still. The Great War came, beclouding
men's minds, instilling passion into their hearts, making
them give out only words of hate and unreason. You remained clear in vision, temperate in speech, loyal to the
core. You voted against the war which was a crime against
America and its every ideal, and in so doing you kept the
American faith. You have kept it ever since. Always you
have been the captain of your soul.

IN these words the editor of *The Nation* began an appeal to George W. Norris, which had its share in
inducing the Senator to reconsider his decision to retire
and again to become a candidate. He was at that time,
December, 1923, not unnaturally depressed. He saw
that the high hopes with which he had entered public

life had come to naught; that the World War had effectively blocked any progress, had bound and trussed liberalism everywhere; that corruption was rife in American life even among the highest; that the public, emotionally exhausted during the war, was determined to be let alone with its pleasures and its prosperity; that there was no powerful progressive or humane sentiment to which to appeal. Weary and downcast, the thought of rest and tranquillity far from the maddening strife of the nation's Capitol wooed him. But when he came to take counsel by himself with his conscience, when he took note of the appeals to remain in public life with which he was flooded, there was only one decision he could reach. He put aside the ease that a man has earned at sixty-two, and was triumphantly re-elected to the Senate.

Yet this was another of the men who was branded as unpatriotic and damned from one end of the country to the other because he insisted on his right to his conscience—a right exercised by John Jay, by Abraham Lincoln, and in 1898 by some of the finest spirits in this land. The whole power of the Government was thrown against the dissenters in 1917 because the Government had a bad conscience and knew that the people but six months before had voted to sustain the policy of peace. Some men it broke, but some it could not. The character of Robert La Follette and George Norris, and others, was not to be wrecked even in that convulsion of hate, and falsehood, and passion which shook the country in 1917. Those men had by their rectitude, their

devotion, and their honour, won a place in the hearts
of their constituents from which they could not be
ousted.

Mr. Norris has himself set forth what happened to
him after his refusal to vote for the armed-neutrality
legislation, in a remarkable letter published in *The
Nation* for January 25, 1928. He was at once the subject "of almost universal condemnation not only in the
Senate but outside"; there were calls from the press of
his State and from many organizations for his resignation. He neither recanted, nor ran away, nor trimmed,
nor sulked in his private office. On the contrary, he at
once wrote to the Governor of Nebraska saying that he
recognized the right of the citizens of Nebraska to have
a Senator in Washington who voted as they wished, but
that he would not have voted for the armed neutrality
bill "even if every voter in the State had demanded it."
He, therefore, asked the Governor to obtain from the
legislature authority to hold a recall election, so that
the people could oust him from office if they saw fit.
The Governor refused to do this, and Mr. Norris rented
a public hall in Lincoln, Nebraska, the capital of the
State, advertised the fact, and stated that on the following Monday he would account for his acts to all who
cared to come and hear him. On his arrival in Lincoln
the day before, he was warned that his meeting would
be broken up and that he would be mobbed—perhaps
killed. Only one reporter called on him to get his views.
His friends were afraid to be seen with him. It did not

seem wise to ask anyone to serve as chairman of the meeting.

What finally happened Mr. Norris described in these words:

Long before it was time for the hall to open, the street in front was crowded with people and, when the doors were opened, this Auditorium, the largest audience-room in the city, was filled to overflowing. Extra chairs were carried in and the aisles were filled. Every seat on the stage was occupied. When I walked out from one of the wings I was met with absolute silence, but I had not proceeded far until I knew that the common sense of the Nebraska people was awake. The first sentence I uttered was that I intended to tell them the truth about the difficulty, and that it would be something that they had not been able to get from the newspapers. That was when the audience broke loose. The people stood up and yelled. I realized then that if an organized bunch of fellows were scattered through that audience, intending to break up the meeting, they rather than I would be the victims of the mob. The audience included members of the legislature and people who had come to Lincoln from 150 miles away. These people had become impressed with the fact that the press had not been fair; that it had not told the truth.

It seemed to me a demonstration that the American mind demands fair play; that it insists that the under-dog shall have his hearing and his day in court; and it demonstrated to me that underneath the deception and the misrepresentation, the political power and the influence, there was, in the hearts of the common people, a belief that there was something artificial about this propaganda, and that so-called leaders of public sentiment, both in and out of public life, were being carried off their feet by misrepresentation and even by falsehood. In that hour I felt repaid for all the turmoil, the agony, and the suffering that I had endured. I would be willing to go through it all again, for a vindication such as I received on that occasion. I was deluged with requests to deliver other speeches on the subject of the Armed Neutrality Bill, but, as my stay in the State lasted only two or three days, I was unable to accept many of them. My experience was the same, however, in every meeting that I addressed while I was in the State.

It is alleged by the *Nebraska State Journal,* in commenting on this letter that Mr. Norris exaggerated the danger he was in and the temper of the people and it suggests that he is of those who are apt to feel, and happy to feel, that they are martyrs. That may be. But no one who went through that period of history and opposed the Wilson policies slept upon a bed of roses. Mr. Norris went back to Washington and upheld its finest traditions by voting against our going into the war.

What that plunge into the maelstrom of European hatreds, jealousies, and rivalries netted the United States Mr. Norris has set forth in an interview he gave on the tenth anniversary of Congress's yielding to Mr. Wilson's wishes, and our entering the war:

We went to war to make an end to militarism, and there is more militarism today than ever before.

We went to war to make the world safe for democracy, and there is less democracy today than ever before.

We went to war to dethrone autocracy and special

privilege, and they thrive everywhere throughout the world today.

We went to war to win the friendship of the world, and they hate us today.

We went to war to purify the soul of America, and instead we only drugged it.

We went to war to awaken the American people to the idealistic concepts of liberty, justice, and fraternity, and instead we awakened them only to the mad pursuit of money.

All this, and more, the war brought us. It is our harvest from what we sowed.

You ask me if I would vote again today as I voted ten years ago. The answer is I would.

This man typifies within himself the best in America: unselfishness, devotion to duty and to principle, absolute fidelity to a trust, courage, and integrity. If ever there was a self-made man, this is he. His illiterate father, dying when George was four years old, left ten daughters besides his son; their mother could barely read or write. His life as a child was embraced "within eighty acres of stumps" in Sandusky County, Ohio. It is only the exceptional spirit that can rise out of such surroundings, such grinding poverty, and overcome such handicaps. Even when they are overcome the marks they leave are too often permanent; too often the bitterness of the struggle hardens the nature, renders callous the spirit. The extraordinary thing about this man is that he came through it all and has weathered the storms of twenty-five years as Congressman and Senator without becoming in the least embittered, or hard, despite his periods of intense depression.

Go to his offices and you will find him accessible, dignified, modest, unassuming, straightforward in his thinking and his acting; a quiet-mannered and low-voiced gentleman who knows what he talks about or else keeps silent. No "side" here; no assumption that his long public service has made him Sir Oracle; but plenty of deep and sincere feeling, the earnestness of a truly religious and devoted character. He is the greatest antidote for pessimism that we have in Washington since the death of Robert La Follette. For he has proved that a man may always be true to the faith that is in him and yet win the abiding support of an American electorate. He constantly revives our belief in the usefulness of legislators in Washington, yes, of Congress itself. It is now the fashion to gibe and sneer at the national legislature; to assert that its members do nothing but loaf and talk, and that the country would be much better off if it met only every other year for five or six weeks, and then went home. It is a falsehood. The amount of business that Congress transacts, and of that which it ought to transact, is truly enormous and, as the issues before the country become more and more economic rather than political, their importance and their difficulty will steadily increase. A comparison between the questions confronting Congress during the first administration of Grover Cleveland and those with which it is endeavouring to grapple today, will cure any hon-

est man of the belief that a congressional job is a sine-
cure.

One can, of course, loaf through two years in Congress or six years in the Senate. But not if one is made
of the same fibre as Senator Norris. Once I asked his
views on a foreign issue. To my surprise he had none.
This was his apology: "For two years I have been absolutely absorbed in the Muscle Shoals problem. It is
so difficult, so far-reaching in its ramifications, that in
order to master it I have had to concentrate upon it and
to exclude from my mind all other matters that were
not absolutely essential." Yet Muscle Shoals was only
one of the gigantic problems which the Senate was compelled to face, problems that can only be solved by deep
and intelligent study of technical points as a rule considered exclusively by technicians and engineers. When
one considers that in this same session the Senate has
also had to grapple with Mississippi River flood pre-
vention, with the Boulder Dam problem gravely involving the future of seven States, to say nothing of naval
policy, of taxation, of foreign affairs, and of the oil
scandals and all the other issues, one comes to recognize that he who sneers at or would ridicule the Senate
writes himself down as ignorant and without understanding of the burdens upon the most interesting, and
educational, and useful institution in our political life.

To return to Muscle Shoals, Mr. Norris began his
study of it six years ago—in 1922—and speedily realized that it was one of the most important subjects be-

fore the country. He became convinced that this great power plant, upon which the United States has expended more than $150,000,000, originally to manufacture nitrate for munitions, presented a problem of vital importance to the nation. After the war it was decided to dedicate it to the making of nitrates for fertilizer and everybody, except Mr. Norris, said: "Oh let's turn it over to the highest private bidder and get rid of the plaguey thing." But Senator Norris discovered that cheaper methods of making nitrate have appeared and that the real possibilities lay in the use of the huge water-power for the manufacturing of electric current —cheap current that would enormously benefit manufacturing and industry throughout that part of the South to which it could be made to minister. Twice Mr. Norris appeared to have lost his fight, first when the House passed a bill to accept Henry Ford's offer to take it all over. But Mr. Norris studied and punctured Ford's plan and, finally, Ford withdrew his offer.

Next, Senator Underwood drafted a bill turning Muscle Shoals over to private power interests, presumably the great Alabama Power Company. In 1926, Congress adopted the Underwood proposal, Senator Harrison of Mississippi fathering it. With his back to the wall, Senator Norris defeated the bill on a point of order after it had passed both House and Senate and a conference report had been submitted! It seemed then, and it seems now, a miracle. In 1927 the Senate Committee on Agriculture favourably reported the Senator's plan, and in 1928 a first victory came to this

great-hearted fighter. The Senate by a vote of 48 to 25
adopted his plan for government control and management. Mr. Norris had been ill for weeks. But he pulled
himself together and went into action, talking for the
better part of three whole days despite his weakened
condition. And won. Yet there are those who would
cloture debate in the Senate! Years of talking, years of
incessant labour, of almost incredibly severe industry,
carried the day. The House of Representatives is yet
to vote—Mr. Norris testified for four hours before the
responsible House Committee with marked effect. The
outcome is still doubtful, but at least the chances are
that it will be a long time, if ever, before Muscle Shoals
goes into private hands.

Like everybody else I admire profoundly Col. Lindbergh's great feat. But when I think of the medals
showered upon him by all the world and think of what
Senator Norris's work in the Senate has meant for his
country, I bemoan the fact that Senator Norris, too, is
not given the highest award within his country's gift.
As I write the Navy Department is seeking to obtain
from Congress a medal of honour for an officer who
bombed some Nicaraguan "bandits" and then stood
their fire while he helped remove our wounded. Will
the world, one asks, never recognize adequately its
greatest heroes?

Well, Senator Norris seeks no medals, and no reward, save that of his own conscience. With him the
fight's the thing. Four times he has seen the Senate pass
his bill to end the so-called "lame duck sessions" of

Congress—the session after an election in which sit the defeated candidates for a year after their defeat, many of them trying their best to bargain offices into their keeping. Four times the House has killed it by order of the Republican clique which controls the House. Eventually it must pass. Senator Norris may not be there to see the victory, but it will come and will be another monument to his pre-eminent public service. Merely to call the roll of the measures he has fought for and sponsored would take pages. Indeed, he began his career of courage and independence by demanding in 1903 a revision of the choking rules of the House of Representatives, upheld by Speaker Cannon, and by taking the lead in that fight although a new member. In this same contest, as told elsewhere, Senator Curtis fought for Speaker Cannon, and today, although a mere rubber stamp for the party, he is a serious candidate for the Republican nomination for the Presidency. The Republican Party which will not think of nominating Senator Borah, its ablest Senator, would still less think of nominating its most high-minded, its most industrious, its most unselfish; in short, its finest Senator —Norris of Nebraska.

So Mr. Norris looks forward to going back to Nebraska in 1931, but not to rest. He has seen another great vision and would like to become Governor of Nebraska in order to make that vision take on reality. He wishes to lead in reforming our State governments now utterly outworn in form, governed by Lilliputian politicians for private or party advantage, pretending to split on the lines of national issues—Republicans against Democrats! Mr. Norris wishes to brush this all aside and to make over State governments at one swoop by creating a one-house legislature of about twenty-five members to be elected, together with a small slate of officials, on a non-partisan ticket. He would consolidate or abolish many of the State officers and put all employees under civil service rules. A dream? No, a perfectly practical, sensible, businesslike scheme, which would be instantly adopted if politics could be banished and our States treated as the simple business entities that they are. It is no more revolutionary than was the city-manager plan when first proposed, and it would do far more good for the country than any single measure for the reorganization of our governmental machinery since the Civil War.

Here let us leave George W. Norris, quickener of our faith in our Congress, yes, more than that, in our country and its institutions. No one can believe that this nation is likely to be wholly submerged by a crass materialism when men such as he can be produced to achieve great things by their own unaided efforts, by their courage, their simple bravery, the force of their unspotted characters. Here is one to offer a wreath of admiration and gratitude to him not after he is dead, but while he still lives and serves his fellowmen—the noblest Roman of them all.

ALBERT C. RITCHIE

Gentleman Governor

STEP up, ladies and gentlemen—not too close, please —but come forward and behold the best-looking, most aristocratic and attractive of Governors, Albert Cabell Ritchie of the Free State of Maryland, where whisky runs as free as water, where prohibition has taken not at all; where the liberty of the individual is as secure as any place in America; where H. L. Mencken finds, and dwells in, an earthly paradise. Behold a candidate for the Presidency who bids fair to be Governor of a State longer than any other man in generations, who is obviously the antithesis of Al Smith. The one bears the marks of his humble origin and hard struggle upwards; the other should be the beau ideal of those who believe that government belongs to the prosperous, the cultivated, the well-bred. Governor Ritchie is plainly "to the manner born," that is, he has behind him generations of means and education—his father was eleven years on the Supreme Bench of Maryland.

See Governor Ritchie in his office or in his spacious and dignified Executive Mansion in Annapolis, and your mind somehow reverts to those elder days when George Washington resigned his commission in the historic room under Governor Ritchie's offices, to the time when courtliness and gentility and knee-breeches and ruffles were the distinguishing marks of our statesmen. Not that he is effeminate, or lacking in virility. He gives himself no airs and indulges in no mannerisms. He is simple, modest, and unaffected; if the word had not been so sadly misused and warped one could speak of him as a notable "gentleman." Were the miracle to happen and were he to be transferred to Washington, he would seem in more ways than one the lineal successor of Jefferson, Madison, and Monroe, and there would again be good manners, dignity, and charm in the White House.

No demagogue here to split the ears of groundlings, and no skilled wire-puller; nor can it be said of Governor Ritchie that he has won his way by wealth and social position. It is impossible to think of his making a whirlwind campaign, or thrilling his audiences with the wit and the *ad hominem* arguments of Al Smith. Passion and Albert Ritchie are strangers. His are quiet, well-delivered, carefully worked-out addresses, intended to appeal to reason. He speaks for the fundamentals of American life, for personal liberties and rights, but he sets no soul on fire when he does so. He has admirably declared, Woodrow Wilson to the contrary notwithstanding, that the Constitution gives no right to anyone to suspend freedom of speech and of the press, whether in peace or in war, but the welkin did not ring when he said it. He was righteously offended when, contrary to American tradition, the Count and Countess Karolyi were banished from America and the Countess Cathcart held in durance vile on Ellis Island. He is op-

posed to every sort of censorship, especially of books
and movies. But these things do not make him step out
of his role of the gentle, reasoning statesman who has
never worked at hard labour or knows what it means to
lose a job and, with empty pockets, hunt another.

Can one be else than placid in the governorship of
the Free State? What are the chief political issues there?
Governor Ritchie took the press into his confidence on
February 7, 1927, and let out the secret—oysters and
gasoline! They were not merely the chief issues—they
were the only controversial ones. This libertarian State
was tortured with doubt only as to whether there should
be private or public leasing of the oyster beds—even
in Elysium the spectre of socialism shows its dreadful
mien! As for gasoline, the contest was over a proposed
gasoline tax and who would actually pay it; which recalls the fact that not long ago the columns of the Baltimore *Evening Sun* were filled with the discussions of
an even more vital controversy— Should or should not
the Nordic tomato yield in Maryland to a low-born
Slavic importation?

Happy the Free State and happier its Governor as
he draws his magnificent salary of $4,500 a year—a
trifle more than half that paid to his underling the Commissioner of Education. Like Al Smith in New York,
having aided in reorganizing the governmental machinery of the State, he, too, sighs for new worlds to conquer. The "best attorney general [of Maryland] in half
a century" has, as Governor, instituted the budget

method of handling the finances of the State, and a model merit system for its employees; has established a State purchasing department; has pushed on the State to build good roads, a larger percentage to the total mileage than any other of our commonwealths; has taken the school system out of politics, and improved the quality of the education offered. More than that, he has revised the State labour and compensation laws, reformed the system of prison labour, breathed new life into the health and welfare departments, put the conservation work of the State on a business basis, and—heed, O business men and the United States Chamber of Commerce—is said to have reduced the State taxes. Why shouldn't a Governor who has done all these things feel that he, having disposed of the fate of Maryland's oysters, born and unborn, and of the gasoline tax, paid and unpaid, can now sit back and declare with Mr. Mencken that all's well on the Severn and the Chesapeake? With a total State debt of only $20,295,000 and its government made over into what Frank Kent calls "the most modern, efficient, and foolproof governmental machine in the country," its remaining problems are obviously administrative, not due to defects of the system. What wonder then that this Executive is placid and that he prefers to think "in those fractions of minutes when men would have him leap to his feet with warm words on his lips"?

Yet this Governor does not lack courage or ability to blaze up if he wishes. When President Harding asked him, with all the other heads of coal-mining States, to order out the militia during the coal strike of 1922 Governor Ritchie sent back a sizzling telegram saying that he would do nothing of the kind. Here the ardent defender of States' rights had his chance and took it. To his courage he added wisdom, for he told Mr. Harding that he would insist that Maryland settle her labour troubles by agreement and not by force. When other Governors were bending the knee before the prestige of the President, Albert Ritchie declared that he would not use troops lest they incite to the very rioting and bloodshed they were intended to prevent—he had not read labour history in vain! Nearly thirty years, he said, had passed since troops had been called out in Maryland in labour troubles. They would not be by him—and there he touched the highwater-mark of his career and gave his partisans the opportunity to say justly that he could get up from his Annapolis easy chair and prove himself every inch a man if the emergency offered.

Similarly, he told the Adjutant General in Washington that he declined to order out the Maryland National Guard for that silly muster day of July 4, 1925, which the War Department soon after abandoned; he also refused to issue a proclamation approving the procedure or to appoint a civilian committee to take charge of it in Maryland. Not that he is anti-military. He has urged every eligible man to attend the civilian military training camps; he believes in preparedness and complete plans for national defence. Here the dull conventionality of office-holders rules with him as it did when he issued a fulsome eulogy of President Harding on the latter's death, as far-fetched then as it is ludicrous reading today.

Another striking act of courage was the Governor's defiance of the labour unions in 1922, when they asked him to adopt the union scale of wages for all State work. No trimming here; he said *"No"* flatly—and told them to take their case to the legislature. Again, he does not hesitate to admit that he has made a mistake, as when he helped to bind the University of Maryland and the State Agricultural College in holy wedlock, and subsequently aided them in procuring a divorce. He vetoes freely, vetoes well, without personal bias, and states clearly his reasons. Politics never enters into them; he has even induced the legislature to print his vetoes as part of the volume dealing with each session's laws. On a single day of April, 1927, he vetoed ninety bills while approving one hundred and seventy-six others —the Maryland Legislature still grinds out its grist of bills, though there is nothing as significant as oysters and gasoline in all of them. His power to commute sentences and pardon criminals he uses with similar fidelity to his trust. For each decision he publishes succinct but clear reasons—it is amazing how often he records his belief that the infallible courts have erred.

But even on the banks of the Severn some of the dangerous bacilli that come with office-holding affect one's blood. Once Governor Ritchie struck out fiercely and wrongly. Mr. H. C. Byrd, assistant to the president of the University of Maryland, denounced the Gover-

nor and the politicians for their alleged failure to support the financial policies of the university in the interest
of the higher education. The gentleman from Annapolis went white and denied to Mr. Byrd "the right to
speak on such an occasion in a groundless as well as
personally offensive way of me as long as I am Governor of the State of which the university is but one department." Even the Baltimore *Sun,* whose editors are
popularly charged with bringing the Governor up by
hand, baulked at this. "There is not room in Maryland," it said, "for this kind of Prussianism," and it
termed the act what it was—a denial of the right of free
speech to a civil official, entirely out of keeping with
the Governor's repeated pleas for free speech and free
assembly. Mr. Ritchie remains to this day unconvinced.
Since it was, fortunately, a first and only offence, we
may justifiably suspend sentence. But it gives a shock to
one who recalls certain changes that took place in
Woodrow Wilson as he continued to hold office, for it
reads like the beginning of the familiar delusions of
majesty to which office-holders are so susceptible.

Now, ladies and gentlemen, how does Governor
Ritchie really stand on the problems vital to liberals?
The answer is that he is of the conservative period of
Grover Cleveland, harping upon the single string of
States' rights. There is no clear-cut lining-up for per-
sonal as against property rights. He has not even de-
clared himself on foreign issues—though he gave a
party allegiance to the Wilson doctrines in 1920, in-

cluding the League of Nations. As to our wrongdoings
in the Caribbean he has been silent—frankly because
he has been steeped in local issues and found no time
for other questions. Unlike Mr. Cleveland, he does not
get excited about our tariff ills—far worse though they
be than in Cleveland's day. For his legal mind the great
issue is the encroachment of the federal government
upon the powers of the individual State, an issue which
died—for the average American—in 1865. That is why
he opposes the proposed federal control of education,
the proposed child-labour amendment to the Constitution, and, like Al Smith, the federal inheritance tax and
federal prohibition. He is a Wet by conviction, but
would, like Senator Borah, have both parties face and
not dodge the liquor issue, since "all human experience
shows" to him that one cannot enforce a uniform liquor
law. For him the future of America is at stake; "the
democracy our fathers discovered [!] seems to me to
rest not on standardized regulations prescribed by the
Union, but strong self-governing States directed by
strong self-governing peoples." He even prays for a
permanent House of Governors in order to uphold
States' rights.

He trembles at the sight of "the mass of liberty-
effacing laws being inflicted on the people" in Washington, thus centralizing all power in the District of
Columbia. He shudders at the thought that if you can
get the votes of 2,316 members of the legislatures
of thirty-six States for a Constitutional Amendment
those thirty-six States can impose their will on the re-

maining twelve, and he wisely demands a State referendum before any legislature shall be allowed to vote
on a proposed federal amendment. He, too, uses the
old slogan of a "government of law in place of a government of men." He protests against the inclination to
"transform the moral ideals of the few into the legal
obligations of all." "Our Government," he insists, "has
become the most regulatory of the Western World,
outside of Russia and Italy." "Inspectors and spies
and official regulators follow the one-hundred-per-cent
American from the day he draws his first nourishment
from his inspected mother's breast." Progressives, he
avers, should achieve their will by "the slow processes
of State action." He opposes the consideration of an
issue on terms merely of morals; it should be in terms
of law and government. Otherwise government "becomes
a scheme for social control and for the regulation of
personal conduct and relations." Most important of all,
he has found that "if we can develop free cities in free
States there need be no fear as to the future of democracy in this free nation." In the growing hostility between city and country and their class-consciousness he
has, curiously enough, discovered the "probable" reason
for the underlying causes of "such movements as that
of the Ku Klux Klan, or Volsteadism, or fundamental-
ism"!

As for business, he stands squarely with Andrew
Mellon and every big-business highbinder in both parties. He trusts (June 10, 1927) the country "may hope
for the dawn of a political era in which business will

write for itself, and share in writing for mankind, a
new charter of safety and sanity, of liberty and human
rights." He wants business freed from political control
—though he believes in rigid regulation of railroads
and other public utilities, and is an advocate of saving
for the people of Maryland their natural resources. But
in May, 1923, he did not hesitate, as Governor, to interfere with one sacred private business by urging a
public boycott of sugar in order to bring down the then
exorbitant price. "Anything that dulls the free enterprise of business is destructive of both social and economic progress." While he admits that combinations of
capital have at times achieved domination over State
and national policies, making it necessary for the State
to interfere, he holds that the pendulum has swung too
far the other way. "Hence, we must"—almost in the
exact words of Andrew Mellon—"take government out
of business except where the great heritage of equality
of opportunity necessitates its presence." Even then
the government "should abandon all business which is
competitive with private enterprises." Finally, after this
playing with words, Governor Ritchie asserts, *ad nau-
seam*, that "that government governs best which governs least."

As a saving grace, Governor Ritchie is realistic
enough to understand the effect upon the public of all
this talking. "Speak of these things," he admits, "and
the average man is likely to yawn and pass it all up as
political claptrap." He confesses that "there is nothing
mysterious in politics except sometimes the flubdubbery

of politicians," and he ingenuously thinks that it is time that both great parties which monopolize the exciting game of humbugging the American people should be convinced that "political hypocrisy, political buncombe, and political cowardice are no longer political assets." When they do it will be quieter than ever along the Severn.

Has Governor Ritchie let his fondness for striking the bonds from the limbs of our enchained and sadly crippled big business affect his administration of the State? Progressives and organized labour charged that he did in the matter of the Conowingo Dam now being constructed on the Susquehanna River, declaring that he sold out Maryland to Pennsylvania and the Pennsylvania Railroad. So Conowingo formed a major issue in the Governor's last campaign. His critics declared that the power should have been used to benefit Baltimore exclusively, to lower rates in competition with the existing company, and to furnish cheap power for industry, and protested against that clause in the charter of the Conowingo Dam project which for ever excluded Baltimore from any benefit from this tremendous development. This charter was sold by one company to another for $4,000,000 which money the protestants felt should have gone into Maryland's treasury. To this the Governor replied that the project would cost $52,-000,000, which would have to be repaid in fifteen years under the Constitution—something beyond the financial powers of Maryland; that two-thirds of the reservoir is on Pennsylvania territory; that current could not be delivered in Baltimore from Conowingo at a price low enough to compete with Baltimore's steam-made power; that there would thus be no saving in money or any increased productivity in Baltimore. For the Governor it was also a case of government ownership versus private ownership. His arguments did not convince his opponents, who still dispute his facts and disagree with the Baltimore *Sun* in its assertion that the voters, whose consent would have been necessary, would never have approved a project for Maryland to go it alone; that if they had there would have been no market for all the power a 300,000 horse-power plant could produce. They also bring out the fact that Frank Furst, a Democratic boss who supports Governor Ritchie, won a contract for $12,000,000 for building the dam and a $5,000,000 one for moving tracks of the Pennsylvania Railroad without competitive bidding. However one feels about government ownership, it is impossible to believe that Governor Ritchie took the position he did for any other than conscientious reasons. He may or may not have erred, but his honesty seems to the writer beyond question.

There, ladies and gentlemen, our inspection of this Presidential possibility ends—we thank you for your attention. Perhaps his own words characterize him best: "I don't claim to be a crusader. I don't want to be fifty years ahead of my time, but I want to belong to that class that is willing to plug along—to do something, to get somewhere, and leave the world better off than if we hadn't lived." You see he must once have gone to Sunday school! He is right about himself. There is no reform leader here, but a man with excellent brains, with his emotions completely under control, and his superficial economic views profoundly affected by his surroundings and his position in life. He is as ingenuous as he is sincere, as kindly as he is candid, and without malice toward his enemies. The latter admit that he has high character, a fine mind, and complete absence of pose. He pretends, they concede, not at all; but they apply to him the stock adjectives "cold, selfish, ungrateful, without real belief in principles"—is there a successful public man to whom they are not applied? Surely most of them are here unjust.

Any President should be proud and happy to have an Albert C. Ritchie in his Cabinet. He stands well, too, when one compares him with the last two nominees of his party, Governor Cox and John W. Davis, and would draw votes better than they. But a Moses to lead the Democrats out of their Slough of Despond; a Grover Cleveland, rugged, powerful, and determined, he is not. No iron has yet entered his soul and no sense of wrong has yet set his generous heart to quivering with an uncontrollable rage to wipe out an injustice. He visualizes no large scheme for human betterment; he has no map of life which equips him to deal with the economic problems that big business is creating under our noses, challenging, where it is not corrupting, the federal government itself.

A. VICTOR DONAHEY

Governor of Ohio

GOVERNOR A. VICTOR DONAHEY of Ohio is as much a man of the plain people as Al Smith himself. If you do not believe it, go hear him pound a mighty fist upon the gubernatorial table in the Capitol at Columbus, and see him spit tobacco juice—like Al again—over the carpet to the accompaniment of many "by Gods" and other liberties with the King's English. Watch him, moreover, settle a difficult problem in the straightforward way which so often distinguishes Governor Smith. Having led plain, simple lives, the approach of both men to trying situations is usually direct and so completely lacking in the guile and finesse of the so-called "higher type" of statesman that observers often believe they have a touch of genius. Governor Donahey shows it particularly when under great stress. Then he acts vigorously, effectively, and, again, simply, so that the people of Ohio think they have a Governor who is on the job and proposes to administer his office with integrity, force, and courage. In consequence they have three times elected this Democrat Governor of a Republican State—the only Governor to have served three times in the history of Ohio. He was elected in 1922, 1924, and 1926, and in 1924 ran 587,093 votes ahead of John W. Davis, the Democratic candidate for President. He is renowned as a vote-getter because Ohio's electorate feels about him as New York's does about Al Smith—that he is a fine administrator who plays the political game honestly and squarely, besides being in himself the personification of the masses.

So it has come to pass that "Vic" Donahey, as he prefers to be known, himself really and earnestly believes that he is just a common, honest servant of the people trying to serve Ohio in a plain and humble way. "Even to intimate friends in his private office," writes one who for years has watched the Governor at work, "he is on parade. To newspapermen who have long known him from the ground up to the top of his six hefty feet, he is constantly making speeches and uttering campaign platitudes. He is ever the avenger of public wrong." But the newspapermen like him, as in New York they like Governor Smith, and for the same reasons, and so he, too, has a friendly and colourful press. The plain man of the people gives opportunity for endless Sunday special articles and equally numerous photographs of Governor "Vic" whittling away at the bird-houses which he makes to give to friends at Christmas, of Governor "Vic" in summer fishing and cooking —he is an expert at broiling steaks and barbecuing— and tramping and talking and laughing with his neighbours on the shores of Indian Lake, where they all live simple lives in modest cottages destitute of plumbing. No golf for the Governor. That would be out of the part, and so would any more fashionable resort than this rather hot one on the banks of a reservoir in northwestern Ohio.

Children? Yes, indeed, and here he is ahead of Al Smith, for he has ten living out of twelve, and three grandchildren, although he is not yet fifty-five years old. What could prove better his complete fitness as a candidate? "Babies is [*sic*] my long suit," he remarked at his last inauguration, when the movie-camera men were taking pictures of him, Mrs. Donahey, and the youngest grandchild, then three weeks old, under specially provided Klieg lights. It would seem also to have been Mrs. Donahey's, although a Governor about to be inaugurated apparently forgets a trifle like that. But those who watch the Governor closely know that Mrs. Donahey's part in bringing her consort to the front is concerned with many other, if less important, things than bringing babies into the world, rearing the entire quiver, and teaching music to her daughters. The Governor did his best day's work when he married his wife. Here again I must quote from a friendly observer: "Mrs. Donahey is a marvel of tireless energy and good taste. She has such a deep vein of sincerity and makes him believe so in himself that he has acquired the habit. She is a charming hostess and modest in her dress and social life." It is she who helped to make his inaugural ceremonies of the simplest and it is she, beyond doubt, who has kept the public from a wider understanding of certain of her husband's foibles and pretences that would lend themselves easily to fun-making and ridicule.

So there in Columbus sits Governor "Vic," favoured of the gods. He, with his Irish name, and all the elements of popularity in him, is actually not a Catholic but a Methodist. That is his supreme good fortune— next to Mrs. Donahey. For there is no greater stronghold of Methodism than Ohio, which, for all its large cities with their foreign population, remains a State of rural communities and small towns and villages with all the hypocrisies and all the conventionalities of Main Street; where frills are few; where there are still deacons to be shocked by the wickedness of the great cities and the horrible Bolsheviks with their loose ideas about marriage. For them it is a source of untold joy that, in a dreadfully changing world, Ohio, personified by her Methodist-ten-child Governor, champion of the home, the family, and the state, faces four-square to all winds and bows to none.

As a public speaker Governor Donahey plays safe, like so many distinguished contemporaries, and takes refuge in the well-known and highly popular platitudes. Here are some excerpts from the speech that he delivered to the National Christian Endeavor Convention in Cleveland on June 3, 1927:

> *It must not be forgotten, however, that liberty does not mean lawlessness. Liberty to make our laws does not give us license to break them. Liberty to make our laws commands a duty to observe them ourselves and enforce obedience among all others. Liberty is responsibility; responsibility is duty, and that duty is to preserve the exceptional liberty we enjoy within the law, for the law, and by the law. The forefathers placed this precious inheritance in our hands for safe-keeping and passed on.*

We, in turn, must place it in the hands of those who follow us, enlarged, of course, but unprofaned.

Therefore we must inculcate in the youth of our land a firm and abiding faith in our destiny and mission as a nation. We must teach them that the greatest responsibility which God in His wisdom has given to His creatures is the responsibility of self-government. We must teach them that self-government is a civil agreement to protect the health, peace, and safety of the people and promote their happiness. We must teach them that self-government means politics, a field in which every loyal citizen should take an active part.

And again, the following nonsense:

We must teach our children that there are four cornerstones upon which to rear a worth-while citizenship—morality, education, patriotism, and discipline. Morality and education should go down life's pathway hand in hand. We must call attention of our young people to the fact that there are three pests afflicting society: The first is an inordinate desire for pleasure; the second is disrespect for law and constituted authority, and the third is easy money without honest effort. These three pests cause the incarceration of 200,000 men, women, boys, and girls in our correctional and penal institutions each year in the United States. We must teach them that the inherent birthright of an American who honestly toils is that he shall receive a wage sufficient to intelligently maintain his family, educate his children, and lay by a mite for a rainy day.

Our boys and girls are our most priceless possessions. The boys and girls of today will be the business men and women of tomorrow. Remember, no community, state, or nation is going to be any better than its boys and girls.

Our boys and girls are our hope for the future. In my opinion the greatest inheritance a boy or girl can have is to have been reared in a religious family.

If this does not put Governor Donahey into the class with Calvin Coolidge as a champion disseminator of platform banality, surely nothing else could. He is one of our greatest propagandists for honesty, simplicity, and fidelity, and has, therefore, no time for controversial questions. Indeed, viewed at this distance, he is but a second-rate opportunist.

Why should not the Presidential lightning strike this man? There would be the best of chances that it would, Ohio being the mother of so many Presidents, good, bad, and indifferent, if only he were a Republican. "Vic" would be an ideal compromise candidate if he were not under the other banner. For he, too, has lived in inexpensive homes, and he, too, is frugal and has all the small-town virtues. He also once called out the militia in a crisis, and is a tremendous devotee of economy in public life. Honestly he believes that modern governments are over-organized, that there are too many boards, commissions, and bureaus, and he has abolished a number of them. Did he not, as State auditor, cut down the $2 meals which State officials allowed themselves to $1.25? Is he not credited with trimming a Lucullan baked potato out of the expense account of an august appellate court judge? Why should the Democrats not turn to this man whom Senator Thomas of Oklahoma declares to be "young, vigorous, honest, independent, fundamentally sound, and a teetotaler"? Has he not a printers' union card in his pocket? And is he not supported by all the religious groups in his State? Besides, Mr. Donahey comes from a pivotal State. How can party managers overlook such a man of all the virtues who, with unemployment abroad in the land, would have every trump in his hand?

As for his record as Governor, it is quite striking. He has consistently carried on a campaign for the reduction of taxes in a way to win the heart of the hardest of financiers. He has vetoed many tax bills as well as other measures—no fewer than seventy-four in 1923, thirty-four in 1925, and thirty in 1927. He vetoed the first gasoline-tax bill passed, although he knew the legislature would pass it over his veto, and it is now on the books to stay. Despite the fact that he is the darling of the deacons and the dominies, he bravely vetoed the bill which was to Christianize all Ohio by compelling the daily reading of ten verses of the Bible in all the public schools of the State, in which thereafter all pupils above the fourth grade were to be birched, if necessary, into memorizing the Ten Commandments. This bill was actively supported by the Ku Klux Klan. It was lobbied through in one of the bitterest religious fights waged in the Ohio Legislature in many years. It was introduced by a farmer, and the farmers, "Vic's" special friends, were all for it, but the Governor killed it with some fine truth-telling about this being a country which was "founded out of the hope and desire for religious freedom." He has never openly attacked the Klan but he has also never truckled to it.

Always he vetoed with a flourish of trumpets, restating his demand for economy and his fears that pay rolls will be padded and public funds exhausted. Only cynics suggest that some of these vetoes are unwise, or that the expenses of the Governor's Highway Department, far from showing retrenchment, are abnormally high. What would you? The Governor vowed that if he were elected he would "get Ohio out of the mud." Here is a campaign promise that has been kept, and every motorist rejoices. Why should anybody, therefore, question the cost? Or notice that road maintenance charges are going up every year? Cannot a good Governor be permitted to be inconsistent and illogical once in a while?

The Governor has been, and is, both inconsistent and illogical—quite often. Like many another—almost every other—politician, he has been accused of instability of purpose, of not knowing his own mind, of failing to keep promises; why does not every public man wear on his person an automatic promise-recorder? A classic example of this phase of the Governor is his pushing through the legislature by means of special messages a bill providing a better and speedier method of recounting ballots in contested elections. He was the saviour of the people. But—when it came time to sign the bill after the legislature had done his much-heralded bidding, he discovered some minor features he disliked and vetoed it. The very next day he wailed aloud and promised by the hairs of his head to reconvene the legislature at once in special session—economy be hanged! Then he found that would get him into trouble on a prohibition issue, and the special session still awaits his call.

But, as has been said, the time comes when the Governor acts with speed and vigour and plain common sense and deservedly gains much praise thereby. Take the rioting at Niles in November, 1924, two days before the Governor's first re-election. Klansmen and Catholics began to attack each other, and for three days the situation became serious. The sheriff called for troops, but the Governor declared that he would send them only when shooting occurred. Press and public waited to see how he would act, with the opening of the polls but forty-eight hours off. The shooting began and the answer came. Troops, mobilized in the interim, were sent at once by the Governor, who had never left his desk by day or night during the crisis. His great majority at the polls proved again how quickly the electorate rewards the prompt and brave acts of a candidate.

An even finer story, which illustrates best of all Governor Donahey's simple, straightforward way of tackling difficult problems, is that which deals with the southeastern Ohio coal-fields. They have been without hope or work since April, 1927, when the mines were shut down, chiefly because of the competition of the unorganized West Virginia fields. There had been little work for months before. The shutdown drove the men to despair. Like all miners they have large families and for years have been earning at best much less than the minimum requirement for an American family. Is it any wonder that after a while the hotheads among those whose children were starving shot at sheriffs and mine guards, damaged tipples, set fire to mines, and planted dynamite? Soon frantic long-distance telephone calls reached Governor Donahey and his adjutant-general, Frank D. Henderson, begging, demanding troops. The Governor sent none; he took a new chew of tobacco and tried something else. Being a man of the people he realized how often the arrival of troops has precipitated hostilities instead of preventing them. What did he do? He sent twenty-one officers to Jefferson, Athens, Hocking, and other coal-fields—not one in uniform, not one wearing a badge of authority, not one showing a revolver or uttering a threat. Each officer entered as a friend of both sides, calling on the starving miners in their desolate shacks, and warning them against violence, and similarly warning mine superintendents against uncontrolled mine guards who might arouse the miners to fury. Then, after a thorough survey, they reported to Columbus the results of their observations: children slowly starving to death; six thousand in dire need; fifteen thousand trying to live on one skimpy meal a day, most of them unable to go to school because of lack of shoes—this in Ohio in the fall of the prosperity year, 1927.

What did the Governor and General Henderson do? Sit back with hands folded like the recreant Red Cross and do nothing? Utter pious wishes and deplore platitudinously this new conflict between capital and labour? They did not. They appealed for food, clothing, and money and sent, not machine-guns but supply trains to feed starving American children who could get food in no other way. The rescuing militia set up stores in the schoolhouses and announced that every child who came to school would receive potatoes, meat, vegetables, bread, and butter. Said that humane soldier, General Henderson: "The children did not come into the world of their own accord. Once they are here, it is the duty of the state to see that they are fed and clothed and put to school. When they see their brothers and sisters slowly starving they are likely to blame the government, saying, 'You exist only for the rich and not for us who are hungry.' We are not asking whether they are miners' children, or what is their religion or colour. All the Governor cares about is that they are fed and clothed. This is not a miners' relief or even a miners' children's relief. It is a children's relief." In a brief time General Henderson established one hundred and three relief stations feeding about 7,500 children daily and supplied 18,000 with clothes—all this done by National Guardsmen performing charitable and social duties instead of practicing battle formations, or policing the property of mine-owners, themselves warm, well-fed, and sleek while starving children faded away. Distinguished service crosses? Not for General Henderson and Governor Donahey. They merely answered the heartrending appeals of little children. But they well deserve the decorations.

Another unusual use of the National Guard by Governor Donahey was in connection with the murder in July, 1926, of Don R. Mellett, the Canton, Ohio, editor who was killed for attacking the alliance of the local authorities and the underworld. "There should be no delay in meting out justice," the Governor declared. "It should be swift and just. . . . Let every one know that the State through my office stands on that basis." He used National Guard officers and State prohibition officials to help unravel the crime because he had no other State employees he could employ. A year later when there were labour troubles at Adena he again refused to furnish troops on demand of the mayor. Instead, he authorized the sheriff to use as many deputies as he needed. The sheriff did so and the trouble soon ended.

As for prohibition, teetotaler that he is, Governor Donahey, too, can dodge issues connected with it. The Supreme Court of the United States having declared unconstitutional the fee system by which judges of certain courts were paid out of costs in cases of conviction, the temperance forces pushed a bill through the legislature the purpose of which was by some hocuspocus to get around this decision. The vetoing Governor Donahey permitted the bill to become a law subject to a popular referendum, while stating that he did not approve of its terms. Thereupon he kept as quiet about this issue as Calvin Coolidge on the oil scandals. His Prohibition Commissioner was one of the protagonists of the bill, but Governor Donahey had nothing to say, not even when by the greatest victory (447,000) ever recorded in an Ohio referendum the bill was buried. On the other hand, when the Governor heard that Governor Smith had approved a bill repealing the prohibition enforcement laws in New York, he roundly declared that he would veto such a bill the instant it was submitted to him.

When it comes to nation-wide issues, Governor Donahey's resemblance to Governor Smith is again marked—both have many blank pages to fill. True, Governor Donahey is known to desire an "adequate navy" —nobody knows what that may be; tariff revision by a bi-partisan board, if such a thing be possible; and rigorous enforcement of all United States laws. For neither man does Europe appear to exist. When it comes to the question of social and political agitation by liberals or "reds," Governor Donahey seems to me to trail far behind his New York rival. I sometimes doubt if he understands that there are liberals and "reds" and that people get excited over social and labour evils. Governor Smith has stood up admirably in favour of the old-fashioned American doctrines. Governor Donahey's position is not as praiseworthy—if it can be praised at all. It was he who shivered in his boots when President Harding died and declared publicly that he "feared that the United States would be swept by a wave of unrest and that there would be grave uneasiness as a result of Harding's death." As will be remembered, only the "Ohio gang" suffered by Harding's timely decease. It was also Governor "Vic" Donahey who in December,

1925, in high dudgeon ordered the Board of Trustees of the Ohio State University to make a thorough house-cleaning because prohibition officials found a bottle or two in the cellar of an instructor's house. The guilty teacher's dismissal was ordered by the Governor without even waiting for a report, and he appears to have concurred heartily in the inquisition to which the Board of Trustees subjected every teacher who was charged with having a mind of his own, which extended to affiliation with liberal organizations, and subscriptions to journals like *The Nation* and the *New Republic*. Of course the Governor does not know that there is such a thing as academic freedom, and that people fight for it and against it.

In this incident the Methodist came out in the good Governor; for the hour he was the *Pontifex maximus* of Ohio. Politically he still is that, and apparently he may continue to be a satisfactory chief executive of the sadly besmirched State of Ohio as long as he wishes to be Governor Why not? Is he not an Elk, a Woodman, and a Knight of Pythias, as well as the teetotaling father of ten children?

THOMAS J. WALSH

A Great Prosecutor

*T*hen there is the Honourable Tom Walsh. We are all
*familiar with the Teapot Dome affair. The Stand-
ard Oil wanted Doheny and Sinclair removed from the
field of competition for valuable government leases
and Tom was put on the job backed by the publicity of
the oil and copper press. Thus Tom was made quite a
hero in the minds of the boobery. But there are some who
remember his Tory proclivities during the war; his
fatherhood of the Espionage Law; his General Leasing
Act of 1920 under which the oil interests looted the public domain; his support of the World Court and other
Wall Street foreign policies and his lead in the fight to
give the valuable Flathead power site to his straw boss
—the Montana Power Company. There is an important
difference between Al and Tom. Al believes in setting
up a State authority to operate and develop the hydro-
electric power sites of New York State. Tom believes in
giving the whole thing to the Montana Power Company.*

Here we have a thumb-nail picture of Senator
Walsh of Montana by a kindly and simple-minded Montana editor. Only a truly simple mind could possibly
believe that the revelation of the oil scandals was nothing more than a neat little Standard Oil plan to down
its rivals. As for the "oil and copper press," if there is
such, it was doubtless, like almost every important daily

in the East, bitterly denouncing Senator Walsh for "emptying the prisons," as the Republican National Committee put it, in order to besmirch such great and good men as Albert Fall, Charles Denby, Henry Daugherty, and Jess Smith. The unfortunate fix in which John D. Rockefeller, Jr., and the Standard Oil interests find themselves by reason of the activities of Harry M. Blackmer, now a resident of France, and Colonel R. W. Stewart is further proof that this group of capitalists was hoist by its own petard if it really instigated the Senate's oil activities.

As a matter of fact Senator Walsh and his Montana colleague, Senator Burton K. Wheeler, were from the beginning attacked by all save a few journals as "cowards," "slanderers," "scandal-mongers," "assassins of character." The New York *Times* accused them of acting like men "who are at heart enemies of lawful and orderly government." Every possible pressure was brought to bear upon them. If Senator Walsh was not indicted on trumped-up charges as was Senator Wheeler, that was probably due merely to luck and to the fact that he was revealing the oil rottenness while Senator Wheeler was probing into the Department of Justice. Both men stuck to their jobs and Senator Walsh is at this writing continuing to reveal new ramifications of the oil scandals, with Senator Nye as chairman of the committee. If ever men were tried and tested by fire these two from Montana were, and they stood the test magnificently. Here are two unpurchasable public servants who cannot be terrorized.

Senator Walsh will, in consequence of these inquiries, go down in history as a great prosecutor, because of his ability, his fairness, his tenacity, his tirelessness, his refusal to be beaten. The spectacular and the dramatic are both lacking in his make-up. Hence the general public never heard of him until 1923; hence his failure to make as much capital out of the original oil inquiry as he might have done. Not until he stumbled upon the incident of Mr. Doheny's paying $100,-000 in a black bag to Secretary Fall did the fireworks really begin to attract the attention of the public. Had he been less modest; had he had a real flair for publicity, Heaven only knows how sensational the matter could have been made. On that side he is totally undeveloped. He is, moreover, scrupulous in his methods as a prosecutor and, if anything, too polite. These traits doubtless account for his leaning over backward when Secretary Mellon was before him, and for his complimenting the Secretary for his refusal to accede to Will Hays's disreputable proposal that he should sell some of Mr. Sinclair's Liberty Bonds and donate the proceeds to the Republican National Committee as if they were his own gift. There were those who saw in this a weakening in the vigour of Mr. Walsh's rapier thrusts and who laid it to his Presidential candidacy. That may be, though proof is lacking. It is a fact, however, that instead of complimenting Secretary Mellon, Senator Walsh should have scored him for concealing Will Hays's proposal from the committee for several years. For this there is no excuse. Unfortunately, the servile portion of the daily press at once seized upon Mr. Walsh's kindly compliment and distorted it to mean that the Montana Senator gave to Mr. Mellon a clean bill of health for the whole transaction.

Perhaps even a brilliant prosecutor must be entitled to one error. It would, of course, be a catastrophe if he should weaken now that the Presidential bee is buzzing around his bonnet—amazing how Presidential mirages lure on the best of men! In Senator Walsh's case it is perfectly true, as he must be aware, that he has many of the qualities a President ought to possess. Whether the public has known it or not, Mr. Walsh has for fifteen years been one of the great lawyers in the Senate, called upon because of his attainments to help in drafting the prohibition and woman-suffrage amendments to the Constitution, and, by his Democratic colleagues, to formulate the case against the seating of Senator Truman H. Newberry of Michigan. It was he who led the successful fight to confirm Louis D. Brandeis as a justice of the Supreme Court upon nomination of Woodrow Wilson, and it is said of his report upon Mr. Brandeis that it "remains a model of persuasiveness and finality." Mr. Walsh was likewise the author of that part of the Federal Reserve Act which compels national banks to subscribe for stock in the Federal Reserve Bank.

This Senator may be a creature of the Montana Power Company, but he happens to be the man who has just made a magnificent fight to have the whole financial status of public-utility corporations, especially

electric- and water-power ones, investigated, not by the
packed Federal Trade Commission but by a committee
of the Senate with, perhaps, himself as chief inquisitor.
The most powerful lobby Washington has ever seen,
with endless money, defeated that proposal—there can
be no question that the Montana Power Company acted
with its brother electric-utility corporations in opposing
the move. But there the Senator stood hour after hour,
making a grand if losing fight. Overborne by the lobby,
he went down firing grape to the end—the admiration
of all who beheld him.

To call Mr. Walsh a creature of the corporations
is an absurd allegation, for he was a bitter opponent of
the all-powerful Anaconda Copper Company before he
entered the Senate, and that company defeated him for
his seat when he tried for it in 1910; he had to wait
until 1912 for election, since when he has served unin-
terruptedly. Never before had Mr. Walsh held office.
He went straight from his lawyer's desk to the Senate
chamber and, thanks to the system of preferential voting in Montana, he owed his election to nobody. Then
he was fifty years old. Today he is sixty-six—near the
deadline for candidates, but obviously at the very height
of his physical and mental powers. See him in action as
prosecutor and you can never forget him. I once heard
him open fire upon a Progressive Senator who had just
arrived that day to take the oath of office. The fledgling
Senator-elect had been outspoken in his criticism of the
Federal Reserve system. The dinner-table conversation
ceased as Senator Walsh took him in hand. A more in-

cisive, merciless, and searing cross-examination I never listened to. In five minutes every man in the room was thanking his stars he was not the recipient of the Montana Senator's attentions. The Senator-elect stood to his guns and, as Mr. Walsh has since admitted, did extremely well. After that baptism of fire his debut in the Senate must have seemed an easy plunge.

As prosecutor for a Senate committee Mr. Walsh is, if anything, more alarming. He has a way of regarding a witness for some moments before putting a question. During this time he stares steadily under his heavy eyebrows at his victim with a concentration of attention enough to make the unfortunate prepare for the worst. He seems to be revolving the matter over and over in his mind, pondering, pondering—and then he strikes with projectile power. Usually he is entirely calm and collected; he does not browbeat or badger. He is the gentleman at all times, never the sensationalist, but you feel as if he had the finality and inevitability of a slow-moving glacier. You do not need to be convinced that here is a man who weighs every argument before making up his mind—only to become immovable when his decision is reached. He has nothing of the muck-raker about him, and no hostility whatever to the corporations or to the existing economic order. The picture drawn of him by the metropolitan dailies as a reckless defamer was as wide of the mark as any shot could possibly go. It would be impossible to find anywhere a more conscientious, a more judicially minded prosecutor. These were all qualities which stood out when he was chair-

man of the 1924 Democratic National Convention, and
they won him the regard and admiration of all the delegates to that political dog-fight. During all those exhausting days he was calm, cool, and spotless, dressed
for the occasion and quite immaculate.

But Senator Walsh's judicial quality is second to
his thirst for facts and his incredible ability to work
relentlessly and unsparingly. Take the Teapot Dome
case. It was Walsh who followed Edward B. McLean to
Florida, and Fall to New Mexico, and who broke down
Fall's alibi by making McLean confess that he had not
lent the $100,000 to Fall. Senator Lenroot of Wiscon-
sin sat as chairman of the committee with every line of
his face and figure showing how deeply he was dis-
turbed by Mr. Walsh's activities; if it had rested with
him precious few facts would have come out. Walsh,
by the mere force of his efforts, threw Lenroot into the
shade. With no help from any individual or from any
department of the government, he created his case day
after day, always relentless, always optimistic, rarely
being thrown off the scent. Those were hours to make
the best detective stories seem tame. When it was all
over Mr. Walsh again summed up the case in a report
which, as Charles Merz has pointed out in the *Independent,* "is a model of fairness, generosity, and good
temper. When the Supreme Court of the United States
wrote its decisions more than three years later, every
fact as Walsh stated it was formally confirmed."

Why, then, is Thomas J. Walsh not available as a
Presidential candidate? He is a Dry; his character, as

we know, is beyond assail; his ability is unquestioned. To this the answer is his age, his religion (he is a Catholic), and the fact that Montana is one of the least important States when it comes to a Presidential election, since it has only four electoral votes—the usual trick is to choose a man whose State is important or pivotal. The Democratic politicians naturally feel that if a Catholic is to be chosen it should be Governor Smith since he is so much better known and is a better campaigner, with a great record as an executive and administrator. The reasoning is sound, yet Senator Walsh has at bottom a better mind and a better trained one, in some respects a wider vision. The one wins respect and admiration; the other admiration and affection and the sympathy of the masses. Both have their records in foreign affairs to make, save that Walsh was a leader in the fight for the League of Nations and the World Court, while Smith has accepted them in perfunctory fashion, doubtless because it was in his party's platform. Beyond that the indications are that Senator Walsh leans toward the imperialist policy—he did and does support the Espionage Act which muzzled the country and will do so again, automatically, whenever the President declares that a state of war exists. This must be offset, however, by his report "unhesitatingly condemning" Attorney General Palmer's raids upon aliens and radicals, that lawlessness by men in high office which Senator Walsh declared to be "the lawless acts of a mob"; "a deliberate usurpation" [of authority].

This report gained in effectiveness because it was written by a Democrat in denunciation of a faithless and lawless Democratic Cabinet officer.

Senator Walsh is, naturally, without Governor Smith's record of wide and effective sympathy for social reforms. But he has struck some telling blows for labour. His first speech in the Senate was on behalf of the bill to make jury trials essential in instances of contempt of court in injunction cases. He deserves the credit for the law forbidding the use of federal funds to prosecute labour unions under the anti-trust laws and he was in charge of the enactment of those clauses of the Clayton Act which specifically exempted all farm and labour organizations from prosecution under the Sherman law. For this, labour ought to be permanently grateful.

It must also be remembered that he, the strict Constitutionalist, has advocated the proposed child-labour amendment to the Constitution which has so horrified the Southern States'-rights wing of his party. Striking, too, is the fact that he heartily favoured woman suffrage; few men of his legal training and type of mind did. He has also been a sturdy fighter for a low tariff. While these things indicate a mind that is far from rigidly fixed, they do not stamp him a great reformer or a great liberal. Radical, as has been said, he is not. His hope is always for bettering the government by adhering to the plan of unveiling the rascals in the hope that the electorate will turn them out. It is doubtful if he knows

much about the great economic currents abroad or realizes the extent to which political government has been
undermined or has broken down.

Enter the Senate any day and you may see at work
this dignified, quiet-mannered gentleman—one can use
this term of a man who came up from the ranks of the
very poor without danger of its being misunderstood.
His speeches you will find replete with facts, packed
with close reasoning, but devoid of the qualities that
appeal to the galleries. Even when he waxes warm there
is an air of diffidence, if not shyness, about him. Yet
when he strikes, his blows are stunning because of his
eternal reliance upon facts. So in the debate on March
29, 1928, when Senator Robinson of Indiana endeavoured to connect the Wilson Administration with the
oil scandals, Senator Walsh immediately riddled his
charges by the most painstaking rebuttal, citing figures,
dates, documents, quotations from speeches made years
ago—facts, facts, facts. Not content with that he characteristically had three great maps of the naval oil reserves hung upon the rear wall of the Senate Chamber
and, so the dispatches reported, "with a pointer, like a
school-teacher, illustrated his points as he went minutely
into the history of the reserves to refute Robinson." Incidentally, Senator Walsh declared in his address that
in Mr. Robinson's place a gentleman would apologize
for his reckless words, and in demanding this, he said,
he did not appeal to Senatorial courtesy. It is a dangerous pastime to fall foul of this high-minded master of
every subject he undertakes to know about!

Puritan in his make-up and his unsmiling personal austerity, Senator Walsh has made his name a synonym for private and public honesty and for ceaseless hostility to privilege and to the control of the government by the masters of big business. Some day a Catholic will—and must—find his way into the White House. The country may consider itself fortunate if that man should prove to be another of the type of Thomas J. Walsh.

CHARLES CURTIS

Jockey and Senator

"THE situation is tapering down to Tim," said
Thomas C. Platt, boss of New York, when asked
once what were Lieutenant Governor Timothy L. Wood-
ruff's chances for the governorship. Mr. Platt was
wrong. The situation did not taper down to Tim, for it
could not; it was too preposterous a proposal. If the
Republican Presidential contest of 1928 should taper
down to Charles Curtis it would simply mean that cowardice, timidity, and moral bankruptcy had done their
worst. His nomination would be the apotheosis of me-
diocrity; Mr. Babbitt would thereby come into his own.

Mr. Curtis is well aware of his own limitations. He
has no delusions of grandeur, no hope or expectation
that by a sudden outburst of oratory or statesmanship
he could force himself upon any convention. He hoisted
his lightning-rod for the Presidential bolt to strike it
because he felt himself in precisely the same situation
that Mr. Harding was in 1920—Mr. Harding had folded
his tents and was stealing away when fate in the shape
of the bosses did him and his country the ill turn of
picking him as the choice of the convention. Mr. Curtis
apparently believed that in their search for a thoroughly
colourless but deserving man who has no enemies the Republican bosses must inevitably turn to him. Does he
not come from Kansas, a farming State, that lives in

history because John Brown spent a few weeks there and because it was the permanent home of "sockless Jerry Simpson"? Is he not the only Senator of American Indian blood? Has he not been the most obedient floor leader of the Senate since the death of Henry Cabot Lodge? What would you have? A man of brilliant parts, colourful attainments, charm, and wide vision? What nonsense! Party candidates are chosen not because they have such qualities but because they are without them. Roosevelt was an accident; Wilson the exception.

Mr. Curtis is well within his rights. History and precedent fight for him. So he sees himself the boy standing on the convention deck whence all but him have fled in dire defeat. His god is the Process of Elimination. Kansas knows that Curtis is a great man; knows that in his sixteen years as a Congressman no Representative ever worked so hard for his constituents, called so many of them by their first names, or mailed as many packages of seeds, or as many letters, necessary and unnecessary, as he—once upon a time he received 1,400 a day and answered most of them by the aid of a devoted sister and three or four form replies. As Senator, too, no one has kept his political fences in better repair. Then why should not unsurpassed industry be rewarded? Is there no sense of gratitude in his party? When he first came to the House there was only one other Republican from Kansas. Now there are eight.

Senator Curtis is as faithful and as devoted to his party as he is dull and dumb. "Yes" and "No" are his favourite answers to queries and he resents questions not put in such a way that he can reply by a monosyllable. He was early told to talk little in Congress and to saw wood. He did both; therefore he was bound to rise, and he rose. Colourful? Only in his ancestry and his early years. He is one-eighth aboriginal American, the Indian Chief Pawhuskie, a Kaw, having been his great-great-grandfather and Princess White Plume, a great-grandmother as well as the wife of a French trader. With French and Indian blood there should have been produced a really high-bred racer; instead of which we have the most patient and plodding of political wheel-horses, one who has never yet sulked or lain back in the traces, or lifted his heels, or tossed his head, or threatened to bolt. Only the crack of the party whip, or the sound of its dinner bell, ever moves him. You could not make him buck or rear if you built a fire under him. Such is heredity! You would swear, if you did not know what strains were in him, that his pedigree read at every generation post "out of Main Street, by Bourgeois."

Is this an undemocratic aspersion of the great lower middle-class? By no means. I admit that the soviet which comprises the Kansas farmer, merchant, post-master, the Elks and Shriners and Moose and Rotarians in good standing, is entitled to its representative in the Senate. The doubt is whether at this precise juncture in American history the hour calls for their Charles Curtis, now sixty-eight years of age, in the White House. As a candidate he runs true to type in that his beginnings were of the humblest. But they were spiced with the

thrill of the race-track! For this darling of the Kansas
W. C. T. U. really was a boy jockey from his tenth to
his sixteenth year—he who as prosecuting attorney at
twenty-four won his way to Congress in the early nine-
ties by enforcing prohibition in his town. He closed
eighty-eight saloons in thirty days and in four years
obtained 103 convictions of criminals out of a possible
108. But he did line his pockets with the godless money
of the race-tracks for seven long boyish years. Then
came his mother, Permelia, a Massachusetts Puritan
by descent, to his rescue. Charley heard her heartfelt
plea for a better life; he left his horses, the ring, the big
stakes, the quick rewards; he bade adieu to the book-
makers, trainers, hostlers, and track-side easy-marks.
Resolutely from that day to this he has trod the straight
and narrow path. One of Marryat's heroes was tattooed
in boyhood with the King's broad arrow to signify that
he was for life the "King's Own." If Kansas had a
broad arrow it would not be needed on Charles Curtis's
shoulder. Kansas and Kansas virtue are stamped all over
him.

So Charles went back to school, quite unsuspecting
that he had exchanged the race-track for the Senate and
that the rewards which are supposed to come to all good
little boys were to be his. The years sped by in deep
domestic felicity and then Charley was back with the
horses—not the race-track, for he remembered his promise to his mother. They were hack horses that lured him
this time, and the reins that he held earned him the

money that paid for his education for the bar. Indeed, this honest and industrious youth was so honest and industrious that he took his way right into Congress in 1893 and there, except for two years when the Democrats tipped him out, he has been ever since. No wonder all the good people of Kansas hold Charley Curtis up to their children as a model of virtue, as the boy who made good far away from home. No wonder they include him in their prayers so that the Almighty may hear how many of the righteous wish Charley Curtis to enter the White House.

If virtue that is Curtis does not get this reward, there is the comforting thought that after all he has a tremendous record of achievement to look back upon—years in the House of Representatives and in the Senate. You can hear him there any day in his swelling periods and the rotund oratorical phrases for which he is distinguished. Here they are: "Mr. President, I suggest the absence of a quorum." "Mr. President, I ask a roll-call." "Mr. President, I rise to a point of order." "Mr. President, I move the Senate do now adjourn." Not his to fill the *Congressional Record* with his beliefs as if he were a Copeland, a Caraway, a Heflin, feeling forty-eight States tuned in to hear. He is as silent as those stoical Indian chiefs who were his ancestors. Yet he can talk, as did they, when the spirit moves. Here are samples given to James O'Donnell Bennett and printed in *Collier's*, sonorous samples of his style, and planks in his platform. Speaking on his favourite theme, "the passing of the political domination of Congress from the East to the West," he said:

> *The chairmanships of nearly all the important com-*
> *mittees are now in the hands of Western men. The Speak-*
> *ership of the House has passed from Massachusetts to*
> *Ohio, and the most urgent problem before the country—*
> *the problem of farm relief—is a Western problem. There-*
> *fore my insistent plea is and will be, "Help the farmer."*
>
> *I hope and expect that this Congress will pass some*
> *reasonable measure of farm relief which will receive the*
> *President's approval and will go a long way toward*
> *ameliorating the conditions surrounding agriculture by*
> *giving the farmers better marketing facilities, greater*
> *assistance in carrying forward the co-operative marketing*
> *principle, and assisting them along other needed lines.*
>
> *I also hope that the committees of the two houses will*
> *agree upon the report to their respective bodies of a meas-*
> *ure which will provide a definite shipping policy, and*
> *that under it our country will be assured the permanent*
> *merchant marine so essential alike to our commerce and*
> *national defense.*

Stirring words these, profound and profoundly wise! But there is no need for him to hold forth often as to his views on any topic. You can always find them in the campaign book and party platform—as soon would he dispute the Holy Bible or the tenets of that Methodism which has carried him so far on the road to greatness as to question his party dogma. He is a regular of the regulars, a cornerstone of the American temple—even the capstone. There must be law and order and men to enforce them by precept and practice. Even Frederick the Great knew that with his ungrammatical: "Ordnung *muss* sind!" Charles Curtis knows it, too, and to it has given his life. Henry Cabot Lodge, his predecessor as majority leader, may have been an intellectual and a Back Bay aristocrat, but he was not as good a collie for the flock as Curtis of Kansas. Curtis knows his master's voice, his master's slightest desire, and his circling of the sheep never ceases, nor his yapping at those who dare to wander.

For he knows his job as the job knows him— majority leader! No temptation to eloquence shall distract him from it. Henry Cabot Lodge had other interests, other tasks. Not Charles Curtis. He is majority leader, heart and soul. For him authority is the final word. Did he not ally himself with Speaker Cannon when, a youngster from the Kaw, he entered the House? Did he revolt against the Speaker and his rules when the upstart Norris of Nebraska began the fight to bind the foremost legislator of Danville, Illinois? Charles Curtis did not! Loyalty is the meat of his bones, fidelity the tune for every beat of his heart. He went down to defeat with Joseph Cannon, but rose again to righteousness and the upper chamber. You cannot keep a good man down—in Kansas or the Capitol. Work is his gospel, work his salvation—fourteen, fifteen, sixteen and more hours a day if need be. Occasionally, rumour has it, he breaks away when Congress is not sitting and then he can be found at a nearby race-track, leaning on the rail, absorbed, a spectator who once rode winners, recalling this hairbreadth finish and that game defeat when he was almost sitting on his horse's ears. Those were the real racing days!

Then, the races over, he is again shepherd of the Republican flock and more than shepherd—detective, supervisor, and controller of all who will be controlled. Not his to reason why. Orders were meant to be obeyed —what a fine soldier was lost in Charles Curtis! Romance may have its way. The pulse may beat faster for one moment. The might-have-been may project itself upon the retina if only for a second. Even in Kansas they dream dreams—sometimes dreams to interest a Freud. But let Charles Curtis enter the White House and mankind everywhere will know that the American home and the American family ideals, best in all this glorious world, have triumphed anew. Every true American will feel a sympathetic thrill. There is in the very simpleness of Charles Curtis something of the soil and the workshop. He is in himself the least common denominator of us all.

WOODROW WILSON

A Supreme Tragedy

And so, once upon a time, there came out of the vineyard to speak brave words one as with a silver tongue. Young and old, rich and poor, stopped their work, gathering in the market-place, saying: "Behold, there is one who tells the truth. Do you not see that he is not of the Philistines? Let us listen and be guided of him." Whenever he spoke men echoed his words, so that more and more came to listen and to revere. When all the tribes of Israel went to war it came to pass that his words winged their way wherever men battled and women suffered; as men lay dying of their wounds they cried out to him to prevail in order that none others might perish like unto themselves. Widows with starving babes at their breasts called down blessings upon his name. Serfs and bond-slaves lifted up their voices before his image, saying: "Lo, He has come again." And when the day dawned when men fought no more, and he went abroad, humble folk kneeled down before him, crying: "Thou art the man!"

Yet one day, falling upon evil companions, his strength and wisdom went out from him and his voice was no longer as the trumpets before Jericho. Conceiving greatly he yielded greatly, doing wrong in the hope that some little good might come. Beholding, the people cried: "He is no longer the Messiah that he was. Do you not perceive how now he strikes hands with those who have misled us?" Soon were heard lamentations throughout the land. Men beat upon their breasts, declaring that woe was theirs, that darkness was now indeed upon all His people, and that there was no light upon the waters. Returning thence to his own tribe, men cast him aside, saying:

"Thou hast no longer the voice of thy other days; we are betrayed and by thee shall we be led no more."

WOODROW WILSON came into the political life of America as if in response to prayer. It was given to him as to no other to step suddenly out of a cloistered life into high office. Then, as today, there was profound distrust of those conducting the government; startling revelations had laid bare both the corruption in big business and the control of the government by those in the seats of the commercial mighty. Neither the spurious liberalism nor the halfway, compromising reforms of Theodore Roosevelt, with his incessant knocking-down of men of straw, had satisfied the thoughtful or cut deeply into our political sores. To Mr. Wilson, as he once remarked in the office of *The Nation* during his governorship, what the country needed was "a modified Rooseveltism"; what he preached was not only that, but a far greater vision of reform, with a far keener and truer analysis of what was wrong. This he set forth with an extraordinary skill and eloquence which placed him in the front rank of American orators of his or of any time—by the beauty of his language, the wealth of his imagery, the aptness of his illustrations, and the cogency of his arguments.

His "modified Rooseveltism" seemed to the business masters of America far more dangerous than the doctrines of Roosevelt himself; they had known how to get around the latter when the pinch came. Wilson was of a different type. There was none of the swash-

buckler and far more of the true crusader in him; his
lips set in different and more dangerous lines; his eyes
blazed with a different fire; here was all the stubborn-
ness of the Scotch-Irishman with a Roundhead's absolute
faith in the completeness of his wisdom and the infalli-
bility of his judgment. Plainly he was not to be trifled
with, and the way he went after the New Jersey corporations with his "seven-sisters" laws boded ill for
big business everywhere. When the election of 1912
came Wall Street was ill at ease. Taft, its favourite,
could not win; so the choice lay between the "wildness"
of Roosevelt and Woodrow Wilson, who, as former
president of one of the staidest and most conservative of
universities, the very citadel of intrenched wealth,
should have been safe and sane, yet was nothing of
the kind. When big-business men examined Mr. Wilson's speeches and his book, "The New Freedom,"
their hair bristled. Here was radicalism indeed. He declared that the government had been transferred from
Washington to Wall Street, whither the President must
go "hat in hand" for orders. He affirmed that the "strong
have crushed the weak," and that therefore "the strong
dominate the industry and the economic life of this
country." "Our government" he asserted to be "under
the control of heads of great allied corporations with
special interests." Again and again he cried out: "We
stand in the presence of a revolution . . . whereby
America will insist upon recovering in practice those
ideals which she has always professed, upon securing
a government devoted to the general interests and not

to special interests. We are upon the eve of a great reconstruction." Since "an invisible empire" had been "set above the forms of democracy," Mr. Wilson demanded an end to the "exploitation of the people by legal and political means," saying "the masters of the government of the United States are the combined capitalists and manufacturers of the United States."

This was treason, and when Mr. Wilson entered the White House the severance between it and Wall Street was complete. The members of J. P. Morgan & Co. were for the first time denied admission to the President's office. So far as Mr. Wilson could make it his was a government of the people and in its interests. To him men rallied in increasing numbers, even of the disappointed bands who had followed Colonel Roosevelt to defeat with a fervent personal idolatry and a religious enthusiasm unsurpassed in our history. Mr. Wilson's followers were actuated less by adoration of him than by admiration for his ideals; yet there were plenty to give him a personal devotion and loyalty such as men are capable of but once in their lives. This kept up even though a change rapidly came over the President. As Governor of New Jersey he had sat in an office where all might see him and approach; in the White House he became less and less accessible. What was probably an unconquerable shyness was coupled with much intellectual pride and relentless bitterness toward all who disagreed. No friendship could survive long when the other party to it criticized the President. It became more and more his habit to work alone. Thus it came about that when the Lusitania was sunk, the note that satisfied the country, yet kept it calm, was written in his closet without personal contact with any members of his Cabinet until it was read to them for their approval only— not for their criticism or advice. In this it resembled many another state paper.

Progress there was. The Federal Reserve system came in time to take up the shock of the outbreak of the war; a system of rural credits was established; there was a real tariff revision downward; a beginning was made of a most hopeful series of arbitration treaties. The whole atmosphere of the government changed for the better. Then came the catastrophe of catastrophes, cutting squarely across the pathway to domestic reform, to end Mr. Wilson's "bloodless revolution." His first steps after the war clouds broke were all good; he commanded for the country a neutrality in thought and deed which he himself at first lived up to. His unusual executive talents were at their best. But the old spell was broken. Declining Mr. Bryan's God-given suggestion for an organization of the neutral countries headed by the United States, to compel respect for neutral rights and then to compel peace, Mr. Wilson gradually violated his own precepts for American neutrality. The powerful note to Great Britain in protest against the seizure of American ships on the high seas—the Solicitor of the State Department declaring publicly at this time that "there was not a canon of international law which England had not violated," a statement whose truth is now admitted by Englishmen—lay upon Mr. Wilson's desk from May, 1915, until November, finally to be sent so emasculated that its author in the State Department could hardly have recognized it. As Mr. Tumulty finally confessed in his book, the scales were no longer held even. Yet when seeking re-election, Mr. Wilson eagerly benefited by the slogan "he kept us out of war," only to violate later this implicit pact with his people.

On January 22, 1917, Mr. Wilson rose to the highest point of his often extraordinary intuition and of his statesmanship. Then he gave utterance to words of profoundest wisdom, acclaimed at the time by almost the entire press of the country—these words that have been justified ten thousand times over by every event since the treaty of peace:

> *It must be a peace without victory. It is not pleasant to say this. . . . I am seeking only to face realities and to face them without soft concealment. Victory would mean peace forced upon the losers, a victor's terms imposed upon the vanquished. It would be accepted in humiliation, under duress, at an intolerable sacrifice, and would leave a sting, a resentment, a bitter memory upon which terms of peace would rest not permanently, but only as upon quicksand. Only a peace between equals can last.*

The crimes of Versailles, the collapsing treaty which has made that name infamous, attest the profound and perpetual truth of these words. There is no other prophecy in history so justified by the event, so marvellous in its tragic fulfilment.

Three months later the breach of faith was complete. America entered the war. Wilson, the champion of democracy, struck it one of the deadliest blows received since the theory of democracy was conceived. That fatal day every reform for which Mr. Wilson had contended lay prostrate. For the first time he found himself congratulated by Henry Cabot Lodge, warmly endorsed and visited by Theodore Roosevelt, for whom there was in his heart the bitterest hate. He was acclaimed with joy by every munition-maker, every war profiteer, every agent of big business, all the evil forces against which he had fought for the "new freedom." To the partners of J. P. Morgan & Co. the White House doors now swung wide open. Positions of the highest responsibility were given to them; they were among his most trusted advisers at Paris. When the war ended the control of the government by big business and the war profiteers was complete—the gift of Woodrow Wilson himself.

What it was that won Mr. Wilson over to the war is not yet clear. It is the great unsolved mystery of his career. Whether it was due to the desire he cherished from 1914 on to be the arbiter and dominator of the peace, whether it was a yielding to the pressure of those who deemed the millions they had invested in Allied securities doomed unless the Allies won, whether an emotional desire to save the Allies from defeat, or sincere belief that no other way remained, is yet to be revealed. In any case Woodrow Wilson sinned against the very ark of the American covenant. Not a civic right of the American but was trampled upon with Mr. Wilson's knowledge and consent. The suppression of free thought and free speech, the terrorization of great masses of loyal Americans, the fettering of the press, the ruthless imprisonment of dissenters, the turning over of the destinies of the people to lawless officials and judges, the filling of the country with the bitterest diatribes of hate and Berserker rage—these Mr. Wilson neither checked nor reproved; they were "necessary acts of war time." He was unable to see that whenever and wherever liberalism links itself with war and war-madness it is liberalism which perishes. He could not perceive that he had struck down as with a dagger the causes he had held dearest. He could not, of course, for all his rare intuition, divine that he himself would be the most tragic victim of the anti-social, anti-democratic, anti-Christian forces which he had unleashed. It was the same Wall Street crowd, the same Henry Cabot Lodges and Theodore Roosevelts, who had applauded him in April, 1917, who were the first to turn and rend him when he had done what they had wished. This they did as soon as we were once more out of the hell of the war in which we Americans made so needless and useless a sacrifice. What honest American citizen who looks upon Europe today can deny that our seventy thousand dead might as well have perished against walls in the streets of New York for all they did to end war, safeguard democracy, or destroy that militarism which today rears its head more ominously than in 1914?

Yet the Fourteen Peace Points, whether they came,

as alleged, from the pen of Walter Lippmann, or from Mr. Wilson's own, lifted the spirits of men; it seemed, if they could be achieved, that a new charter of liberty, a new world order would be mankind's. Mr. Wilson went to Europe exalted on high; he *was* the Messiah. And if only he could have met his supreme test he would rank today in the minds of men next after Jesus of Nazareth. The kneeling, praying masses before whom he passed, prayed and kneeled in vain. It was to Orlando, to Foch and Clemenceau, to Lloyd George, in whom the good and evil demons struggled hourly for control, that the victory went. Hate, revenge, and brutal force, the lust and avarice of the conquerors prevailed. It was indeed "a victor's terms imposed upon the vanquished," "accepted in humiliation, under duress, at an intolerable sacrifice," with the result that today the next great war looms upon the horizon. To Paris Mr. Wilson went unprepared, ignorant, by his own confession, of the secret treaties widely published in the United States ten months before his departure, which were the key to all the Allied acts from the day the war began. They were the explanation of the Allies' motives and the charter of their real aims so skilfully hidden behind altruistic assertions that the Allies were the anointed of God and their cause entirely unselfish and righteous. So. Mr. Wilson was not on guard in Paris against aims as self-seeking and as godless as those of the enemies he had defeated in the war. Nor was he able to cope with what then confronted him. The evil habit of compromise, which came upon him in Trenton

and in the White House as on many another, making
him accept doctrines which he had previously declared
that he never, never would, beset him here. His personal weaknesses, like his compromises, fell upon him
and disarmed him; his very taking counsel of himself
became part of his undoing. But above all it was foreordained that the truth that good shall not come out of
the evil of war should remain beyond challenge wherever men walk.

Now for truth's sake it must be written down that
when Mr. Wilson passed the curtain fell upon the greatest tragedy in our history. William Dean Howells once
declared that there were but two great tragic and dramatic figures in our past, John Brown and Abraham
Lincoln. Surely we may add Woodrow Wilson as well.
For what could be greater tragedy than to have ruled
eight years and to have left so few enduring marks upon
our institutions; to have preached visions and ideals to
one's countrymen for eight years, only to yield office to
the most material, the most corrupt, the most sightless
Administration ever to hold its sway in America. If
Mr. Wilson could but have learned from John Bright
that *"War is the grave of all good, whether in administration or legislation,* and it throws power into the
hands of the most worthless of the class of statesmen!"
he could not have betrayed America and her democracy
as he did by going to war. There is no treason in our
history of similar magnitude and the evil thereof will
endure for generations to come. Probably only an Æs-
chylus could do Woodrow Wilson justice today. Cer-

tainly no element of the sombrest Greek tragedy was lacking in Washington when Woodrow Wilson left office.

Upon these things will the historians of the future pass, each according to his bias and to his interpretation of state papers now sealed, documents now hidden, events yet to take place. Philosophers will always wrangle as to whether that man's offence is worse who deliberately destroys the rights and liberties of a people or the crime of him who exalts the spirits of men by a glorious vision of a new and inspired day, only to let the uplifted sink back, utterly disheartened and disillusioned, into the darkest slough of despond. As to the merits and demerits of Woodrow Wilson books will be written to the end of time. Those who worship him will continue to keep eyes and ears closed to facts they do not wish to hear; those whose very souls he outraged and betrayed will judge as through a glass darkly. But one fact no one can deny: Aspiring to the stars he crashed to earth, leaving behind him no emancipation of humanity, no assuaging of its wounds, only a world racked, embittered, more full of hatreds, more ready to tear itself to pieces today than when he essayed the heavens. The moral of his fall is as immutable as the hills, as shining as the planets. If humanity will perceive and acknowledge it that will be Woodrow Wilson's priceless legacy to the world he tried to serve so greatly.

COLONEL E. M. HOUSE

His Nakedness Self-Revealed

*T*HE *Intimate Papers of Colonel House,*[1] by the
Colonel and his editor, Professor Charles Seymour
of Yale, do more than tear the mask from the face of
the most amazing character and the most interesting
lesser personality of the Wilson Administrations. They
strip him to the buff. No more extraordinary self-
revelation can be found in the memoirs of statesmen
and public men, and it is the more remarkable because
of the unconsciousness of the revealing. What could
have induced Colonel House thus to show his hand and
to step out of the character of the man of silence and
mystery which he played upon a world stage is not
clear, unless it was that he felt the necessity of replying
to the letters of Walter Page. To him the Colonel *has*
replied, and in doing so he has demolished with a few
rounds of grape the elaborate structure of glorification
lately set up about the former Ambassador to Great
Britain. But he has also bared himself, retaining not
even a fig-leaf, and the picture is not one to enchant
in so far as his political activities are concerned. True
this Texas comet, which suddenly shone in the diplomatic heavens and made its rapid and brilliant way
through that celestial sphere, cast a bright light while
it travelled on its way. It did illumine the heavens; it

---

[1] Houghton Mifflin Company.

did focus upon itself the attention of all astronomers and observers. But when it faded out it left the heavens exactly as they had been and thereby only accentuated the remoteness and the dullness of the professional statesman-stars across whose orbits the comet had flashed.

Beyond doubt here is an engaging personality. Shrewdness, the ability to draw others out, a tremendous power of sympathy and quick understanding, of eager friendliness, of apparent unselfishness, of profound interest in world problems—all of these combined, in addition to his personal attractiveness, to fit Colonel House for the role of king-maker and of king-director. As to this we have the testimony of Viscount Grey, who yielded on sight to the Colonel's charms. "It was not necessary to spend much time in putting our case to him. He had a way of saying 'I know it' in a tone and manner which carried conviction both of his sympathy with, and understanding of, what was said to him. . . . I found combined in him in a rare degree the qualities of wisdom and sympathy. In the stress of war it was at once a relief, a delight, and an advantage to be able to talk with him freely. His criticism or comment was valuable, his suggestions were fertile, and these were all conveyed with a sympathy that made it pleasant to listen to them." H. N. Brailsford adds this to the picture: "House had a way of impressing his personality with some unconscious magic on those with whom he talked. He seemed curiously modest. He talked very simply. One felt . . . his courtesy and sincerity." But this work has not proved him to have been entirely sincere or disinterested. It makes it clear that if he waved aside high public office, such as the Secretaryship of State, it was because he wished to be President or nothing—"nothing less than that would satisfy me . . ." Aside from that, he obtained precisely what he wanted, namely, the position of being the power behind the throne, and it flattered his vanity and caressed his ego far more than would have been the case had he accepted the Secretaryship of State and been held accountable by the country and the press for his official acts—had he been compelled to face constant press criticism.

Public men, office-seekers, press men—whose editorials and dispatches he constantly dictated—came to him for aid, for news, for a thousand different things. He was errand boy, court chamberlain, buffer extraordinary, minister plenipotentiary, chief justice, writer of presidential notes, opinions, and speeches, chief of the secret service, the perfect counsellor, and finally the self-appointed arbiter of the world's destiny. There is nothing like it in the political history of the United States, and nothing like it in the history of the modern world. Foreign diplomats took their orders from him— Spring-Rice came to House's heel when called like a well-trained setter. On one occasion, writes the Colonel to Wilson, "Spring-Rice wished to know if he was doing anything wrong or everything to please the State Department. It was rather a staggering question, and I had to tell him that some of his methods might be improved upon. *He promised to do better.*" Even when so big a man as Franklin K. Lane wished to find out if he was doing well as a Cabinet official and pleasing the President he went not to the President but asked Colonel House. There can be no doubt that no other private citizen ever wielded greater power; and it, of course, could only have been wielded by a wily and able man. This he did by the consent of the President, conscious and unconscious. It is safe to say that such an arrangement would have been tolerated by no other personality than that of Wilson, whose shyness, aloofness, and embarrassment in meeting people, as well as his laziness and procrastination, made him only too happy to have in Colonel House a friend who kept away hundreds of bores, saved the executive offices from conducting much correspondence that otherwise would have poured in upon it, and relieved him of endless labour.

There is no denying that in these volumes Colonel House and his editor, Professor Seymour, reveal constantly a very great satisfaction with the achievements of Edward M. House. To them it is not only an all but impeccable record but the most magnificent credited to any man among all the leaders of all the nations which were drawn into the war. Others might err—even President Wilson could blunder—but it is not often that Homer is allowed to nod. They are right in taking satisfaction in it, and the hidebound partisans of Woodrow Wilson are equally justified in gnashing their teeth over this record. They cannot deny that Colonel House helped to force Bryan upon the President, made up the Cabinet, and furnished ideas for it. It was the Colonel who, we now learn, originated all or a good part of that magnificent program of social and economic reform which made the first two years of Wilson's regime so brilliant in achievement. They cannot deny that when it came to foreign affairs House took the lead, that he conceived policy after policy, and that Mr. Wilson accepted them and constantly wrote to him asking him for advice and aid as to how he should reply to a letter or a note or what policy he should institute or follow. Here is proof that House composed some of Wilson's most important speeches.

Besides the Cabinet officers, Colonel House chose the ambassadors—a sorry job he made of it, too—and actually notified them of their appointments and told them how they were to behave. The most amazing thing about it all is the way the Cabinet officers and the diplomats submitted to this government by an irresponsible individual. The Secretaries of State were apparently willing that they should be ignored and the public business conducted by Colonel House on secret instructions of which they were ignorant. Cabinet officers reported to him; they frequently could not communicate with the President or see him for weeks at a time—Lane alone was allowed to discuss with Wilson the Lusitania note before it was written, and that only over the telephone. The more the President lost faith in some of his Cabinet and his diplomats, and he lost that faith quickly in several cases, the more he was willing that Colonel House should take them off his hands. How Walter Page with any self-respect could have retained his position as Ambassador to Great Britain is beyond explanation; he must have been supremely dense not to have suspected that House was in London because the President, who often did not answer his letters, had no further use for him, and not to have insisted upon his resignation when he found that he could not take part with Colonel House in urging mediation upon the Allies.

Now, with all respect to both House and Wilson, the role assumed by Colonel House was one that could only result in disaster, as it finally did in the irrevocable break between the two men. This was due apparently to the feeling of the President that his Cardinal Wolsey had been faithless to his god in the White House, just as once before the relations between Colonel House and the President were summarily broken off—something not recorded in the volumes before us. Moreover, the position that House assumed compelled, I am inclined to think, insincerity and double-dealing, and more so as time went on. He became more and more Machiavellian. Thus, he claimed to be a pacifist—Professor Seymour even dares to say that this man who approved the slaughter of men, women, and children at Vera Cruz, the lawless invasion of Mexico by Pershing, and the murder of over three thousand Haitians under President Wilson's orders, "was himself, perhaps, the most sincere pacifist in America. . . ." Well, if deceiving the pacifists who came to him in good faith and belief in his sincerity makes House a sincere pacifist, he is entitled to the credit. His real attitude he reveals when he boasts that he stirred up a controversy between a group of pacifists *"as usual . . .* which delights me."

Again, at the very time that he was making the pacifists believe that he was one of them he was working with General Wood in the interest of preparedness and plotting how he could bring the President over to all of General Wood's plans for armament. Similarly he was for ruthlessness in dealing with any disturbing elements in the country. He wanted Congress to give the President more power for the immediate deportation of "hyphenates," he consulted with chiefs of police as to how drastically disturbing elements should be handled if it came to disorder. "I urged Baker to use a firm hand in the event trouble should manifest itself in any way. I thought it was mistaken mercy to temporize with troubles of this sort"—in which attitude he again unanimously agreed with his friend the Kaiser and once more showed himself the "sincere pacifist." Subsequently he always appeared to sympathize with those who came to him protesting against the infringement of American rights and liberties after the outbreak of the war, and particularly against the maltreatment of conscientious objectors, and to regret those official excesses. It is impossible now to believe that he was else than a complete hypocrite, that he was not in thorough accord with what actually took place—to the nation's dishonour.

His job compelled him to be all things to all men, compelled him to toady, compelled him to play one group against another, the Germans against the English, the French against the British. It compelled him more and more to devious ways which he herein sets forth in complete nudity, as, for instance, when he proposed to the British Cabinet a plan to get the United States into the war on the side of the Allies through a set of terms phrased in such a way that the Germans would fall into a trap. If the Germans refused to bite, he, Edward M. House, an unofficial citizen of Texas, promised the British Government that the United States would enter the war on the side of the Allies! [1]

Here we have the most startling revelation of all. This official-unofficial intriguer had grown so great in his self-esteem and his power by 1916 that he did not hesitate to gamble with the lives of American citizens as if they were his pawns. He cites Gerard's indignation with the Kaiser for speaking of the German, Russian, and English people as if they "were so many pawns upon a chessboard," but on his lone authority House brushes aside the Congress of the United States and repeatedly notifies Sir Edward Grey that in certain contingencies the United States will join forces with the

[1] "It is in my mind that, after conferring with your government, I should proceed to Berlin and tell them that it was the President's purpose to intervene and stop this destructive war, provided the weight of the United States thrown on the side that accepted our proposal could do it. I would not let Berlin know, of course, of any understanding had with the Allies, but would rather lead them to think that our proposal would be rejected by the Allies. This might induce Berlin to accept the proposal but, if it did not do so, it would nevertheless, be the purpose to intervene." (House to Grey, October 17, 1915, Vol. II, pp. 90–91.)

Allies. As Professor Seymour puts it: "House promised that if the Germans refused to accept the terms he had outlined, the United States would enter the war. This tentative understanding, of course, was to be dependent upon the approval of the allies of Great Britain." Nothing said about the approval of the White House, although Mr. Wilson was at that time entirely opposed to our entering the war—House felt sure the President would obey him! Nothing said about the Congress, the war-making power in the United States. Nothing said about the American people, who might have been expected to have some say as to whether their sons should be swept into the war. So it went right along. House promised from the beginning that the United States would enter the League of Nations, forgetting to his cost the existence of the United States Senate. Yes, even as far back as 1913, before the war, he had the effrontery to offer the Kaiser, whom he was so soon thereafter to call a bloodthirsty wretch, an alliance with the United States. "I spoke of the community of interests between England, Germany, and the United States, and thought if they stood together the peace of the world could be maintained." On January 11, 1916, he records that he told Balfour and Grey that Wilson would throw over our historic policy of no entangling alliances with Europe and would enter into an agreement with the European nations in matters such as navalism, militarism, etc.—George Washington supplanted by Edward M. House! On February 7, 1916, he records: "I again told them

[Briand and Cambon] that the lower the fortunes of the Allies ebbed, the closer the United States would stand by them."

Curiously, while he was doing this he was bewailing the fact that the destinies of the people of Europe were being settled by their leaders without their knowing anything about it. Thus he wrote on June 23, 1916: "It is not the people who speak, but their masters, and some day, I pray, the voice of the people may have direct expression in international affairs as they are beginning to have it in national affairs." This from the man who, without official authority, was, with Woodrow Wilson, the master of the fate of the American people—who were, for all House's pious wish for democracy in international affairs, permitted by him and by Mr. Wilson to know nothing about what was going on behind the scenes. Professor Seymour recalls with satisfaction that the purpose of House's most important trip to Europe offering mediation never reached the press of the United States.

The history of statecraft surely contains no record of anything approximating the *naïveté* and the innocence and the self-conceit with which House tackled the European problem. Never having had anything to do with foreign affairs in any capacity theretofore, he assured the Kaiser on June 1, 1914, that the President and he "thought perhaps an American might be able to better compose the difficulties here and bring about an understanding with a view to peace than any European, because of their distrust and dislike for one another." "*I had undertaken the work,"* he continued, *"and that was my reason for coming to Germany,* as I wanted to see him first"—a kindly consideration that must have gratified His Majesty. House of Texas was in the field to compose differences and dislikes rooted in a thousand years of peace and war! But that is merely one sample. What could surpass his writing to Woodrow Wilson on June 17, 1914, that the French "statesmen dream no longer of revenge and the recovery of Alsace-Lorraine. The people do, but those who govern and know hope only that France may continue as now"? At the very moment that House penned these lines, Poincaré was plotting a world war and, a month later, left for Russia to complete those negotiations for the attack upon Germany which came to naught only because Serbia struck first. House was so ignorant of the actual causes of the war as to do England the gross injustice of saying she went into war "primarily . . . because Germany insisted upon having a dominant army and a dominant (*sic*) navy" (June 29, 1916). It is no wonder that the Germans smiled behind Colonel House's back when he first came to Berlin in 1913, and said: "Er ist zu einfach"—he is too simple.

And simple he was all the way through. He would suggest his mediation scheme to the French ministers and the fact that they listened earnestly to him and said "how interesting" convinced him that he had impressed them with his cause. Despite his natural sagacity and power the British Cabinet strung him along for months so that he could write the most encouraging letters to

Mr. Wilson, and then it all came to naught. Naturally, he blames the British Cabinet ministers, even his friend Grey a bit, and bewails their inability to seize upon the golden opportunity: "Colonel House was naturally and bitterly disappointed," writes his Boswell. Often he was delightfully fooled by the British ministers, as on February 14, 1916, when he had a long talk with Lloyd George, Balfour, Grey, and Asquith: "We all," he says, "cheerfully divided up Turkey both in Asia and Europe." But as Professor Seymour points out in a footnote his hosts did not take the trouble to tell House about the secret treaties which these same four gentlemen had already signed partitioning the Turkish empire as part of their unselfish war for liberty and the rights of small nations and the self-determination of peoples. Finally, what could surpass in incredible, overpowering egotism House's writing to the President on February 13, 1916: "In my opinion hell will break loose in Europe this spring and summer as never before; *and I see no way to stop it for the moment. . . .*"?

Yet curiously enough, while being fooled by individual ministers, House at times showed that he did understand the motives and the character of the governments with which he sought to cope. The Germans he sized up admirably; he took their measure well and gauged their weaknesses, strength, stupidities; their political follies; their self-suicide. On May 17, 1916, he wrote to Wilson: "The more I see of the dealing of governments among themselves the more I am impressed with the utter selfishness of their outlook. Gratitude is a

thing unknown, and all we have done for the Allies will
be forgotten overnight if we antagonize them now"—
incidentally a delightful admission that the United
States *had* been helping the Allies during the very time
when President Wilson had officially called upon his
countrymen to be neutral in thought and deed! On April
30, 1916, he was even franker: "What the Allies want
is to dip their hands into our treasure chest. While the
war has become a war of democracy against autocracy,
not one of the democracies entered it to fight for democracy. . . ." Again, writing on May 24, 1916, he said:
"It is evident that unless the United States is willing
to sacrifice hundreds of thousands of lives and billions
of treasure we are not 'o be on good terms with the
Allies. . . ." House was always properly and righteously expressing his abhorrence of German militarism,
as when he wrote to Grey that Germany must be taught
its futility. But when it came to the pinch he was equally
ready to suggest that we do precisely the same thing that
the Germans had. Thus he regrets constantly that we
did not arm to the teeth the minute the war began so
that we could have compelled England and Germany
to yield to us, and he does not see that that was precisely
the Kaiser's philosophy of using might to do what he
thought was right. In the event of the failure of his
mediation he for a time believed we ought to arm on
sea and on land to the limit and then retreat into our
shell and sit waiting for anything to turn up that might.
In other words, he was as bankrupt of rational remedies
as any of the European statesmen whom he criticizes.

He wanted his League of Nations only, apparently, if we could enter the war in such a manner that we could dictate the peace.

And how he wobbled as to whether we should or should not enter the war! Immediately after the sinking of the Lusitania he declared: "America has come to the parting of the ways, when she must determine whether she stands for civilized or uncivilized warfare. We can no longer remain neutral spectators." On August 22, 1915, House urged the President to send Bernstorff home at once, although he believed that it meant war, but Mr. Wilson refused to be convinced. Every now and then the President did refuse to follow the dictates of his mentor and Colonel House confesses that he overplayed his hand on occasion. By January 6, 1916, House told Sir Edward Grey that he was advising the President against actually breaking with Germany and thus recorded his opinion: "I thought it far better for the democracy of the world to unite upon some plan that would enable the United States to intervene, than for us to drift into the war by breaking diplomatic relations with the Central Powers. . . . I confess having advised the President against an actual break with Germany at this time"—an entire change of front. By July 16 of that year he had swung around once more and it is written that he felt that ultimate co-operation with the Allies in the war was "inevitable."

But when it came to the Presidential election of 1916 Colonel House was all for trumpeting the fact aloud that Mr. Wilson had kept the country out of the

war and for concealing the fact still further that he
[House] had done his best at times to put the country
into it and still believed it inevitable. Politician that he
was, he knew well that the mass of the plain people
was utterly opposed to our going to war, and so he
cynically recommended to the President that he play
up to that sentiment—even Professor Seymour finds it
necessary in a foot-note to gloss over this inconsistency.
"The keeping the country out of war, and the great meas-
sures you have enacted into law, should be our battle-
cry," wrote House to Wilson July 5, 1916. Assidu-
ously the cry of "He kept us out of war" was spread
all over the country, and it undoubtedly won the election for Wilson, because the multitudes of mothers who
voted for him did so because of the implied promise in
that slogan that Wilson would continue to keep the
country out of war. Let anyone who questions this re-
read the keynote speech of Governor Glynn of New
York at the St. Louis convention which renominated
Wilson. That speech of Governor Glynn's was read and
edited by House and Wilson before it was delivered—
"The President and I will aid him [Glynn]," wrote
House, "in preparing the keynote speech. I agreed to
take charge of it, and after the speech is finished I am
to send it to the President for criticism." Yet Professor
Seymour thinks it would have been "rather Quixotic"
for House to fail to take advantage of this peace-
desiring American mood, although he "had himself
advocated a plan" which, if accepted, "would have
brought us into the war." This is what happens to the

morals of certain types of idealists when they get into politics and have power placed in their irresponsible hands—to say nothing of the editors of their writings!

Thus runs this chronicle of egotistic futility to the very end. House could see clearly the weaknesses of the Allied statesmen, as when he wrote: "My observation is that incompetent statesmanship and selfishness is at the bottom of it all. It is not so much a breaking down of civilization as a lack of wisdom in those that govern; and history, I believe, will bring an awful indictment against those who were shortsighted and selfish enough to let such a tragedy happen." And yet he had no other vision than to drag America into the mess, and when he and his chief reached Paris (his views as to Paris we shall doubtless get in a later volume) they were checkmated, overwhelmed, routed by the very shortsighted, incompetent, selfish statesmen whom he so denounced—and by their own lack of wisdom and force. Lowes Dickinson has written of these statesmen: "What little puppets, knocking away, with Lilliputian hammers, the last stays that restrain the launch of that great deathship, War." When it came to docking that ship and putting it out of commission again, House's little hammer was not even as efficient as that of the other Lilliputians. He could see clearly that if the Germans won "the war lords will reign supreme and democratic government will be imperilled throughout the world." But he could not see that the abandonment of his and his chief's soundest position that there should be "peace without victory," "no victors and no vanquished," insured the similar imperilment of democracies by the complete victory of the United States and the Allies, so that today democracy is dead in Italy, Russia, Greece, Hungary, Poland, and Spain, and totters in as many more. House had a conception of compelling peace, but he wanted to do it alone with Mr. Wilson, and he declined the safe way urged by Secretary Bryan (whom he called a mischief-maker), namely, the rallying of all the neutral nations to demand the cessation of the war, a practical and entirely wise proposal urged again and again, but in vain, upon House and Wilson by the smaller neutrals. So the Colonel's triumphs turned to ashes. The unbiased historian must declare him as discredited as any of the other war lords if measured by his achievements and the results of his policies. Colonel House will not be judged by the record of this book alone. The Wilsonians will have the next inning and there are many letters omitted from these volumes which will then see the light of day. They will be certain to bring into sharper relief his self-contentment, his frequent errors, and the extent of his frailties.

On all counts the record must not be allowed to stop here. Nemesis, the Nemesis of stark Greek tragedy, awaited the Colonel at Paris. Nothing came of his plan for dictating the peace, beyond the League of Nations. The friendship which was the most valuable thing in the world to him again came to an abrupt end and this time was not restored. Colonel House was never again allowed to see the President he helped to make and so largely inspired. That President went into the war against his better judgment. He knew that "it would mean that a majority of the people in this hemisphere would go war mad, quit thinking, and devote their energies to destruction. . . ." "Once lead this people into war and they'll forget there ever was such a thing as tolerance." He knew that a peace dictated by the victors would rest upon quicksand, for he said so January 22, 1917.

By this his own record there rests upon Colonel House's head a large share of the blood guilt for those 70,000 American soldiers who were done to death in France in considerable degree because of House's unofficial administration of our foreign affairs—as uselessly done to death as if they had been shot down on the prairies of Nebraska in cold blood by their own fellow-citizens, so far as the realization of the Fourteen Peace Points or any of the American ideals in entering the war is concerned. For the condition of Europe today is infinitely worse than in June 1, 1914, when Colonel House turned up in Potsdam, calmly assured the Kaiser that only an American could solve Europe's troubles and end her rivalries, and added: "Kaiser, I am here."

ROBERT M. LA FOLLETTE

A Great American

ROBERT M. LA FOLLETTE was American to his finger-tips. No other country could have produced a man just like this nor one truer to his convictions and his principles. It seems to me that he was closer to the people and closer to the soil of America than almost any other great politician since Lincoln. He knew what they wanted in a public servant and he gave it to them, and they who knew him and saw him at close range in return clung to him with a fidelity and devotion which were not in the least shaken by the unjust storm of abuse and calumny which burst upon him in 1917 when he dared to vote according to his beliefs on the matter of the declaration of war. Thereby he kept untarnished the oath he took when he became Senator. Thereby he kept his conscience clear, his soul his own. It is idle to prophesy what history will or will not say about such a figure, but if that fickle muse writes truly of him it will assign to him one of the noblest places in the annals of America—the man who deliberately chose what seemed political death and perpetual contumely rather than yield one iota of convictions. Like Bright and Cobden, Campbell-Bannerman and Ramsay MacDonald, he survived the attacks upon him for opposing his country's going to war. He died stronger in the affection of the masses of the American people than ever before. Time has justified almost his every stand. The tributes, however grudging, paid him by the hounds of daily journalism, who for years snapped at his heels at their masters' behest, are proof that in the final test even the most vindictive must yield in respect to a character that knows no fear and is true to itself.

A very great American he was. Not in the sense of statesmanship. From the Old World standpoint he would hardly be classed as a statesman. His range of vision, until his later years, was too narrowly circumscribed by domestic issues, so that he was long debarred from profiting by European knowledge and experience. In Wisconsin he fought the devil with fire—he played the local political game with the bitter partisanship he had learned from his enemies. They gave no quarter, and he followed suit; in Wisconsin political enmities are almost as deadly as in Kentucky. He used the public offices and patronage of every kind to build up his machine. This was as natural a step in the process of political evolution as had been, until La Follette broke their grasp, the mastery of the State by corporations and the bosses whom they created and owned. He broke their hold not only by taking a leaf out of their book. He card-catalogued the State; he wrote to thousands upon thousands, establishing personal relations with them. Thus he offset the hostility of the daily press and established his own leadership. It goes without saying that that leadership, however established and maintained, could not have continued for a long political lifetime had he not been buttressed by principle, had he not been genuinely devoted to the popular welfare, had he not been absolutely selfless in giving himself to his causes. This it was, together with his understanding of them, that gave him that hold upon the plain people which nothing could shake, which made nearly 5,000,-000 voters acclaim him in 1924 as their national hero.

Not even Lincoln was so beloved in Illinois, prior to the Presidency, as La Follette in Wisconsin. Whenever he spoke people flocked to hear him, undismayed by his interminable speeches—he once spoke for nineteen hours without a stop, against the Aldrich currency bill. It is related of him that on one occasion he began to speak in the "opera house" of a small town at seven o'clock. Long before that every seat was taken and all the standing room. Outside a long queue of patient people stood waiting. At 8:30 Mr. La Follette paused, drank a glass of water, and announced that the first phase of his talk was over. He had discussed corporations in general; next he would take up the railroads. If anyone wished to leave this was the opportunity. Nobody stirring, Mr. La Follette spoke for an hour on the railroads. Again he paused to rest and said: "I know some of you folks have come in from the farms and you've a long drive before you and you have to get up very early. I shall understand if a lot of you want to go." Not a person arose; outside, after two and one-half hours of waiting, the line was intact. Again Mr.

La Follette spoke for an hour and then when he paused, two farmer folk arose and said: "Bob, we don't want to go but you was right, we've got a long ways to go and a lot of cows to milk!" Their places were immediately taken by those at the head of the line and the speech continued until nearly midnight.

This was not an exceptional incident; it was part of the patient drudgery of the man who could find no other way to offset the wealth of his adversaries and their control of the press. He literally talked himself into the hearts of the people, not by the arts of the demagogue—he had few of the arts of the orator, though he had the histrionic manner and an enormous voice which could fill any hall—but by his persistent appeals to them on the basis of reason and common sense, backed by extraordinary reservoirs of knowledge upon the subjects he discussed. These were reservoirs that could be drawn on by the hour yet never ran dry. His plain, straightforward, year-in-year-out presentation of his facts won the people. They watched him like hawks and found that, if he played politics as it had always been played in Wisconsin since its first settlement, he none the less held to his faith and fought his main fights without compromise. They could not fail to be convinced that he was unselfish in his advocacy of the State's taking control of its affairs out of the hands of its rich men and its corporation managers. They had seen too many Progressives go over into the enemy's camp and live thereafter lives of ease and plenty. Had Mr. La Follette wished to take retainers from the other side, he would have been rich overnight, and the very men who declared him to be a person of small parts would suddenly have discovered in him a statesman of great powers, fit for the highest office.

Endless physical and mental labour Mr. La Follette's course called for and the sacrificing of his own and the family's comfort. Zona Gale has drawn a touching picture [1] of the way that extraordinary family pulled together—Mrs. La Follette, young and beautiful, abandoning the profession of the law to walk with this man over the inevitably long and stony and thorny paths that lead toward freedom. "Over and over she campaigned the State with the Senator, daunted by no condition of roads, or hours on trains, or status of hotels, because 'the people must understand.'" She and her husband "left their children free only if they used that freedom in the social struggle. . . . To the La Follette family the human family was 'the human being.' The La Follette family was never merely a family, it was an idea in action." That idea bound them together in ties of unsurpassed devotion and affection. When the present "Senator Bob" was desperately ill, his father spent the greater part of a year by his boy's bedside; it was the only time anyone could accuse the veteran Senator of letting a family situation take precedence of public affairs. The freedom the parents gave to their children has brought the richest dividends in free individual lives and their wisdom has been repaid by completest devotion. This was the man, this father, whom

[1] *The Nation*, February 15, 1928.

multitudes, blinded by war hate and passion, declared to be faithless to his country.

Yet it cannot be denied that the Senator constantly stood in his own light. Accused of vanity, of being a poseur, he cared so little about himself and what people thought about him as to be the despair of his friends. He not only spurned opportunity after opportunity to advance his fortunes and to trumpet abroad his virtues, he was far too indifferent to falsehood and slander. Not until a year after the Associated Press's abominable misquoting of his words in his St. Paul speech (by which he was made to say that we had *no* grievance in the sinking of the Lusitania, whereas he said directly the opposite) did he seek to set the public right although he could have recovered heavy damages from the Associated Press and its affiliated dailies. During that year the writer of these lines sat on the board of directors of the Associated Press in ignorance of the wrong. When it was finally brought to his attention he demanded and obtained a complete retraction, but the injury had long been done; the correction could not overtake the lie, for it never does. Once, a brilliant journalist joined the Senator's office force for the express purpose of challenging misrepresentations of Mr. La Follette and getting the truth about him before the public. In vain; after some months the journalist resigned because he could not get the maligned man sufficiently interested in himself to make the task worth while. His causes alone interested him; they carried him through the slough of despond of war days. They were his life, but his absorption in them to the extent of being utterly indifferent to the charges against him was a misfortune for him, and therefore, for the causes which he championed.

Again, Mr. La Follette's judgment frequently erred when it came to choosing lieutenants and associates, and so he was often the victim of treachery and deceit. This made him more than ever determined to put only tried and trusty friends on guard, which policy, in 1924, nearly wrecked the Senator's Presidential campaign. The kindly, loyal, and devoted Wisconsin Congressmen who took charge of the national headquarters proved totally unfit and utterly lacking in political and executive ability, and so did State chairmen and other officials whom "Bob" chose because he trusted them. Without money or the knowledge how to raise it, betrayed by some of the venal unions which had pledged money and votes, the La Follette headquarters floundered helplessly and hopelessly, cheered only by the discovery that the other two party headquarters were just about as incompetent and inefficient, despite their plethoric treasuries. In a number of States there was no La Follette organization at all. None the less, nearly five million votes were cast and counted—how many uncounted will, of course, never be known—for this "wild man" from Wisconsin, this "traitor," this political renegade. It is my deliberate opinion that no greater tribute was ever paid to an American candidate, for in many places people could vote for La Follette only with the greatest difficulty or in the face of social ostracism—in New York State alone 500,000 men and women voted for the

Senator although in many towns not a printed or spoken word helped on the cause during the entire campaign.

It was the custom in this campaign, as in all the others in which he took part, to decry Senator La Follette as a man without constructive ideas, a merely destructive force—always the first charge of the empty political pate. As a matter of fact there was no man in public life in his time who had a finer record of constructive achievement. In 1908 he first began going into the Republican conventions demanding planks which were regularly refused him. At convention after convention he presented his minority platform only to be ridiculed and howled down. Yet, in 1924, Representative Cooper of Wisconsin, speaking to the Republican Convention in Cleveland, pointed out that of the thirty-one demands which Mr. La Follette had made during those sixteen years, only to have them contemptuously rejected, no less than twenty-six had been finally adopted by the party and been enacted into law. It would be hard to find any other public man who even approached this. By this statement Mr. Cooper did not mean that Senator La Follette had originated the thirty-one measures, only that he had tried to force them upon his party when he was so far in advance of the times that he was denounced as a wild radical, derided, and ignored. He early favoured woman suffrage, prohibition, and the unsuccessful child-labour amendment to the Constitution. He was foremost in advocating a parcels post, the postal savings system, the creation of the Federal Trade Commission, and the establishment of the Department of

Labour. One of his greatest achievements, which rightly bears his name, is the La Follette Seaman's Act, which has been called the Magna Charta of our merchant sailors. Never was legislation more bitterly assailed, especially by ship-owners and operators. Yet there is today no measure more firmly established in our code of laws. Even the ship-owners have come to accept it, and would modify it today only at minor points. More than that, it has become a lever by which the conditions of sailors have been improved in various other countries. It was truly international legislation, although passed by the Congress of the United States.

But this was only one of the measures that he sponsored in the interest of labour. He helped to obtain the eight-hour day for government employees, improved employers'-liability laws, and a measure limiting the hours of railroad workers. In the international field he fought the ratification of the Treaty of Versailles, saw nothing in the League of Nations but "a sham" and "a fraud," and opposed our latter-day policy in the Carribean and Central America by declaring that the American flag should not follow the "speculative investments of its citizens in the countries where the governments are weak." He was in the forefront of those who denounced our unconstitutional wars upon Russia, Mexico, Haiti, and Santo Domingo. It must be always written down to his credit that in addition to voting against the World War he opposed conscription and the villainous Espionage Act under which Americans were deprived of liberties which they have not yet altogether regained.

It was not only that he had a constructive mind; he had that rare quality in an American public man—the willingness to let everyone know just where he stood and why he took a given position. No man ever buttressed his speeches with more facts or greater wealth of argument.

In reviewing Mr. La Follette's political doctrines, however, it is undeniable that he never had a thoroughgoing political or economic philosophy. He was like most of us in that he attacked one evil after another as it presented itself, with little understanding of the basic facts, their relationship to one another, and the necessity of applying fundamental remedies rather than legislative palliatives or prohibitions. Senator La Follette, too, merely groped his way—as nearly all the world is doing today as it seeks to find solutions for the unending list of evils of our highly capitalistic system. His final platform, that of the 1924 Presidential campaign, was anything but thoroughgoing. He was against privilege, but failed to see that the tariff is the greatest bulwark and creator of privilege that we have; he opposed corruption, but he voted regularly for the tariff system which for generations gave rise to more political corruption than anything else. He was opposed to war, but he was not a pacifist—he could not see that he who compromises with this evil and refuses to break with it at all times, under all conditions, merely helps to continue it—helps it more than does the outright advocate of war. He believed in co-operation, yet lacked the vision to see what enormous benefits the whole nation would derive if it were made of paramount importance. In the matter of monopolies and the trusts, he based his last campaign upon conditions and policies which time had outlawed. He was only a recent convert to government ownership of railroads, and he permitted the putting into the platform of the proposal to curb the Supreme Court, which, although it was precisely what Lincoln had urged as President, yet gave to his adversaries one of the two handles they had to frighten people into believing that the platform was dangerously radical. It was, of course, not a whit more so than the Roosevelt platform in 1912 with its recall of judges; even Mr. Wilson, it is known, had come to government ownership of railroads shortly before his death.

Calling Mr. La Follette's platform *radical* aroused the laughter of all foreign observers on the ground. Mr. La Follette was not a real radical in the European sense —perhaps because he was so entirely unfamiliar with European conditions and the development of European thought. It would have been rather depressing to see him put the outgrown question of curbing the trusts to the front had his last effort not been so gallant against such terrific odds. The rank and file of the workers could not understand why the Senator was so slow to begin his speaking, he who always spoke from sunrise to sunset in his local campaigns, and why he made so few speeches. They knew vaguely that he was in the doctor's hands, but only a few of those nearest and dearest to the Senator realized that his appearance on the platform at all was an act of supreme heroism. He took his life in his hands every time that he spoke, for the disease that carried him off had already progressed far. Despite the wonderful reception given him at the historic Madison Square Garden in New York he could not hold all of his audience; it drifted out, as listeners did out of the meetings of Coolidge, Dawes, and Davis. Yet the stricken Wisconsin veteran fought on, cheerful and uncomplaining, eager to spend himself utterly then and there, chafing at the physicians' limitations of his activities, keenly aware how poorly the organization was functioning, and how much the whole campaign depended upon him and the valiant Senator Wheeler. Talk about battlefield heroism! There was never anything finer than this lion-hearted effort and no one who witnessed it and knew the odds can ever forget it. Here was a *true* prophet, who at least had all honour in his own country of Wisconsin; who visioned aright and fought to the end.

But the high point of his career remains his opposition to the war. In voting against it, he merely exercised his historic right. Never before had it been demanded of a Congress that it should unanimously approve the recommendations of an Executive that the country go to war. Abraham Lincoln opposed the Mexican War while a member of Congress and while the struggle was on, thus laying himself open to the charge so freely used during the Philippine and World Wars that he was stabbing our soldiers in the back while they were facing enemy bullets. In 1917 the government, knowing that a large majority of the American people were not for the war, that our entering it was a breach of faith on Mr. Wilson's part with the millions who had voted for him because he kept us out of war, utilized all its powers of denunciation and propaganda, the appeal to stand by the flag, to be patriotic, in order to drum everybody into line. The country had to be taught to hate, and from the head of the government himself came the first attacks upon the "Wilful Twelve" who refused to go with him on the armed-ship bill, who dared to put their consciences and their judgment above his imperious will. In those days, and when the final vote on our going to war came, many envied the courage of La Follette and Congressman Lindbergh, the father of the flying marvel, and the others who dared to vote contrary to the President's wishes. A secret ballot would have made an astonishing difference in the voting. Mr. La Follette's own colleague from Wisconsin assured him a day or two before that he would stand by him, and then he voted for war; from then on his moral collapse went on apace while Senator La Follette stood erect and knew that his soul was his own, that he had been true to his faiths and his beliefs.

Miss Gale has given us two excerpts from a private letter which reveal the Senator's state of mind on January 5, 1918, when, as he wandered alone through the halls of Congress, men whom he had known and who had admired him for years, dared not be seen speaking to him in public; when he was denounced by a crazed press, which failed to realize that it was he more than anyone else who was upholding America's ideals and standards, the historic American right, yes, the historic Anglo-Saxon right, to differ with one's government in time of war. The first quotation is this:

> *May I say to you that in the midst of this raging storm of hate I am withal very happy in so far as my own future is concerned. I would not change places with any living man on the record as it stands today.*

There spoke a true hero. And the other extract from this remarkable letter is this:

> *War is a terribly destructive force, even beyond the limits of the battle front and the war zone. Its influence involves the whole community. It warps men's judgment, distorts the true standards of patriotism, breeds distrust and suspicion among neighbours, inflames passions, encourages violence, develops abuse of power, tyrannizes over men and women even in the purely social relations of life, and terrifies whole communities into the most abject surrender of every right which is the heritage of free government.*

Today no man with sane judgment can deny the truth of this statement, this analysis of what the war did to America, just as it is of record from Mr. Wilson's own lips that it was not a war for a humbug purpose to end war, or to free the seas, or to safeguard the rights of small nations, but a war whose causes were purely economic, plus historic military and naval rivalries.

That vote of nearly five millions of fellow-citizens for La Follette in 1924 showed, under the circumstances in which it was cast, what a large part of the electorate thought of him. Had he lived a little longer he would have seen the fog of hate and bitterness conjured up by hysteria, and lying, and misrepresentation rising faster from the earth and rapidly disappearing. But in the darkest hour he was not lonely, this outcast. That he could never be because of his devoted family and the host of friends who adored this warm, this intense, this absolutely honest personality. Here was a leader of men, here a patriot.

"I don't know how the people will feel toward me," he said to his son, Robert, as he lay dying, "but I will take to my grave my love for them which has sustained me through life." Never were truer and never were more sincere words uttered by a public man. Somehow we have no fears for Robert La Follette's posthumous fame. Historians may write what they please; in the hearts of the plain people Robert La Follette is safe, for their love echoes back to his.

WILLIAM J. BRYAN

Cabinet Officer

"**H**E is obviously lacking in taste, breeding, and knowledge of the world, despite his travelling." These words in an article of mine in the New York *Evening Post* of May 17, 1915, hurt William J. Bryan to the core. The next time we met, which happened to be in front of the White House, he burst out with a vigorous denunciation of the article and its author, and voiced the emphatic assurance that his family and his breeding were infinitely better than those of the offending journalist. He then left me to enter the White House where he saw President Wilson and complained about the article. That afternoon the White House asked me in a friendly way for an explanation of the whole thing. This happened a day or two before the excited Mr. Bryan resigned as Secretary of State.

The offending words would not have been penned had it occurred to their author that they would pain Mr. Bryan who, prior to that time, had been called every name in the category—"liar," "forger," and "blasphemer," were some of the epithets hurled at him by the New York *Tribune*. For no one really wished to hurt Mr. Bryan when he was Secretary of State. There was something so well-meaning, yet so pathetic about him; one felt so sorry for him in the position in which he found himself, that everybody with a spark of decency in him had the instinctive desire to shield and defend him. So, in the very article to which Mr. Bryan objected, there were also many words in praise of him, and a genuine effort to put him in the most favourable light possible. Thus, there were stressed his loyalty to President Wilson under extremely difficult circumstances; his willingness to subordinate himself to the President in the conduct of his Department, and his readiness to do anything to serve his party, his President, and his country. Beyond that the Secretary of State was represented as being devoted to principle, forceful and earnest, yet humble in spirit; as having won the affectionate regard of his colleagues in the Cabinet, however often they might disagree with him; and as making genuine contributions to such Cabinet discussions as took place. "Nor is there," I wrote, "the slightest evidence of any selfish desire to make capital for himself or to stay in the limelight"; nor was there, I added, any desire on Mr. Bryan's part to advance his own political fortunes.

Yet to make the picture complete and truthful it was necessary to say that Mr. Bryan's weaknesses as Secretary of State were chiefly due to his lack of education, to his lack of administrative experience, to an inability to win the respect of all those with whom he came into contact, or to uphold his own personal dignity. However much one might respect his sincerity and the integrity of his life, one always had the impression of uncouthness, of a certain amount of unattractive commonness as distinct from that wholesome self-respecting commonness so often to be found in the work-shop, on the farm, and in earnest self-made men. These were serious deficiencies in one who was nominally in charge of our foreign affairs, who was in daily contact with the diplomatic corps, and with the representatives of the press. It must be remembered that the time of which I speak was the period just after the sinking of the Lusitania when the country found itself in a genuine crisis.

Never in my journalistic career have I seen anything as pitiful as Mr. Bryan in his daily conference with newspaper men. One blushed to be of the profession when one listened to the deliberate and studied effort of some of the correspondents to ask Mr. Bryan impertinent and embarrassing questions, some of which could no more be answered than the famous one as to whether you had stopped beating your wife. Needless to say no one ever thought of asking such questions of Mr. Wilson, or of the other important members of the Cabinet. The Hearst journalists were the worst offenders, and as Mr. Bryan stood in the Secretary of State's office, trying to ward off these snapping wolves of the press, I could only think of him as an old, nearly worn-out, and very shaggy buffalo trying to drive away the pack by much lowering of his head, and many menacing lunges. Unfortunately, Mr. Bryan had laid himself open to these attacks, for though there was a time in his earlier life when he thought that no one should amass, or be allowed to amass, more than a hundred thousand dollars, he was himself eager for money, and would therefore not give up his public speaking for a price. It had been for so many years the very breath of his nostrils; he hungered so for the excitement of the platform and the thrill of the applause which he received that he could not abandon going the rounds of the nearby chautauquas. Undoubtedly it was a great strain upon him to live on the small salary of a Cabinet officer, as it was upon all the others who were without personal means. Still Mr. Bryan had a good many financial reserves, yet he could see no clash between the dignity of his official position and his appearance as a platform speaker. He was inordinately proud of the large sums he made by an evening's talk, and was not unhappy that it was known that he received $400 or $600 or $800 for single appearances.

So it was the habit of the malicious journalists to begin the daily newspaper conferences by asking Mr. Bryan: "Well, Mr. Secretary, what is the arrangement tonight, $300 and half the gate money, or fifty-fifty straight?" This would be varied by asking him whether he would appear between the Swiss bell-ringers and the world's greatest saxophone artist, or whether he would follow the Siamese jugglers upon the program. Try as he would, Mr. Bryan could not stop these impertinences; sometimes the questions obviously flattered him. Then there would follow diabolical inquiries, cleverly framed to make him betray the secrets of his Department, whether he answered yes or no. After one of those disheartening conferences which had resulted only in mortification and had yielded no news for those honestly in search of it, he called me by name and asked me to remain after the others had gone. He then proceeded to lecture me for what he considered a dereliction on my part, the publishing of a "beat" which had been given to me by a member of his own Department with permission to make it public. Mr. Bryan declared that I must choose between two horns of a dilemma: I had either betrayed an official confidence, or I had dishonestly acquired the news that I had published. He was much astonished when I told him that I had to grasp neither horn of the dilemma, and reminded him that as I had been sending correspondents all over the world during the previous twenty years for the daily which had the highest journalistic standards in New York, it was not within his province or his power to instruct me as to the behaviour or the responsibilities of a correspondent.

The Secretary of State showed no resentment. On the contrary, he suddenly melted and began to tell me his tale of woe. He charged the newspaper men not only with the offences that I have described, but with deliberate breaking of their word, and violation of the confidences with which he entrusted them. I asked him whether he had not thought of summoning the steering committee of the correspondents and consulting with them. He had not thought of it. When we next met I suggested to him that to relieve himself of this intolerable nuisance and these undignified scenes he transfer the whole unhappy duty of receiving the correspondents to Mr. Lansing, or some other subordinate. It was then that he broke into a fury and went off to see the President in high dudgeon.

His final interview with the correspondents was pathetic to a degree. Said he: "I have been like an old hen with a lot of chicks. The chicks were my secrets, which I tried to keep under my wings, while you were trying to get them away from me." It was hard for the men to keep their countenances, it was such a perfect description of what had been going on. None the less, they did, and all of the earnest men who were there felt a real touch of sorrow on parting with him, just as did his fellow-members of the Cabinet. One of these, Franklin K. Lane, had written of him a couple of months earlier that "Bryan is a very much larger man, and more competent than the papers credit him with being." He was able to testify warmly to the genuine feeling which marked the good-byes when Bryan made his last appearance in the historic Cabinet room, and went from there to a farewell luncheon with his associates of the Cabinet.

So far as Mr. Wilson was concerned, between him and Mr. Bryan, who was so dissimilar in training, in antecedents, in mental processes, there sprang up a genuine and affectionate friendship. If I may quote again from my notes of the time, there was on Mr. Bryan's part "the profoundest admiration for his chief, whose superiority in ability and in literary and political skill he most generously concedes. On Mr. Wilson's side there is genuine regard and sincere gratitude for great aid freely given, not only in the matter of the currency bill, which stands largely as Mr. Bryan's personal contribution to the fine record for achievement of the Wilson Administration, but in other legislative matters, indeed, in all matters." As a matter of fact Mr. Bryan gladly took the impossible position of becoming the diplomatic errand boy to Mr. Wilson with the result that he was often represented in the press as being put aside and ignored, as being out of touch with what was going on. This was often true, yet as a matter of fact he was usually no more in ignorance of what was happening than were the other members of the Cabinet. Mr. Wilson constantly ignored them in vital matters as in the preparation of the notes to Germany during the summer of 1915, until, after his final return from Europe and his illness began, the Cabinet was kept in utter darkness as to what was happening. A man of different type from Bryan, one of lesser loyalty and of higher spirit, could not have consented to being made an under-secretary in his own Department. But here Mr. Bryan's humility came into play, for he recognized his own limitations, and frequently took the minor notes and messages which he sent to foreign governments, or to our diplomatic representatives abroad, to Mr. Wilson for revision. His admiration for the skill with which Mr. Wilson by a few strokes of his pen could convey the exact meaning which Mr. Bryan had unsuccessfully endeavoured to put into words, was convincing testimony to his lack of jealousy, his inability to take offence, and his all-embracing desire to help his President.

Yet, from his own point of view, his resignation from the Cabinet was a very great error. So far from relieving the President by ending the stream of criticism which poured in upon them from the Republican and imperialistic press, Mr. Bryan's going at just that hour made Mr. Wilson's task more difficult in that it encouraged the Central Powers to believe that there was a rift in the Cabinet over the Government's policy in regard to the Lusitania. It seemed to all the world a sign of weakness when a united front was needed. Mr. Bryan had of course no thought of this when he resigned. The exact reason was never quite clear; but the break supposedly came because of a difference between his pacifist views and those of the belligerent members of the Cabinet. If this was the reason, it was characteristic of him that he could not see that that was the very time that he should have remained in the Cabinet and should have fought with his full authority for the course which he thought the United States ought to follow. He often had excellent ideas and policies. It is my belief that it was he who originated the idea of calling a conference of all the neutral nations of the world to insist upon their rights which were being more invaded by the Allies than by the Germans. Such a conference, controlling as it would have the raw materials which both sides were obtaining—the Germans received many cargoes carried in British bottoms to Scandinavian ports— could have insisted upon freedom of the seas and a genuine effort to obtain a negotiated peace based upon the *status quo ante*, in line with Mr. Wilson's subse-

quent doctrine of January 22, 1917, that there should
be neither victors nor vanquished. Mr. Wilson toyed with
the idea for some time, but finally abandoned it when
Mr. Bryan was no longer in the Cabinet to fight for it.

His resignation was characteristic of Mr. Bryan.
He frequently failed utterly to fight things through. He
was at first going to fight for free silver, and to free
men from slavery to gold just as long as he lived; he
abandoned that after a while. He came back from
Europe in 1906 and championed government ownership
of railroads—not by the United States, but in some
mysterious way by the individual State without interfering with interstate commerce—only to abandon the
plan when he found that it did not take. He was an outspoken pacifist until the war of 1898 came, when he
became a ridiculously inefficient and speech-making
Colonel of a Nebraska regiment, which fortunately
never had to go under fire with Bryan in command.
Again, he was opposed to our entering the World War,
and then he offered himself as a private, a position for
which he was obviously physically unfit, and when he
died he was buried by his own wish in the military
cemetery of Arlington as Colonel of the Third Nebraska
Infantry.

Of all the men I have seen at close range in thirty-
one years of newspaper service, Mr. Bryan seemed to
me the most ignorant. He may have read books in his
youth, but in his later years he never read anything except magazines and newspapers. His excellent emotions
and desires were never supported by clear-cut thinking,

or by logical mental processes. Yet beyond question he powerfully influenced great masses of his fellow-Americans, and his decision to enter the Wilson Cabinet was in itself a tremendous contribution to the causes for which Mr. Wilson was then fighting, for as Mr. Lane then put it, Bryan "really represents a great body of moral force and opinion." As late as January, 1920, Mr. Lane repeated his opinion, saying "he [Bryan] has been, and will continue to be as long as he lives, a great force in our politics. People believe that he is honest, and know he is sympathetic with the moral aspirations of the plain people. They distrust his administrative ability, but on the moral question they recognize no one as having greater authority." It was, therefore, all the greater misfortune for Mr. Bryan and the country that just because of lack of knowledge, of personal dignity, and of ability to utilize to the utmost the moral authority within him, he could not live up to his opportunity or drive through to success many of the causes for which he stood, in which he fought for the advancement of the masses. It always seemed to me as I observed him that he constantly failed to think things through, partly again because of ignorance and of lack of knowledge of the precedents which might have aided him.

His mistakes of judgment were numerous, but his mistakes of taste were worse in their effect. He who had travelled so much, who knew, therefore, the value of foreign representation, who had learned between his first and second visits to England to drop the business

suit and soft hat for ceremonial occasions, could see no
reason why he should not stuff the diplomatic and con-
sular services with unworthy political henchmen, or
superannuated ministers, or even drunken Tammany
toughs. They were his friends or his supporters; therefore, they were good enough to represent the United
States abroad. The final unveiling of his abysmal ignorance of science and modern thought came during the
Scopes trial in Tennessee at the very end of Mr. Bryan's
life. But there was no time during his career when a
similar cross-examination would not have revealed similar ignorance of other lines of human thought and activity.

There have been plenty of other men in our public
life who were ignorant of history and literature, but they
were able to triumph over this shortcoming by their
native intuition, their common sense, and their instinctive
understanding of what lay at the bottom of many of the
problems they confronted. They had no better birth or
breeding than Mr. Bryan, but nobody ever dared to
enter their presence and to make derogatory remarks to
them. Nor did they when they retired from a high
office continue to appear on little country platforms
between bell-ringers and jugglers, or lend their prestige
and their oratory to boomers of real estate in return for
solid cash, as did Mr. Bryan at the close of his career.
He was for a time a great apostle of democracy; he was
able to rouse the masses although not to overcome their
enemy. He could at times preach against imperialism

and for the freedom of peoples in chains, and then vitiate it all and throw doubts upon his sincerity by taking part in a ruthless invasion and slaughter in Vera Cruz, and in pulling down the century-old independent Republic of Haiti, and fettering it with the chains supplied by the very bankers of Wall Street against whom he had inveighed so long. He could see, moreover, in these acts of imperialism abroad nothing out of harmony with his negotiations of what were at that time excellent peace and arbitration treaties with many of the nations of the world.

Mr. Bryan owed his strength in large measure to the fact that he was of the people, that he was clean, honest, and above-board in his life, and that he was devoted to temperance and to all the homely virtues. Over that devotion the journals of the great cities made merry, but it counted very largely with the masses of his fellow-citizens. No mistakes of taste or of judgment could ever shake the popular belief in him and the rectitude of his purposes. Often he was a lap or two behind the times and even of the developments among his own kind. Often he was hurt and puzzled by criticism, and unable to understand the public fault-finding with him. None the less, he typified a great hope with multitudes of his fellow-citizens; he was their champion, as he was the defender of their faith and of their trust in immortality. He remains a monument to the need of sound education and sound mental processes in public men. We need the prophet and the apostle of liberty beyond all others. But if the torch of liberty is really to be handed on, the torch-bearers must know whereof they speak, and not rely merely upon sincerity, generous emotions, and a kindly heart to point the way.

FRANKLIN K. LANE

Public Servant

"LIFE is just a beautiful adventure, to be flung away for any good cause," Franklin K. Lane once said to a group which was endeavouring to keep the country out of war. One could easily challenge that statement, but no one can challenge the fact that its author was one of the finest prophets and one of the greatest public servants the United States has produced. Had Mr. Lane not been born in Canada and had he retained his health, he would have been President; the nomination would have been his without question in 1910 or 1920, and sooner or later he would have entered the White House. For here was a poet, an orator, a philosopher, a statesman, a noble spirit, whom nature intended for the highest posts. It is difficult to write of him save in superlatives, yet the truth demands them. Among all the Cabinet officers whom I have seen pass into and out of the Cabinet in forty years, Franklin Lane stands out as one unsurpassed in his fidelity, in the purity of his own life, in his foresight which at times was something uncanny, and in his breadth of vision. He was as nearly the ideal public official as we shall probably ever see.

Here was a great personality and a great American. He himself bewailed the fact that his was an Irish temperament and that he had not been made a "stolid, phlegmatic, non-nervous, self-satisfied Britisher, instead of a wild cross between a crazy Irishman with dreams, desires, fancies—and a dour Scot with his conscience and his logical bitterness against himself—and his eternal drive." But the fact remains that he was American to the core. It makes no difference that he did not cross the Canadian border until he was seven years of age; he took root in American soil the minute that he reached it. He needed no teaching of Americanism. In its best sense it flowered in him at once; not a worship of mere forms, but of the spirit which underlies our institutions and our Constitution, something all too often confused by the native-born. He knew from the beginning that, as he himself wrote, "our government is not our master but our tool, adaptable to the uses for which it was designed; our servant, responsive to our call." He had early in life "a consciousness of the deep meanings of our national experiences." He could wish that these might be taught where they had not been taught, but he was not to be had for any jingo exaltation of our country and its social system. "America," he once wrote, "gives men nothing—except a chance." He knew that our institutions were far from perfect, and he felt that out of the World War must come far-reaching economic changes which would alter the whole emphasis of social life. He refused to bow down to the great God Property, and he was not at all sure that anyone had a natural right in property except those who held it in trust to use it well. He was even not afraid to foresee a day when there might be nationalization of some industries if people did not mend their ways. He admired Roosevelt, among many things, because Roosevelt was correct in declaring that it was not he who was compelling government control of railroads and of business, but the masters of business themselves.

Always Mr. Lane was devoted to the public service. He remained in it for twenty-one years until the absolute necessity of earning more money drove him out of it—in debt even for the tickets to take his family home, for he who had not a dollar of private means had to live like a Cabinet member on a Cabinet member's salary. Everything about the government service he adored. He shrank at first from the Secretaryship of the Interior, when Mr. Wilson offered it to him, because of the extraordinary conglomeration of duties and responsibilities it comprised. But the longer he was there the more the variety of it won him. He found he could deal with big issues and leave the details to others. Everything in it and about it appealed to him. He could not even be content with his tasks, but created new ones. He was perhaps the first Cabinet officer to concern himself intimately with the employees in the big building of his Department. He knew that they were human beings and not automata; that their nerves of energy and initiative were likely to be atrophied in a few years. He found them part of the government—yet its orphans—citizens without a vote since they lived in the District of Columbia; employees without employee representation, without anything in the form of self-government. All their

creative energies were throttled by a dull routine, with
no vents for self-expression, without even the opportunity for social intercourse among themselves.

The latter Mr. Lane quickly remedied, so far as
the Department of the Interior was concerned, by form-
ing the Home Club to which all were eligible, to which
he and Mrs. Lane came, not in a spirit of condescension,
of the lord visiting among the lowly, but with the frank
recognition that they were all public servants together.
The club soon had seventeen hundred members, gave
entertainments every night in a fine old Washington
residence, with dues of only fifty cents a week. Most
naturally his reward for this and other "concerns" for
his subordinates was their loyalty. They knew he worked
for longer hours than they, that he was industry,
honesty, and probity personified. They soon learned
that if they came to him they received the same attention
as if they were co-heads of departments; that he played
no politics and no favourites. They realized his bigness
and were proud of him. Like everyone who knew Franklin Lane they understood that he was not Secretary because he wanted a job, or was lazy, or could not make a
living elsewhere, but because he felt there could be no
greater honour than to be a part of the government for
the purpose of making it better—not of worshipping it
as a pagan god.

Of course he liked his job in handling the Indians,
he who always said he must have friends, men, women,
people, about him. His idea of earthly misery was to be
alone with nobody to talk to, to compare human experi-

ences with, to find out how they looked upon life, its shams, and hypocrisies. Of course, he liked to be head of the irrigation service and deal with waste lands and to run the national parks, he who loved the great plains and hills and the vastnesses of the West. Was he not a Westerner to the end, full of the breeziness, the reckless-ness, the love of humans and of nature that invariably mark the true Westerner? To all of these and many other duties he brought a rarely constructive mind. It was well that he did not live to know that the second man after him to sit as Secretary of the Interior turned a traitor to his country and sold it out, once for $100,000 in a black bag, and again for $300,000. That would have broken Frank Lane's heart, as it would have drawn from him the blistering oaths of which he was capable, which in their variety again stamped him the Westerner, this absolutely honest personality.

Always he was that rare thing, a genuine personal-ity, warm and affectionate, with an impulsiveness which sometimes broke in on his loyalty to his friends, for he was of those who put friendships below loyalty to prin-ciples and causes. Yet, he would often swing back to his friends, and he was incapable of believing, as did Theodore Roosevelt, that a protagonist was a weakling or a crook because he disagreed with him. Indeed, Lane could go out of his way to aid a man, like the writer of these lines, if he found his rights as an American jeopardized, although he differed totally from him on all the issues of the hour. Perhaps it was his Scotch inheritance that made him so tenacious of individual rights under the Constitution. The average American, if he sees one of those breached, shrugs his shoulders. It is too bad, but it will soon be forgotten; what of it? Mr. Lane looked underneath a lynching and saw what it signified; witnessed a case of suppression of the liberty of the press and knew that it was a nail in the coffin of the American democracy. He could see no good in the Russian economic revolution and its social changes and accepted the current falsehoods about its achievements. But he recognized clearly that the twentieth-century problem is chiefly one of distribution of produce and of wealth, and he did not hesitate to say that the United States was "the most backward and conservative of all the democracies of the world," and that its politically static condition—after Mr. Wilson lost interest, because of the World War, in his domestic reform program—boded ill.

As for his relations to President Wilson we do not yet know the full extent of his feelings toward his chief, though there are a number of outspoken utterances in such of his letters as have already been published. He never saw or knew Mr. Wilson until after he was appointed to the Cabinet and, like so many others, he was at first charmed with the man and believed that those who, in Western parlance, had called Mr. Wilson "a cold nose," were entirely in error. But like others in the Cabinet, while he still admired Mr. Wilson's great abilities he became more and more conscious of his great defects which led to the eventual disaster. Mr. Wilson's secretiveness; his yielding to the blandishments of men

like Mr. Tumulty (who, Mr. Lane suggests, kept up in
Mr. Wilson during the last years illusions of grandeur)
and Mr. Burleson; his playing a lone hand in foreign
policy; his reduction of the Cabinet meetings on many
occasions—when it met at all—to a story-telling affair;
his constant wobbling—all these often grated deeply on
Mr. Lane's nerves. Even at the Cabinet meeting of October 15, 1918, just before the Armistice, the Cabinet
was not allowed to see the second note of the Peace
series which Mr. Lansing had already given to the press
for release at four o'clock that day, so afraid was the
President of adverse criticism. Yet a week later when
Germany came back with an acceptance of his terms he
appealed to the Cabinet for aid, for once saying: "I do
not know what to do. I must ask your advice. I may have
made a mistake in not properly safeguarding what I
said before. What do you think should be done?" When
Mr. Wilson refused to consult with any of his Cabinet
in regard to his first Lusitania note, Mr. Lane alone demanded over the telephone his rights as a Cabinet counsellor, and was invited to submit his views in writing.
He did so promptly.

Mr. Lane was straightforward, accustomed to hitting
from the shoulder, of saying just what he meant and
looking, as he said it, straight at you through his wonder-
fully searching and honest eyes. Probably if Mr. Lane
had been Chief Magistrate he would have blundered,
through hasty impulse and warm-blooded rage. He would,
however, have been accessible, open to argument, without that stubborn egotism and pride of opinion which

marked Mr. Wilson. Months before Mr. Wilson was
inaugurated Mr. Lane correctly wrote of him "he is apt
to prove one of the most tremendously disliked men in
Washington that ever has been here." But Mr. Wilson's
faults were offset in Mr. Lane's eyes by his achievements and those of his Administration. There he was
a biased witness, for, though he inveighed against Burle-
sonism and must have resented the scandals in connection with the airplanes and the Alien Property Custodian's office, the suppression of personal liberty, the
throwing men into jail because they put conscience above
country, Mr. Lane declared that nothing that the Wilson
government did was else than noble and great. The
"heroic mood" of the country during the war thrilled
him, although that mood was largely compounded of a
stupid berserker rage, bitterness, and endless and incredible lying, falsifying, and the suppression of truths
the American people were entitled to know.

"Courage," Mr. Lane wrote, "is oxygen, and Fear
is carbon monoxide. Wilson, be it said to his eternal
glory, did not fear." Yet he distinguished between the
"Little Wilson" and the "Great Wilson." When the
Administration was branded and finished by the knock-
out blow delivered by the electorate in 1920, Mr. Lane
wrote truly enough: "The American-born did not like
Wilson because he was not frank, was too selfish and
opinionated." Like Lansing and Houston, and Garrison
who did, Lane wanted to leave the Cabinet: "I came to
the brink when the President blew up my coal agreement [intended] to save three or four hundred million

dollars for the people. But I was stopped by the thought, 'Give no comfort to Berlin.' " He was also not blind to Mr. Wilson's "ego-mania." Once he wrote to his brother: "I have served with [Wilson] long and faithfully under very severe circumstances. It is hard for him to get on with anyone who has any will or independent judgment. Yet I am not given to forsaking those to whom I have any duty." But when the Armistice came he recorded that "the world is at his [Wilson's] feet, eating out of his hand! No Cæsar ever had such a triumph!" That was the summit; the descent was rapid and Mr. Lane could not help to check it, much as he wished to. He and the Cabinet were kept in ignorance of Mr. Wilson's condition and did not know whether he was insane, paralyzed, or merely suffering from a nervous breakdown. That was really a dreadful period for Mr. Lane. He could not get over the Harding triumph. Finally he wished that it had been unanimous so that the country could start all over again with a new deal, divided into Conservatives and Radicals. He saw what was in store for the Democratic Party, for, as he wrote to Mr. Lansing, "all possible leaders have been submerged, squelched, drowned out in the last eight years." Mr. Wilson could barely tolerate big figures like Mr. Lane near him; he could not rally to himself, as could Roosevelt, a host of young men and enthuse them for policies and for leadership.

During the war Mr. Wilson had no more belligerent supporter of him and his policies than Mr. Lane. On August 31, 1915, long after the sinking of the Lusitania, Mr. Lane was astonished that a friend of his in Italy should suggest that we enter the war. But he was already leaning toward universal military service, that hateful German invention which was at the bottom of all their militaristic development. From then on he became more and more bloodthirsty, demanded preparedness, headed the Council of National Defense, and set it to work with all his matchless administrative ability and personal force long before hostilities were decided on. Mr. Wilson's notes to Germany were all too weak for him, and he actually persuaded himself that America itself was in danger, that if the Germans won we should have a German army policing Canada—a million of them under arms on our border and that, he gravely pointed out, would mean that 30 per cent to 40 per cent of every American's income would be devoted to armaments to keep the Germans in Canada at bay. He died too soon to read, in 1927, the report of the Secretary of the Treasury that, although we won the war and kept the Germans out of Canada and Paris, we are spending no less than 80 per cent of our total income for past wars and preparedness.

This inconsistency in this great liberal I cannot explain. He was so rational, so farsighted, that he, just as well as Calvin Coolidge, must have known that armaments cannot keep a country out of war or insure victory if war comes, but on the other hand invariably lead to war. A mind so full of history and constructive plans as Mr. Lane's must have realized that war kills liberalism and every civilian ideal and blocks progress for years and years. Curiously enough he did realize it.

When an editor of the New York *World* wrote to him for an interview on the spiritual benefits to America to come out of the war, he declined to play the hypocrite like many others but wrote (italics mine): "This would be sheer camouflage. Of course, we will get some good out of it and we will learn some efficiency—if that is a moral benefit—and a purer sense of nationalism. *But the war will degrade us.* That is the plain fact, *make sheer brutes out of us,* because we will have to descend to the methods that the Germans employ. So you must go somewhere else for your uplift stuff." But he wrote with pride that his son had killed one German and bombed others. And he was of those who, without the slightest sound reason, wanted to end the war far in German territory; it was nothing to him that that would cost at least 25,000 more American lives. Yet at the same moment he assured a friend: "I am not for revenge or their [the Germans'] paralyzing"—further proof of the power of war hatreds to make utterly inconsistent an extraordinarily strong mind.

Perhaps it was again the Westerner in him that made him so eager for war. He had seen one man hanged and others meet their deaths in peculiar Western ways. That in turn may have affected him. Even when we were after Villa during the Mexican troubles he could only believe in force. He wrote to the President: "My judgment is that to fail in getting Villa would ruin us in the eyes of all Latin Americans. I do not say they respect only force, but like children they pile insult on insult if they are not stopped when the first insult is given." Well, he and Mr. Wilson did not get Villa and it was not their failure which has ruined us in Latin America, but their armed intervention in Haiti, where the Wilson Administration killed 3,500 Haitians who had never injured us, together with the subsequent invasions of Nicaragua. Villa's was not the only other case in which Mr. Lane's judgment and influence in international affairs were all wrong. In his attitude toward Japanese and Chinese he was on the side of the worst passions of the Pacific Coast. Looking at the Russian Revolution he quite calmly remarked that it was "a good thing for us in one way. *It will cost us perhaps a million lives,* but it will prove to us the value of law and order." History does not record a much worse guess. Then he was quite willing—he the believer in the sacredness of the Constitution—to carry on an illegal and unauthorized war in Siberia and at Archangel and when he wrote those words probably intended to spend a good share of the million American lives in conquering the Bolsheviki—he shuddered when Wrangel was defeated. At last when the war was over, while he deemed war perpetual, he wished the nations to join "in rivalry of progress rather than in a competition in the art of scientific boy-murder."

The extraordinary thing is that this was the same mind that could see that we "ought to make over our system of life"; which could cry out: "Damn all your politics and partisanship! Humbug—twaddle—fiddle-dee-dee, made for lazy louts who want jobs and bosses who want power"; which could cut to the bone with his declaration that "the White Man's Burden is the weight of the load of sin, disease, death, and misfortune he has dropped on the happy ones who never knew a Christian creed. We have given them bathtubs in exchange for cheerful living." Mr. Lane could even perceive that the call for socialism or communism is "generally a call for more justice and of honesty and of fair dealing between men." He penned one of the finest analyses of what America ought to be; yet in this matter of force and arms he invariably played into the hands of the same sinister forces against which he threw all his power throughout his life.

If Franklin Lane did nothing else he proved that in the best of men in public life there apparently must be the grossest of contradictions in point of view and conduct. How else could the same human being calmly contemplate sending a million Americans to their deaths and then declare that he had never wronged any man, and write this exquisite and utterly pathetic note to his daughter: "I think that we have got to see each other somehow, somewhere, because life is passing awfully fast and there is one best thing in it—supremely, overwhelmingly best—and that is affection. I've chased around for fame and work for others, but I just wish I had spent pretty much all my time loving you and Mother and Ned and let everything else come way down the list. The people who really love us are so few, aren't they? Lots of them like us, lots of them are glad to be with us, but few can be counted on 'world without end amen.'" If there is an Elysium Franklin Lane is there and he has surely learned that one "supremely, over-whelmingly best thing in life" is also the solution of international problems—not by murdering millions of boys and depriving them of their right to spend "pretty much all their lives" loving their mothers and Neds and Nancys.

One turns back with joy to the man in place of the statesman, to this big-hearted youth who declared three weeks before his death: "I am the youngest thing in-side that I know; in my curiosity and trustfulness and my imagination, and my desire to help and my belief in goodness and justice. I want to strike right out now and see the world and having found the good bring it back and distribute it." Naturally he felt that the longer one lived the more convinced one must be that it is our duty to be light-hearted and gay, and that the big things that count are love and goodness and un-selfishness. He had them all; he had a poet's soul which thrilled even to oil-wells and water-powers. He wrote so well that if he had not gone into politics he must have become one of our greatest writers. His use of words was extraordinary. He could be whimsical, gay, grave, ever-moving and altogether amusing. His letters are priceless if only for their humour.

I defy anyone with a heart to read dry-eyed the documents and letters that he wrote during those last ter-rible weeks and days when he cried out against the ironic God who had decreed that he who had led so restrained, so selfless, so blameless a life must suffer such anguish, such torture. Always he was struggling for the solution of the riddle of life, envying his wife the serenity of her faith, and willing to try anything, Christian Science, Mohammedanism, anything, for a complete belief, often referring to God, pleading for a spiritual rebirth by the power of a great spirituality, wishing that faith might be taught, but always groping, groping. He rightly considered himself deeply religious. "We pray," he said to a friend, "we do things for the good of men and women —but we do not properly relate ourselves to the Great Enveloping, Permeating Spirit." He had previously asked the same friend: "Could it be that there is no soul except the one that we make for ourselves by fighting?" To another he said: "Doesn't it, after all, come just to this—*to spend and to be spent*, isn't that what life is?" Again he found his best solution in the joy of struggle: "There is no way to make the fight excepting to believe that the fight is the thing—the one, only, greatest thing. (To deny this is to leave all in a welter, and drift into purposeless cynicism—blackness.) To determine that this is the way, the truth, and the life, is to get serenity. Then the winds may howl and the seas roll, but there can be no wreck." There are worse creeds in the world; many another has come to this.

When the final struggle came he faced it with magnificent courage for all his questioning, jested about his operation and his abominable gall-bladder, and his nurses and doctors, and recorded it all with perfectly extraordinary power, fidelity, originality, and soul-recording in letters to friends. Where are their equals? He clung to life because he wanted so greatly to provide for the loved ones he had "neglected" for the public service. "But this is so interesting an old world that I don't want to leave it prematurely because one does run the risk of not coming upon one equally interesting." For physical death he had no fears. After his death there was found in his own hand this fragment written the day before he undertook the Great Adventure, when he still believed that he was not to die then. It has been printed before but, like his apostrophe to the American flag, it deserves reprinting a thousand times, not only for its own extraordinary worth, not only because it was written with nerves racked by dreadful suffering, but because it pictures for all time the beautiful nature out of which it came:

And if I had passed into the other land, whom would I have sought—and what should I have done?

No doubt first of all I would have sought the few loved ones whose common life with me had given us matter for talk, and whom I had known so well that I had loved dearly. Then perhaps there might have [been] some gratifying of a cheap curiosity, some searching and craning after the names that had been sierras along my skyline. But I know now there would have been little of that. It would not have been in me to have gone about asking Alexander and Cromwell little questions. For what would signify the trifle which made a personal fortune, that put a new name up upon some pilaster men bowed to as they passed? Were Aristotle there, holding in his hand the strings and cables that tied together all the swinging and surging and lagging movements of the whole earth's life—an informed, pregnant Aristotle,—

Ah! there would be the man to talk with! What satisfaction to see him take, like reins from between his fingers the long ribbons of man's life and trace it through the mystifying maze of all the wonderful adventure of his coming up. The crooked made straight. The "Daedalian plan" simplified by a look from above—smeared out as it were by the splotch of some master thumb and made the whole involuted, boggling thing one beautiful, straight line. And one could see, as on a map of ocean currents, the swing and movements of a thousand million years. I think that I would not expect that he could tell the reason why the way began, nor where it would end. That's divine business, yet for the free-going of the mind it would lend such impulses, to see clearly. Thus much for curiosity! The way up which we've stumbled.

But for my heart's content in that new land, I think I'd rather loaf with Lincoln along a river bank. I know I could understand him. I would not have to learn who were his friends and who his enemies, what theories he was committed to, and what against. We could just talk and open out our minds, and tell our doubts and swap the longings of our hearts that others never heard of. He wouldn't try to master me nor to make me feel how small I was. I'd dare to ask him things and know that he felt awkward about them, too. And I would find, I know I would, that he had hit his shin just on those very stumps that had hit me. We'd talk of men a lot, the kind that they call the great. I would not find him scornful. Yet boys that he knew in New Salem would somehow appear larger in their souls than some of these that I had called the great. His wise eyes saw qualities that weighed more than smartness. Yes, we would sit down where the bank sloped gently to the quiet stream and glance at the picture of our people, the negroes being lynched, the miners'

*civil war, labor's hold ups, employers' ruthlessness, the
subordination of humanity to industry*————

Can such a soul not be immortal? Franklin Lane
would have been the first to ask the question.

They have named a great mountain peak for him
in Rainier National Park. For once the honour is just,
for here was a mountain peak among men.

ROBERT LANSING

Secretary of State

ROBERT LANSING as Secretary of State pleased neither the anti-war, nor the pro-war liberals, nor our militarists and imperialists. Most liberals held a poor opinion of Mr. Lansing; they believed that he was a conventional and an imperialistic diplomat and were not deeply moved when he was dismissed from the Cabinet, although they felt that he had been a victim of outrageous ingratitude on the part of Woodrow Wilson, and that he was punished for taking exactly the right course in one of the most trying situations in our recent history. Liberals are, of course, grateful that he was opposed to the treaty of peace and let it be known, and they admit that if the negotiations in Paris had been left to him we probably should have had a better and more consistent result. On the other hand, the militarists and imperialists felt that Mr. Lansing was not strong enough, that he should have pressed for a much more vigorous policy both against Germany and against Mexico.

It is perhaps because I had the opportunity to see something of Mr. Lansing at close range, both when he was counsellor of the State Department and Secretary of State and a peace commissioner in Paris, that I have a more favourable opinion of him than that held by many critics of the Wilson government. There are still matters relating to Robert Lansing that came to my cognizance during the pre-war and the war years that I am not free to put on paper. But I do know and can say that his intuition and foresight were often startlingly correct. How accurate his judgment could be is clearly shown by this admirable analysis of the abortion which the Paris Peace Conference gave birth to and called a peace treaty. Writing in his diary on May 8, 1919, he said of this document:

> *The impression made by it is one of disappointment and of depression. The terms of peace appear immeasurably harsh and humiliating, while many of them seem to me impossible of performance. . . . It must be admitted in honesty that the League is an instrument of the mighty to check the normal growth of national power and national aspirations among those who have been rendered impotent by defeat. . . . This war was fought by the United States to destory for ever the conditions which produced it. These conditions have not been destroyed. They have been supplanted by other conditions equally productive of hatred, jealousy, and suspicion.*

To this he added his belief that the League was simply an alliance of the five great military Powers, that justice was secondary and might primary in the settlement, and that the treaty could not bring peace "because it is founded on the shifting sands of self-interest." "Mr. Wilson," Mr. Lansing declared, "won a great personal triumph, but he did so by surrendering the fundamental principle of the equality of nations. In his eagerness to 'make the world safe for democracy' he abandoned international democracy and became the advocate of international autocracy."

Nothing can be added today to this characterization of the treaty or to this analysis of the League. Mr. Lansing quickly saw that, instead of the League's being created as an agency to prevent war, it was chiefly to be an agency to carry out the terms of peace. He was utterly opposed to the interweaving of the Covenant of the League with the Peace Treaty. Indeed, Mr. Lansing in this connection directly charged Woodrow Wilson with misrepresenting facts to the American people when on March 28, 1919, the President assured the public that it was not true that the drafting and interweaving of the Covenant was responsible for delaying the peace. "Why attempt," wrote Mr. Lansing in his diary (which in Paris had a lock upon it besides being always locked in a drawer), "to refute what is manifestly true?" He admits, however, that the President's action might have been due to his having failed to appreciate the exact situation in Paris—an alternative not complimentary to the President's acumen, though such alternatives present themselves at other points in Mr. Wilson's career and compel the honest historian to choose between falsehood and ignorance.

Mr. Lansing's ability to read the future appears clearly on more than one occasion. As far back as May 20, 1916, a year before America went into the war, in a letter to Mr. Wilson he opposed the doctrines of the League to Enforce Peace, declaring with rarely prophetic vision that "popular opinion, as well as the Senate, would reject" any treaty which limited our independence of action to the will of other nations across the seas. He did not believe that America should bind itself to fight wars abroad at the behest of an international body and leaned to the opinion that the use of force in compelling acceptance of a decision could be avoided by a resort to economic compulsion. He wanted to obviate the necessity of forcing nations to abstain from invading other countries by asking the nations to give a mutual understanding not to impair the territory or the sovereignty of any state. Just as Senator Knox argued that we should build on the Hague Tribunal, so Mr. Lansing wanted the basic principle for the new organization to be judicial settlement. From the beginning he had valuable constructive criticisms to make. He found, to his grief, on the way to France, that political expediency and diplomatic adjustment "tinctured with morality" were to be the President's basis for the settlement of international controversy. In Paris he laid before the President a memorandum on the "constitutional power to provide coercion in a treaty," in which he declared that any attempt to contract by treaty to create a state of war upon certain contingencies would be unconstitutional, "null and inoperative." But as was frequently the President's habit in dealing with Mr. Lansing, Mr. Wilson neither acknowledged receipt of the covering letter nor of the memorandum, and he did not consult with his Secretary about the matter. Mr. Lansing thinks that Mr. Wilson's distrust of him came originally from the fact that he is a lawyer. At the conference of the American Peace Commissioners on January 10, 1919, Mr. Wilson bluntly told Mr. Lansing that he "did not intend to have lawyers drafting the treaty of peace"—although the Covenant of the League had been largely drafted by an inconspicuous lawyer, David Hunter Miller, of New York, and Mr. Wilson was himself a lawyer by training and some years of practice. Thereafter Mr. Lansing, and with him Mr. White and General Bliss, were left in outer darkness; they were not consulted, did not see Mr. Wilson for days on end, and were studiously ignored by their Chief who was also their President.

How wide the breach was between Mr. Wilson and Mr. Lansing appears from each successive chapter of Mr. Lansing's memoirs of Paris.[1] The Secretary of State wanted a carefully thought-out American program to take to Paris; Mr. Wilson took none—he admitted he had not even read the secret treaties which were the key to the whole political side of the struggle. Then they disagreed on self-determination, Mr. Lansing believing that if applied to every case it would become a source of political instability and rebellion. Mr. Lansing was also absolutely opposed to the system of mandates, originated by General Smuts, and he charges that the Allies set afoot a deliberate propaganda to induce the United States to accept mandates over Constantinople and Armenia, both of which would be a heavy burden to the mandatory Power, while reserving for themselves

[1] The Peace Negotiations, by Robert Lansing. Houghton Mifflin Company. Boston, 1921.

rich and prosperous territories. Those who engaged in this propaganda did so, Mr. Lansing says, for the purpose of taking "advantage of the unselfishness of the American people and of the altruism and idealism of President Wilson." Then Mr. Lansing opposed the President by favouring the speedy negotiation of a preliminary treaty which should contain a set of declarations as to the League of Nations and an agreement for a future international conference to draft the details. Had this policy been adopted and vexed territorial questions left to later negotiation the whole situation of the world would be vastly better today and hundreds of thousands of people would have been saved from death by slow starvation.

To the proposed "triple alliance" treaty with France and England Mr. Lansing, General Bliss, and Mr. White were entirely opposed, and the fact that this treaty, which would have bound us to spring to France's rescue *in perpetuo*, has never had serious consideration in Washington bears out the correctness of their position. Mr. Lansing declares that this proposed treaty was agreed to by Mr. Wilson solely in order to do away with the French demand for an international military staff and for the creation of an independent Rhenish Republic.

But the classic example of the way Mr. Wilson was betrayed by his expediency and sacrificed everything for the Covenant still remains—Shantung. Mr. Ray Stannard Baker, it appears, went before the Chinese delegation after the President's surrender and said to its members that the President was very sorry that he had not been able to do more for China but that he had been compelled to accede to Japan's demand "in order *to save the League of Nations*." Not unnaturally Mr. Lansing describes this in his diary as an "iniquitous bargain" and "a flagrant denial of undoubted right." Mr. Lansing points out that it was the result of secret diplomacy, because the "arguments which prevailed with the President were those to which he listened when in secret council with M. Clemenceau and Mr. Lloyd George." So murder will out. Mr. Lansing declares that the Japanese threats were "nothing but bluff," but the President yielded before them as he threw overboard, one after another, all of the Fourteen Points. Even members of the British peace staff bewailed the fact: "they had counted on him to stand firmly by his guns and face down the intriguers."

It is the President's secret diplomacy in Paris that Mr. Lansing most severely criticizes. When the writer of these lines left the Crillon after the indignation meeting of the American correspondents on its becoming known that Mr. Wilson had surrendered on the open covenants of peace, William Allen White, the Kansas editor, prophetically remarked to him: "It's all up with Mr. Wilson. Lloyd George, Clemenceau, and Orlando will now take Mr. Wilson into a private chamber and rob him to their hearts' content, and the outside world will not even hear his cries for mercy." Mr. Lansing on January 29, 1919, remonstrated with the President, declaring that his *private conferences* were "making a bad impression everywhere." The President heard him in silence. On March 29, Mr. Lansing told his faithful diary that "Secret diplomacy is reaping a new harvest of execrations and condemnations. Will the practice ever cease?" The record of the Paris proceedings he later declared to be one of "the abandonment of principle, of the failure to follow precepts unconditionally proclaimed, of the repudiation by act, if not by word, of a new and better type of international intercourse."

None the less, with complete inconsistency Mr. Lansing not only signed the Treaty of Peace, but joined Mr. Wilson in urging its acceptance upon the Senate. The reason he gives is not in the least bit convincing. "So long," he says, "as the President remained inflexible and insistent, its ratification without change seemed a duty to humanity." In other words, because Mr. Wilson was an obstinate person who had blundered badly and had helped to write a treaty which Mr. Lansing thought was abominable, the United States should have yielded to his obstinacy, and approved the abominations that he, Mr. Lansing, denounced. This is perverted loyalty, indeed, and so was his position in regard to himself and his two disaffected associates on the Peace Commission. General Bliss was so disgusted with the whole performance and his treatment by Mr. Wilson that he wrote a letter of resignation. Mr. Lansing mistakenly persuaded him to withdraw it. If all three had thrown down the gauntlet to Mr. Wilson and demanded that they be treated as something else than dummies, under penalty of immediate resignation and a public statement if they were not so treated, something would have happened.

Similarly, a united front by all three of them on such an outrage as the Shantung decision would likewise have accomplished something. Instead, they swallowed their pride, permitted themselves to be made the wonder, if not the laughing-stock of the army of newspapermen in Paris, and, when they returned to the United States, defended the treaty or kept silent about it. Mr. Lansing appeared before the Senate Foreign Relations Committee on his return from Paris, but concealed the facts as to what had actually happened and was correspondingly vexed when Mr. William C. Bullitt of the Peace Commission Staff told the whole truth as to what Mr. Lansing really thought and felt. This seemed to Mr. Lansing an outrageous breach of confidence—we have again the old problem as to how far loyalty to one's crowd or one's chief shall be allowed to cut a man loose from his ethical moorings. There can be no question that Mr. Lansing compromised with his conscience, which is one reason why he does not stand as high as he should, and why he was compelled in his book to defend himself as to his attitude in Paris and the paradoxical and, it seems to me, indefensible position that he took when he returned to the United States.

Mr. Lansing's ousting from the Cabinet was not due to his differing from his chief in Paris and thereafter as to the Treaty of Peace, but to his action in calling the Cabinet together when Mr. Wilson, having suffered his stroke, was incompetent to govern the country. It was a highly dangerous situation for the country, and one that is not provided for by the Constitution or any laws. Mr. Wilson's condition was concealed from the public; the Presidency went into the hands of the regency composed chiefly of Mrs. Wilson and the President's physician who kept up the pretence that the President was capable of transacting business and thereby perpetrated a swindle upon the American people. Mr. Lansing was the senior member of the Cabinet. Had he been willing to sit idly by and do nothing under these circumstances he would have been open to the charge of callous indifference to a situation which gravely menaced the very government itself. As it was, the Cabinet took no action of moment; it chiefly discussed the situation and watched events; the members jointly exchanged their views. When Mr. Wilson was enabled once more to take charge of the situation, the reports he received of Mr. Lansing's patriotic and entirely justifiable action led to his demand for Mr. Lansing's resignation and the public dismissal of the man who out of loyalty to Wilson had swallowed his dissent from the Peace Treaty. Thus was Mr. Lansing's violation of his conscience to aid Mr. Wilson by preserving a united front in the American delegation in Paris rewarded by the beneficiary of Mr. Lansing's acts.

Again, it must be set down to Mr. Lansing's credit that, after becoming Secretary of State, he felt that the United States should hold the scales evenly between the contending forces in the World War. Mr. Wilson and Colonel House pretended that they were doing this; Colonel House's reminiscences as edited by Professor Seymour show the complete falsity of the pretence. Mr.

Lansing felt that the government should be just as much in earnest in calling England to account for its violations of international law during the war as in scoring the Germans for their sins. For instance, there was a note prepared before Mr. Bryan resigned, to be sent to Great Britain as soon as the first Lusitania note had gone to Germany, taking issue with England for various infractions of the laws of war, particularly as they affected neutrals. Mr. Cone Johnson, then solicitor of the State Department, was responsible for the statement in the corridor of the State Department to a delegation of business men from New York that there was not a single canon of international law that England had not violated up to that hour; and it was beyond doubt true that England at that time had not only thrown all possible difficulties in the way of our dealing with Germany but was holding up our ships destined for neutral ports. For instance, on May 20, 1915, there were twenty-four American cotton ships, all bound for Scandinavian or Dutch ports, held up in England in deliberate violation of British pledges that all cotton for which contracts of sale or freight engagements had been made before March 2, 1915, would be allowed free transit provided the ships sailed not later than March 31. Mr. Lansing was one of those who thought that just as stiff a note should be sent to England about these matters as had been sent to Germany about the Lusitania, and when the President reached New York on May 18, 1915, on the Mayflower, to review the fleet, such a note was placed in his hands by a special messenger from the State Department. With the drafting of that note Robert Lansing had a good deal to do.

Unfortunately for the country, that note was not sent to England until nearly five months later, during which time its effect was weakened for several reasons. In the first place, it came too late to have that effect upon Germany which it was hoped it would have— namely, of relieving the German suspicion that America was playing the Allies' game. In the second place, it was very much toned down in its language and was not nearly so sharp an indictment of Great Britain as its projectors had intended. In the third place, much water had gone under the bridge in the interim. But at least here is the fact that at that time Mr. Lansing was for dealing out an even-handed justice, was for vigorously upholding the rights of the American flag upon the high seas in accordance with American traditions, and was determined to stand by the tenets of international law which had been so hardly won by decades and centuries of slow juristic development. To my mind, this was the turning-point of the war. Had Mr. Wilson been true to his own policy of being neutral in deed as well as in thought the American public would have realized how lawless on the high seas and in their destruction of international law were both sides to the struggle, and the United States would never have gone into the war out of which it has gained nothing beyond obtaining the ill-will of the entire European world. Certainly, if the American people had been told by Mr. Wilson that American ships bound from New York to Norfolk in ballast had been captured by a British war vessel and taken into Halifax with the British flag hoisted above the American, there is no question as to the indignation which would have swept the country from end to end.

It was a quiet-faced, self-controlled, able, and dignified man, immaculately clad in the cutaway of statesmanship, who met the correspondents, myself among them, in the office of the Secretary of State during that trying summer of 1915. It was the same grave, dignified presence, distinctly greyer and more worn, who received the correspondents in the Hotel Crillon in Paris, and it was the same grave and dignified personality that took leave of official life when the President's indefensible message compelled his resignation. Mr. Lansing sincerely desired a better world as a result of the war, and fought hard for it, despite the fact that he was hampered by the conventionalities of diplomacy, by the natural conservatism of the international lawyer, and the hidebound loyalties of the place-holder. But he stood for a broad, liberal, generous, and forgiving policy toward those who in this country dared to disagree with the government's going to war, and in Paris he fought for a humane and just policy toward Russia and a wise and sensible and Christian attitude toward the Central Powers. Certainly, had his program been followed it would have spared America the disgrace of having participated in the starving to death of hundreds of thousands of German, Austro-Hungarian, and Russian women and children. It is the final fact that had he, like Wolsey, served his God as he served his country in Paris, had he refused to compromise and to lend himself to the deception that was practised upon the American people by Woodrow Wilson as to what had actually happened in Paris and what the treaty signified, Mr. Lansing would never have been in need of any defence, and, in his shining righteousness, would have been one of the great patriotic figures of the country.

PHILANDER C. KNOX

Dollar Diplomat

"FOR a good many years now," wrote a Washington correspondent in 1908, "the demand for Philander Chase Knox has greatly exceeded the visible available supply. Mr. Knox is five feet five inches high and shares with Elihu Root the distinction of being our most highly finished domestic product. The incoming, like the out-going, Secretary of State has made a specialty of brains. The thing Mr. Knox does best is to accomplish what he sets out to do. It has become a habit." From 1901 until his death in 1921 Mr. Knox was Attorney General in the Cabinets of McKinley and Roosevelt, Secretary of State under Mr. Taft, and thrice Senator from Pennsylvania. During that time he twice declined appointment to the Supreme Court of the United States and refused the Governorship of Pennsylvania. More than that, he came much nearer to being nominated for President of the United States at the convention of 1920 than all but a few people understood. For instance, had Senator Johnson of California been clear-headed enough to realize his defeat at that convention and thrown his strength to Knox before the early morning conclave which nominated Harding, and had Senator Penrose not been kept away from the convention by ill health, Senator Knox might easily have been the

nominee and the United States been spared the most
disgraceful administration in its history.

Curiously enough there were many liberals and
progressives in Chicago who earnestly hoped that
Senator Knox might be chosen even though during a
large part of his career he had been anathema to them
and had borne the brunt of many an attack upon the
conservative wing of the party. In the first place this
"sawed-off cherub," as Mr. Roosevelt once dubbed him,
was, like Mr. Root and Mr. Spooner and many another
lawyer-leader of the Republicans, a product of big
business. His wits were sharpened in their workshops,
his experience acquired over their briefs. They counted
him their own when he entered McKinley's Cabinet and
later rejoiced that he was to be a "steadying influence"
when the "wild man," Roosevelt, came to Presidential
power by the accident of an assassin's shot. Mr. Knox
was, and for a long time had been, of Andrew Carnegie's
counsel when he took office, and Mr. Carnegie testified
that he urged William McKinley to make Mr. Knox his
Attorney General at the same time that he put Mr. Reed,
Mr. Knox's law partner, into the directorate of the
United States Steel Corporation. But if Mr. Carnegie,
or anybody else, expected that that would make things
comfortable for big business, he experienced some sad
shocks. When President Roosevelt asked Mr. Knox if the
elder J. Pierpont Morgan could not be omitted from the
list of defendants to the Government's suit against the
Northern Securities Company, Mr. Knox replied: "Well,
Mr. President, if you direct me to leave his name out

I will do it, but I want to say plainly that in that case I will not sign my name to the bill. I do not propose to have the lawyers of the country laugh at me." Mr. Morgan became one of the defendants, and Mr. Knox signed the bill.

During this same episode this corporation lawyer, whose practice was said to net him $350,000 a year before he entered public life, had the nerve to tell the firm of Morgan over the telephone that "the stock ticker did not tick in the Department of Justice." Previously, in 1897, he had shocked his corporation clients by a speech in which he boldly asserted the then new and revolutionary doctrine that the Government has the right and power to control great combinations of capital; and when he entered Mr. McKinley's Cabinet he warned the President that he would make it his business to test the value of the Sherman Anti-Trust Act, which he felt was constantly violated. This from a man who, according to James J. Hill, had "cleaned up $600,000 in the organization of the Steel Trust"! When Mr. Knox took the oath of office it was no form with him; soon his old associates were gnashing their teeth over his "betrayal" of those who "had made him"; he began vigorous attacks upon large corporations; and he justified Roosevelt's faith that his Attorney General was, by reason of his intimate knowledge of large corporations, just the one to bring them to book. Set a trust-maker to "busting" trusts!

The historian of Mr. Roosevelt's Administration will not have an easy task to say how much of the credit for the Roosevelt corporation policies belongs to Mr. Knox. It is certain that his Pittsburgh speech of 1902 ushered in a new era in the relations of the Government and the large corporations, which was bitterly resisted at the time by the latter. The Northern Securities case was started and won. The Beef Trust prosecutions were begun and the first moves made against Standard Oil. It was because he was particularly the agent of Roosevelt that his nomination as President was urged by a number of newspapers in 1908. It may well be asked now how effective this anti-trust campaign really was. Not only have the dissolutions of the Standard Oil and other trusts failed to check abuses, but in the latest railroad policies we are moving directly in the opposite direction from the Northern Securities decision and are even trying to put together the very Pacific railroads Mr. Knox separated. By many it has now been recognized that our economic evils call for much more radical remedies than the Sherman Anti-Trust Law. None the less, Mr. Roosevelt and Mr. Knox are entitled to great credit for a course which, at the time, called for personal and political courage.

Mr. Knox was never afraid to talk back to the impetuous President he served. Mr. Roosevelt once said in his presence that the Attorney General could give a complete criticism of Gibbon's "Rise and Fall of the Roman Empire" in three hundred words. Quick as a flash Mr. Knox replied: "And of recent Presidential messages in less!" In the middle of the Panama theft— which Mr. Knox subsequently defended on the ground that the "interests of the world imposed upon this government an imperative mandate to build the Canal"—he was asked by Mr. Roosevelt for his advice. "I am sorry that you have asked for my opinion," replied Mr. Knox, "because, up to the present time, the proceedings have been free from any taint of law!" In 1912 Mr. Knox naturally stood by Mr. Taft in whose Cabinet he sat and said of his former chief, Mr. Roosevelt, that he would be defeated "unless the Republican Party has become the plaything of one man, prompted by his whims, his imperious ambitions, his vanities, and mysterious antipathies." On October 2, 1904, Mr. Knox had taken a very different view of Mr. Roosevelt. Then he found him to be one "endowed by the Creator" with "high mental and temperamental qualifications for his great office," "a peculiarly fit public servant," who had achieved "lasting benefits to the nation and to humanity."

As Attorney General Mr. Knox made himself so obnoxious to the corporations that three corporation magnates, A. J. Cassatt, president of the Pennsylvania Railroad, John D. Archbold, of Standard Oil, and Henry C. Frick, of the Steel Corporation, paid $500,000 to have him appointed to the vacancy in the Senate caused by the death of Senator Quay. He was too effective a "trust buster" for these men and so they took up notes of the managers of the State machine, aggregating a half million dollars, which notes were held by the estate of the then recently deceased Henry W. Oliver of Pittsburgh. In return Mr. Knox's appointment to

the Senate was immediately made and James J. Hill
had no hesitation in declaring that "Knox was made
Senator of Pennsylvania by the Eastern railroads." No
one has ever charged that Mr. Knox was a party to this
transaction or knew of it until later. The three men in
question must have been angry indeed when, in 1906,
this Senator from Pennsylvania wrote and introduced
a Senate bill to bring the railroads completely under the
control of the Interstate Commerce Commission in the
matter of fixing rates, with, however, the right of a court
review.

Quite as puzzling from a liberal's point of view
was Mr. Knox's career as Secretary of State. First he
proclaimed the era of "dollar diplomacy" by which the
foreign policies of the Government were to be subordinated to helping the business man to make money
abroad, than which no policy is of greater danger to
the peace of the world, or to the sanctity of weak
or backward nations. To it may well be applied the
words of Adam Smith in denouncing a British proposal
to found a great empire for the sole purpose of raising
up a people of customers: "a project altogether unfit
for a nation of shopkeepers, but extremely fit for a nation whose government is influenced by shopkeepers."
But he was very proud of his policy and, defending it in
an article in the *Saturday Evening Post* of March 9,
1912, he declared that the promotion of American commerce was "one of the first duties of American diplomacy." He also felt it his duty to "encourage the use of
our abundant means in assisting less forward countries

to develop their resources and to advance reforms necessary to national stability and progress in regions aspiring toward a higher civilization." Partly as a result
of Mr. Knox's acts our naval guns have dominated the
political life and subordinated the liberties of Santo
Domingo, Haiti, Costa Rica, Nicaragua, and Honduras,
and we have menaced still other nations. In several of
these countries our financiers are gobbling up land and
natural resources in a way to store up trouble for us
for generations to come. Yet Mr. Knox sincerely believed that "the capital of the more advanced nations
of the world would be better employed in assisting the
peaceful development of those more backward than in
financing wars. . . ." He was never able to realize that
more than half the trouble in the world today is due
to this invasion of the "backward" countries of the
earth by dollar diplomacy.

Mr. Knox also defended this policy from the charge
of pure materialism by declaring that he had prevented
or terminated a war between Ecuador and Peru, a war
between Haiti and Santo Domingo, and one in Honduras, and had prevented strife in Costa Rica and
Nicaragua. He was also responsible for an American
President's taking "the world's greatest step toward universal peace through the French and British arbitration
treaties." Under his incumbency of the office of Secretary of State there were, according to his own words,
"more resorts to arbitration and more peaceful settlements of just claims and more brushing away of mis-
understandings than seem to have occurred in any other

corresponding period." More than that, at the very time
when he was responsible for our improper and unworthy
financial and political intervention in Honduras and
Nicaragua he was urging the establishment by the great
Powers of an international court of arbitral justice at
the Hague with jurisdiction over nearly all questions
between nations. It is interesting at this time when the
struggle over our entrance into the World Court at
Geneva is still going on to note that he believed that the
establishment of the Hague Court would reduce armaments the world over. More than that, he agreed with
most pacifists that this court's decrees and decisions
could and would be carried into effect merely by the
force of the enlightened public opinion of the world.
Yes, he, the champion of dollar diplomacy backed by
naval guns, had actually come to believe that there must
be no international police force to uphold the decrees
of the Hague Court. He wanted no international army
and no international navy. He even felt that the outlawry
of war was possible and practical and he wanted that
outlawry *now* and not a hundred years hence. Finally,
Mr. Knox is entitled to great praise for having put into
his arbitration treaties a clear and accurately defined
jurisdiction in place of the vague and indefinite terms
of the then existing pacts. He insisted that under those
treaties neither the honour nor the vital interests of the
United States can be imperilled unless we assert them
against another nation's rights.

When it comes to the Far East the contradictory in
Mr. Knox again appears. Just as he was the author of the

arbitration treaties and as he urged the international
court which the world must and shall have, and then made
American capitalists masters in Central America, so he
tried to induce Russia and Japan to neutralize the Man-
churian Railway, and then turned around and joined
the Six-Power group for the financial exploitation—and
aid—of China. President Wilson promptly took us out
of the Six-Power group declaring—how odd it sounds!
—that there should be "no entangling foreign alliances
even in respect to arrangements for supervising the financial compacts of weaker governments . . . the responsibility of the United States in the Six-Power group is
obnoxious to the principles upon which this government
rests." (That master of inconsistencies, Mr. Wilson,
later joined the Four-Power group to do the very thing
for China which Mr. Knox proposed and Mr. Wilson
denounced in the above language.) Mr. Knox was always
friendly to the Japanese and the Chinese. A group of
reporters on one occasion asked him whether he favoured a war with Japan. "I do favour it," he replied,
"provided, however, that there are no soldiers on either
side except newspaper reporters." The London *Times*
once remarked that there was a marked conflict "between the American people's high ideals of humanita-
rianism and justice, their ready response to any noble
cause, their almost quixotic impulses of altruism and
the inevitable result in practical politics of their vigorous nationalism and ambitions of expansion." Under
the false liberal, Woodrow Wilson, it was precisely this
conflict of aims and impulses which has got the United

States into such trouble both abroad and in the Caribbean. Sometimes one asks whether, until we reach the day of a square deal in international relations, we should not be better off in the hands of an honest imperialist like Philander Knox than of a faithless liberal.

For his fight against the Treaty of Versailles Senator Knox deserves the highest credit because, despite the charges to the contrary, he made his fight against it not on partisan or merely nationalistic grounds but on principle, and because of a deep sense of outrage at the entire Versailles treaty—yes, because of a genuine idealism. The drafter of the Senatorial round robin which correctly served notice on Woodrow Wilson in February, 1919, that the treaty would never be ratified if intertwined with the Covenant of the League of Nations, Mr. Knox was one of the three or four men to whom belongs the chief credit of having kept the United States from the dishonour of ratifying a treaty which history will surely record as the self-inflicted defeat of the Allies and one of the greatest disasters to humanity. Mr. Knox's legal skill, his parliamentary experience, his natural acumen and ability, the power of his speeches, all contributed enormously to the result of what seemed at first a hopeless fight against impossible odds. Probably no liberal could have accomplished as much in some directions. Certainly it made the business and political world take notice to find a rich conservative like Philander C. Knox voicing sentiments that came also from such "flighty" Senators as McCormick, Reed, La Follette, Johnson, Norris, and Borah, and were so singularly like those advanced by such "dangerously radical" journals as *The Nation* and the *New Republic*, albeit from a different point of view.

What gave Mr. Knox even greater power was his ability to formulate constructive suggestions. His opposition to the Versailles Treaty was not merely opposition; he had alternatives. It is now permissible to say that the constructive plan for an alternative to the League of Nations, published in *The Nation* of November 17, 1920, was, save in one or two respects, identical with a memorandum prepared by Mr. Knox and held in reserve by him for use at a future time. This was the case whenever he was in opposition; his portfolio always contained an alternative proposal.

It is finally to be pointed out that on all the great social issues, on the vital questions of labour and capital, Mr. Knox either expressed himself not at all or voted with the standpatters. If he had a program for domestic social reform, or a plan for our economic regeneration, the world is as yet ignorant of it. Nor did he make any fight for our gravely jeopardized personal liberties or the Constitution which is daily spat upon by the constituted authorities sworn to honour and respect and enforce it. Yet the disappearance from the Senate of this intellect was a genuine loss to the nation and not merely because there are now few Senators of first-rate intellectual ability and distinction. So it happened that Mr. Knox's untimely death was mourned alike by conservatives and by all the liberals who knew and understood him and valued his downright honesty and courage.

HENRY CABOT LODGE

A Scholar in Politics

THUS Henry Cabot Lodge was hailed when first he
entered political life—a scholar in politics. A man
of more than comfortable means, he had taken his A.B.,
LL.B., and Ph.D. at Harvard, had been for three years
editor of the *North American Review*, for two years
editor of the *International Review*, a member of the
Massachusetts House of Representatives, and had
written several excellent biographies, besides a useful
short history of the English colonies in America—all
this before he was thirty-three years old. Men like Carl
Schurz, Edwin L. Godkin, George William Curtis, and
Governor Boutwell looked with profoundest satisfaction
upon Lodge's coming into public life as they did upon
the political debut of his friend Theodore Roosevelt.
Together with others of the same calibre, their appearance gave rise to the hope that a new and golden era
in our politics was at hand. It was a delusion for those
who placed ideals above party loyalty, for both Lodge
and Roosevelt, after fighting staunchly at the Republican convention in 1884 against the nomination of
James G. Blaine because of his unfitness, after declaring
that they would bolt if he were chosen to lead the party,
finally decided that they would make their fight for
reform within the party and violated their consciences

by swallowing the man they had declared hopelessly blemished.

Not unnaturally, the then editor of *The Nation* could not refrain from pointing the moral when the news came that Henry Cabot Lodge had been defeated for Congress at the 1884 election, which placed Grover Cleveland in the White House. His words are worth reprinting for several reasons:

> *The defeat of Mr. Cabot Lodge for Congress in Massachusetts is to be regretted because he would undoubtedly have made a good legislator; but it is to be rejoiced over because it is a distinct discouragement to his kind of politician—we mean the kind furnished by nature and art with every assistance in being better than they are, but who refuse it vigorously, and insist on being bad or mediocre. It is the special function of such men to make a good show of moral fibre at great crises, and when they fail there is really nothing left of them. It was undoubtedly due to Mr. Lodge's influence that Mr. Theodore Roosevelt threw away the admirable position he had acquired in the politics of this State last spring, by not only coming out for Blaine but going back on Governor Cleveland. They put their heads together and thought they would show the theorists a wonderful "wrinkle" in the way of practicalness, and now they are both out in the cold, and their natural friends and allies are not sorry and the real "practical men" are laughing at them. It is, however, never too late to mend.*

The hostilities thus established never ended during Mr. Lodge's lifetime. As long as he was editor of *The Nation* Mr. Godkin lost no opportunity to use shell upon the renegade scholar from Massachusetts—and there were plenty of good opportunities, for Mr. Lodge was elected to Congress in 1887 and immediately began to make himself felt. In that year he defended the sale of the governorship of Rhode Island to a rich New Yorker by the gang of corrupt politicians who then, and for many years thereafter, controlled that State. "The American stump has seen many strange things," wrote Mr. Godkin, "but nothing stranger than a man of fortune and a scholar, a Harvard graduate and quondam instructor, and an author of some repute, perorating publicly against the people who object to this degrading [Rhode Island] spectacle as 'guilty of a mixture of sham morals and false issues which is revolting to any honest-minded man.' " Mr. Lodge's apostasy to the cause of tariff reform which he had championed in his biographies of Hamilton and Webster and his final swallowing of the extreme protection doctrine similarly brought down upon him the editorial thunder, and so did his extraordinary vagaries in the matter of the gold standard and in the field of international politics.

Strange as it may seem, this man, who was in his later years voted an Anglomaniac, began his political career as a most deliberate and determined tail-twister of the British Lion, in which pastime no Fenian exceeded him. He was for war with England not once but a dozen times. As far back as 1895 he announced in the Senate that we were "a part of the European balance of power. As in 1778 and 1812, we shall find ourselves in practical alliance with Russia and France, and in practical hostility to England and the Dreibund [Austria, Germany, and Italy]." His reason for this was that "Halifax is a menace to us, Bermuda is a menace to us, and so is Kingston. . . ." Therefore we must enter an alliance with France and Russia "because, so long as Great Britain remains a Power on this continent, in Canada, we can be nowhere else" than hand in glove with Paris and St. Petersburg. When Grover Cleveland sent to Congress his amazing and still inexplicable Venezuelan Message which so nearly precipitated war with Great Britain, Senator Lodge fairly threw himself into Cleveland's arms—up to that time he had assailed and maligned him at every opportunity. They became brothers before the war-god. Curiously enough, his change of opinion as to England came while he was writing his "Story of the Revolution" in 1897. At the outset the book abounds in the conventional violent abuse of England's conduct as the ruler of the American colonies. "When he began to write," a reviewer declared, "it was the fashion to curse England, and he cursed her soundly. When he ended everyone was falling on England's neck, and he fell, blubbering with the rest."

Until that conversion Senator Lodge injected his hatred of England even into economic and monetary discussions. Incredible as it will now seem to Wall Street, Senator Lodge was for years an ardent pro-silverite and opponent of the gold standard. To oppose the latter he wanted on April 6, 1895, in a speech in the Senate,

to boycott England, if not to war upon her. These were
his words—not the words of Bryan:

> *The gold monometallic policy of Great Britain, now
> in force among all great civilized nations, is, I believe,
> the great enemy of good business throughout the world
> at the moment. Therefore, it seems to me, if there is any
> way in which we can strike England's trade or her
> moneyed interest, it is our clear policy to do so in the
> interest of silver.*

All of which did not prevent the Senator from Massachusetts from joining, *just fifteen months later*, in the hue
and cry over William Jennings Bryan for taking the
same position. Nobody could have been more unctuous
than Henry Cabot Lodge or held up his hands in holier
horror over the rude and violent Nebraskan whose sole
offence was that, like Mr. Lodge prior to the Democratic
nomination, he did not want humanity crucified on a
cross of gold. Commenting on Senator Lodge's Carnegie
Hall speech on September 28, 1896, *The Nation*, after
quoting from the *Herald* that Mr. Lodge received the
ovation of the evening for his "terse and scathing arraignment of the sponsors of the silver movement,"
pointed out that "he should have included himself in
the arraignment, for no man has ever been more reckless or shameless in pandering to the silver party and
inflaming it to the point of desperation."

Indeed, so superficial is the usual thinking among
our financial and social leaders that such lapses in
Senator Lodge as well as his inconsistencies and his
deliberate turning his back upon traditions and standards

to which he was pledged by birth, antecedents, and
training were hardly noted by the powers that be in Massachusetts. True, a vigorous minority of conscience ever
fought him, and in his last campaign for re-election he
won by a mere handful of votes. But State Street and the
Back Bay could find nothing wrong when he backed the
Force Bill in 1889 and 1890 and declared that he was
willing if necessary to place a file of United States soldiers at every polling-place in the South. When he sought
to gerrymander the State of Massachusetts in the most
outrageous way in his own interest it seemed to them
the right thing to do. They found no fault with his bel-
ligerency against England, his persistent imperialistic
policy in regard to the Philippines, the South American
countries, and the rest of the world. They were certain
that the interests not only of New England but of the
whole country were safe in his hands, and so he became,
with the lapse of years, one of the leaders and dictators
of the Republican Party, a chieftain of the Old Guard,
a maker of Presidents, and the bosom friend and adviser of more than one. No one could question his ability,
his political skill, his historical knowledge, or his
power.

To the average politician he remained the cold
intellectual, the "highbrow." And yet they came to value
him as one of the greatest window-dressers of their party
and defenders of its misdeeds. Take, for instance, the
postal scandals in 1903. His defence then reads exactly
as would have read his defence of the scandals of the
Harding Administration had his health permitted him

to take part in the Coolidge campaign. Thus, he was certain in July, 1903, that the postal scandals could only have a favourable effect upon the fortunes of the Republican Party. He did not, of course, dwell upon the fact that a gang of Republican rascals and thieves had been enriching themselves at the expense of the government, but, like Calvin Coolidge in 1924, he stressed the fact that some of them had been found out and that the party was in the process of punishing them.

When the war came Mr. Lodge was once more compelled to throw himself into the arms of a Democratic President whom he loathed. He who wanted for so many years to war against England warred side by side with England with all the enthusiasm he had lavished upon his efforts to force us into hostilities with her. His war speeches, now separately published, give the Wall Street side of the war to perfection and the British case in all its passion and all its falsity. He was then a regular of the regulars—until the Treaty of Versailles. As to that, politics never made stranger bedfellows than the cause which put under the same blanket Senator Lodge and the editors of *The Nation*—he hated it as much as they. Of course Lodge's personal dislike of Wilson had much to do with his opposition to the treaty, but there was sincerity in it, too. He acted according to his lights and he readily stood his ground, though he came in, for the first time, for a tremendous amount of personal abuse, some from old friends. All of which he received with characteristically sharp cynicism. It was his last great fight and he enjoyed his triumph to the brim, believing that he rendered to his country his greatest service. Some will never forgive him for it; to others it outweighs all his many sins committed in the name of party and party creed.

But as the years passed by some things did happen to Henry Cabot Lodge which must have made many of his triumphs turn to ashes in his hands. True, he remained the darling of the Back Bay. There were men, like the late Professor Barrett Wendell of Harvard, and John T. Morse Jr., who believed to the end that Henry Cabot Lodge was the finest modern product of American statesmanship. His hold upon big business was never shaken until 1924. The great mill-owners, protected manufacturers, and banking houses knew he was theirs, so much so that they did not have to tell him what they wanted. He knew instinctively. Was he not one of them? But when he favoured the soldiers' bonus, and voted for it even over the veto of President Coolidge, State Street rose in anger and Mr. Lodge knew what it was to experience popular ingratitude, or rather ingratitude at the hands of those whom he had served most faithfully. It is the irony of fate, too, that this blue blood of the blue bloods, this Brahmin of the Boston Brahmins, this pillar of Harvard University and the church and every other venerable institution, this worshipper of the god of things as they are, should have been edged out of his commanding position in the party by another Massachusetts man—Calvin Coolidge—his very antithesis in breeding, training, and tradition. At his last Republican convention Henry Cabot Lodge was a pitiful figure. He was occasionally called to the platform publicly for consultation, but he was a feeble old man whose power had so evidently passed that his fall was the subject of various letters by correspondents who witnessed it. This veteran pilot of his party President Coolidge dropped, sent over the side, knowing full well that the pilot had lost his skill and his strength and that he was at the end of his career. It was the farmer's boy who gave the final push to the scholar in politics.

What is the moral of it all? What encouragement is there to be drawn from the achievements of this scholar in politics? Precious little for those who believe that all would be well in America if only all the offices could be filled with aristocratic gentlemen of ancient lineage, men of wealth, writers of pleasant essays, representatives of success in business, favourites of "society." There is nothing in Henry Cabot Lodge's career to furnish a text to youth, to inspire young men. He was a compromiser of compromisers; for office and party loyalty he sold himself not once but endless times. On the side of the privileged and the larger battalions he, save only once, invariably trimmed his sails to favouring breezes. Men will read his books, a few his speeches; they will find nowhere the divine afflatus and never will it be truthfully claimed for him that he broadened the range of American idealism, or brought the achievement of our ideals an hour nearer, or advanced in any way the brotherhood of man.

LEONARD WOOD

Military Administrator

WHEN General Wood died as Governor General of the Philippines on August 7, 1927, it was universally admitted that he was an able and highly distinguished administrator. His critics could, and did, differ with his philosophy of government and of the relations of a great Power to its overseas wards. They were disappointed that he could not agree with Abraham Lincoln that "no man is good enough to govern any other man without that other man's consent"; they, like the Filipinos, heartily disliked the "cavalry cabinet" with which he surrounded himself in Manila, but they cheerfully admitted his integrity, his readiness to work by day and by night, and his desire to aid the Filipinos just so far as his political philosophy and his limited faith in democracy permitted him to do so. As for his personal followers, of whom there were many, they adored him. To them he was Kitchener and Lord Cromer combined, the finest exemplar of the military-trained administrator on the English model whom the United States has ever produced. That Leonard Wood never became President appears to them—especially to the Harvard contingent, which was large indeed—as an inexplicably wicked failure of Providence.

For the rest, Leonard Wood had a distinguished

bearing, a reticence which could, and did, pass for wisdom, and a personal charm which, while not as engaging as that of his comrade in arms, Theodore Roosevelt, none the less profoundly affected those with whom he came in contact. He, too, had the good sense and the power to draw young men of a fine type to his service and drilled them in the way that he thought they should go. He became in time an excellent disciplinarian and drillmaster. There was no doubt that he was a very able soldier in peace time—we do not know what he could have done in handling large bodies of troops under fire. President Taft once told the writer that General Wood was by far the ablest and most active of the generals he had in the Philippines. Wood rose with the sun, was early in the saddle, and gave a great deal of personal attention to the drilling and handling of his troops, unlike the other generals most of whom were about sixty years of age and could not rid themselves of the old army idea that the sole duties of a general were to sit at his desk year in and year out and sign official papers. General Wood was then about forty-five years of age and this alone gave him an advantage over all of the others. I gladly record, too, the fact that when I was in France in 1919 the almost universal testimony was that the division which Leonard Wood trained at Fort Leavenworth was the best drilled and the best disciplined of all our troops that went to France.

Why was it then that General Wood was not al-

lowed to command that division in France? He had had
far more administrative experience than other generals;
he aroused great enthusiasms not only among his staff,
but among the soldiers of his command. He had hosts
of devoted friends in social and political life, and had
by his talents and his industry completely overcome the
jealousies and antagonisms created in the army itself
when he was pitchforked from a captaincy in the Medical Corps to a line brigadier-generalcy. He had, moreover, been one of those generals selected to take a course
of instruction in France as soon as we got into the war.
When he was relieved from his command just as his
troops were leaving for France, there was a perfectly
understandable outcry. President Wilson, it was declared, was playing politics, was seeking to make it a
Democratic Party war and therefore denying to General
Wood the chance of a lifetime, the opportunity for
which his whole service had been but a training, lest
he emerge from the war a greater figure than Wilson
himself. Taken with the refusal of Mr. Wilson to permit
Theodore Roosevelt to raise an independent division for
service in France, it seemed proof positive that Mr. Wilson proposed to allow no one to dispute with him the
front pages of the dailies.

Much was, therefore, written about Woodrow Wilson's arrogance and petty jealousies, General Pershing's envy of General Wood, and Newton D. Baker's
malice, until the following letter was published in the
New York *Times* on February 4, 1924:

The White House
Washington, June 5, 1918
To the Editor of the [Springfield] Republican:
I hope you will not be surprised to know that I sub-scribe almost in its entirety to the inclosed editorial from the Republican.

I am keenly aware of and keenly sensitive to the im-plications which will be drawn out of the fact that I am not sending General Wood to the other side, and I want personal friends like yourself upon whose approval I de-pend for my encouragement to know why I am not send-ing him.

In the first place I am not sending him because Gen-eral Pershing has said that he does not want him, and in the second place, General Pershing's disinclination to have General Wood sent over is only too well founded. Wherever General Wood goes there is controversy and conflict of judgment. On this side of the water we can take care of things of that sort because the fighting is not being done here, but it would be fatal to let it go on at or anywhere near the front.

I have had a great deal of experience with General Wood. He is a man of unusual ability, but apparently absolutely unable to subordinate his judgment to those who are superior to him in command. I am sorry that his great ability cannot be made use of in France, but at the same time, I am glad to say that it is being made very much use of in the training of soldiers on this side of the water, a task for which he is eminently well fitted and which he is performing with diligence and success.

With sincere regards, faithfully yours,
(signed) Woodrow Wilson

This tells the whole truth as to the greatest weak-ness of Leonard Wood. He had hardly reached France

as a student general when intriguing began—his whole
career was concerned with intrigue. It is but right, therefore, that the facts should be set forth, if only in justice
to Wilson, Baker, and Pershing themselves. So marked
was this failing that two Secretaries of War before Mr.
Baker assured the writer of these words that General
Wood was so often guilty of insubordination that they
could readily have court-martialed him, but that they
did not wish to make a martyr of him. If his record
could be published as it is in the secret files of the War
Department, there would perhaps be found several official rebukes. But General Wood never denied the insubordination; if reports are correct he gloried in it. It
was set forth in his behalf that if he had not been in-
subordinate the country would not have been prepared;
that the Plattsburg camp would never have been established which gave training to so many of our officers of
the American Expeditionary Force. If this statement is
correct, General Wood's memory will undoubtedly profit
by it. But the fact remains that one of the tests of the
true soldier is to set to his subordinates an example of
obedience. It was certainly not the act of a loyal soldier to bring to Plattsburg Theodore Roosevelt and to
incite or to permit him to make a violent attack upon the
Commander-in-Chief, President Wilson, in a speech to
the officers and men in the training corps. This was what
General Wood did in the summer of 1915. Secretary
Garrison would have been justified in retiring General
Wood from duty at Plattsburg after this; instead he
sharply reprimanded him.

General Wood's failure to get to the front did not dampen the ardour of the General's friends. The war over they were as determined to put him into the White House as if he and not Pershing had headed the armies in France, and to that end they raised huge sums which were, together with the misuse of Governor Lowden's fund, the scandal of the prenomination campaign. The General, according to sworn testimony before the Senate investigating committee, was present when it was agreed to raise $500,000 to win the nomination for him and also attended a later meeting at which it was decided to raise $1,000,000 for this worthy purpose. His friends exceeded their pledges; in all the staggering sum of $1,252,919 was raised, of which Colonel William Cooper Proctor advanced $731,000. They were, however, the rankest amateurs in politics. When the early morning hour came in which, at the Hotel Blackstone in Chicago, the half dozen party big-wigs met to pick "the choice of the convention" they gave not a moment's thought to General Wood, but selected the complaisant Warren G. Harding. That citizen of Ohio, little dreaming of the fate before him, had closed his headquarters, packed his bag, and was about to depart for his home when he learned that the "party" unanimously desired him to accept the nomination and the Presidency—the oil conspiracy was from that moment under way. Even this disaster did not quench General Wood's ambition. As late as 1922 he was still hopeful that the lightning would strike him in 1924.

Whenever it came to talking politics General Wood

was hopelessly out of his depth. His speeches in the 1920 campaign bordered on the ridiculous; he outdid all the other candidates with his generalities. Indeed, if the American sense of humour had survived the war, he would have been laughed out of court. Take, for instance, his statement that he was for reservations provided they really Americanized the peace treaty. What delightful pussyfooting! He paraded himself on the stump in soldier's uniform contrary to the precedent of Grant, Hancock, Garfield, and others, but he had not the courage to take a single strong position except against the Reds. He even wobbled as to the size of the regular army we ought to have, saying 100,000 one day and 200,000 the next. As for a program of social reorganization, General Wood, of course, had none. Had he been nominated and elected his backers would have found him an industrious executive, they would also have discovered that his brain worked slowly and that he lacked vision and background, and that he was ill-informed as to what was going on in the world. An officer who travelled with and served General Wood for more than a year was asked by a university professor what the General read as they wintered and summered together. "Why, the *Army and Navy Journal*," was the response.

General Wood was destined by fate to be the centre of controversy from the very beginning of his spectacular career. There was, for instance, the question of the bestowal upon him of the medal of honour, the highest decoration for gallantry in action, and prior to the

World War the only one bestowed by the United States Government for heroism under fire. It was for services rendered while Dr. Wood was attached as Assistant Surgeon to Captain Henry W. Lawton's troop of the Fourth United States Cavalry, during that officer's famous campaign against the Indian Chief Geronimo in Arizona that Wood received the medal, together with the other officers of the troop. But a fellow-officer of the troop, Lieutenant Colonel Harry C. Benson, repeatedly stated over his signature, once in the *Army and Navy Register,* on July 3, 1919, that Leonard Wood received and retained his medal although he *never heard a hostile shot fired throughout the entire campaign.* In no other army could an officer have remained in the service after such a charge without applying for a court of inquiry, for obviously either General Wood wrongfully obtained the medal or Colonel Benson told falsehoods. But curiously enough the charge was never investigated, not even by a board of officers constituted during the World War for the express purpose of examining into cases in which officers were charged with improperly receiving the medal of honour.

In the complete transformation of Dr. Wood from an inconspicuous military surgeon into a general with a record for administrative reconstruction in Cuba four men figured largely: Theodore Roosevelt; the same Henry W. Lawton; a chain-gang convict under the alias of "E. G. Bellairs," and a retired officer of the army, James E. Runcie. Theodore Roosevelt picked Leonard Wood to be the regular army nurse of the Rough Riders because of their common tastes for strenuous outdoor pastimes and their close Washington friendship. When Leonard Wood was promoted to brigadier-general, Roosevelt succeeded to the command and brought the regiment back to Montauk Point. If Lieut. Col. Benson is correct the only hostile shots General Wood ever heard were those at Las Guasimas on one day (except for those he heard on his visits to the Allied fronts as a student-general). Testifying before the Senate Military Committee on December 3, 1903, the late Major General James H. Wilson reported the following conversation with Theodore Roosevelt at Sagamore Hill:

> *He began then in rather extravagant terms of praise of General Wood, whereupon I said to him: "Governor Roosevelt, I think you are perhaps mistaken about that. If I am correctly informed, General Wood never was under fire in his life until the Spanish War began, either in the Geronimo campaign or at any other time. In the Spanish War he was never in but one battle, and that at Las Guasimas, where, but for his rescue and support by the colored troops, he would have been badly handled." "Oh, yes," said Mr. Roosevelt, "he was at San Juan." To which I replied: "I beg your pardon, he was not. You know that he was in the rear looking for ammunition."*
>
> *"Yes," said he [Roosevelt], "but do not tell anybody."*

It is only fair to add that the President thereupon denied the conversation and elected General Wilson to the Ananias Club which was at that time so popular by reason of Mr. Roosevelt's nominations, but General Wilson was never court-martialed for maligning the

President. In its issue of July 12, 1919, the *Army and Navy Register*, a reputable Washington service publication, asked General Wood three questions: whether he was ever in a fight with armed men prior to Las Guasimas; where he was during the battle of Santiago; and whether he had ever commanded troops in a fight since then. So far as recorded, General Wood never answered the questions of the *Register*.

When the fighting at Santiago was over, Henry W. Lawton, who later fell in battle in the Philippines, then a major general who had fought his command admirably at Santiago, was made governor of the evacuated city. He chose his former surgeon, Leonard Wood, as second in command. Now Lawton had one weakness, occasional intemperance, which in the eyes of all who knew him detracted little from what was otherwise a most estimable character. But somebody, a subordinate, or someone else, reported to the War Department that General Lawton had been seen on the streets of Santiago in an improper condition. General Lawton was recalled, General Wood's career as a Cuban administrator began, and there came to the front Bellairs, ex-convict and Santiago correspondent of the Associated Press, as press agent for Leonard Wood. No more amazing story than the actual career of "Edgar G. Bellairs," forger, has ever been penned, or put upon the stage. Of good family he early took to crime in England whence he soon drifted to other countries in his criminal career. I had reason to believe that he had served in the British army in Egypt and on the strength of his knowledge of military affairs

I selected him in April, 1898, as a war correspondent for the New York *Evening Post* as the result of an introduction from Dr. Fabian Franklin, then an editor of the Baltimore *News*. For deceit and financial irregularities Bellairs was later dismissed by the *Evening Post,* only to be employed by the Associated Press.

For Leonard Wood, Bellairs conceived, as he himself assured me, the profoundest admiration. Up to that time the brilliant but unfortunate Valentine Baker, in whose army Bellairs claimed that he had served, had been his beau ideal. "I would lie down and let General Wood walk upon me," he declared. Never did Associated Press dispatches carry such fulsome praise as came out of Santiago from the pen of Bellairs. Melville E. Stone, the head of the Associated Press, has published his belief that the "bias" was taken out of the dispatches in the New York office of the Associated Press (*Collier's Weekly,* April 3, 1920), but others will not agree with that belief. There soon developed a movement to remove General Brooke, then Governor General of Cuba. At that time an article by Major J. E. Runcie appeared in the *North American Review* attacking General Brooke's administration of the island. It resulted in Brooke's retirement and General Wood's succession—the purpose for which it was written. This promotion the General primarily owed to the reputation created for him by Bellairs, coupled with his own energy and ambition. Thus, first Lawton and then Brooke disappeared from the path. To Havana came Bellairs almost in the *entourage* of the new Governor General and there was certainly no evidence of any hostility to Wood in Bellairs's dispatches. As Melville E. Stone discreetly puts it: "Once more there seemed to be insidious references in his [Bellairs's] service which caused remark. Then I received a letter from Florida suggesting vaguely that I look into Bellairs's record. I set out to do so, when the General appeared on the scene and vouched for the man's character in unmistakable terms. He assured us that Bellairs was the victim of malice and was wholly trustworthy. Finally, there was a transference of both men to the Philippines, and again apparent fulsome praise of his friend on the part of the correspondent was noted." Then and not till then was Bellairs investigated and removed. Meanwhile, he had represented the Associated Press with the American Boxer expedition to Peking, and his poisoned news was all that the great bulk of the American public received from China.

Yet the Bellairs who held such a position of trust and power had been in one prison after another; during all this time his picture and a full description of him appeared in Inspector Byrne's "Professional Criminals of America," page 220. He did not even take the trouble to grow a mustache or a beard. Other aliases were Cheriton, Cameron, and Elaine, his real name being Ballentine. He had swindled persons in every country of the globe, always playing the part of a society confidence man, and he was sentenced in Tampa, Florida, in 1891 for seven years.

When Bellairs left Manila he was given a farewell dinner at the Army and Navy Club. The handsome sou-

venir menu lies before me as I write. There were ten
toasts, each celebrating Bellairs, the forger and chain-
gang man; among the speakers were General Chaffee,
General Jesse M. Lee, Commander Knapp of the Navy,
Morgan Shuster, Mr. Fergusson of the Philippine Commission, and Martin Egan, now of J. P. Morgan & Company. Leonard Wood was not among the fifty-one guests
—he had not yet arrived—but he should have been. For
he owes more to Bellairs than to any other man he has
ever met except Theodore Roosevelt. Toward the latter
Wood was savage in 1900. "The Rough Riders" had appeared in which Roosevelt took all the credit for himself.
General Wood told me that he had received letters "from
Maine to California" asking him to denounce it. Should
I print some things which General Wood said to me at
that time about Roosevelt they would not be believed. He
asked me if I had seen the Rough Riders at Montauk. I
said that I had. He asked me what I thought of them. I
told him frankly I had never seen anywhere so irregu-
lar and undisciplined a body of men. "That," he said,
"began with the day Colonel Roosevelt took over my
regiment." But the breach was easily healed later.

As for General Wood's long service in Cuba, Mr.
Root and Theodore Roosevelt, when President, made the
most extravagant statements about it, the latter declaring
that it equalled the work of Lord Cromer in Egypt. The
speedy collapse of the Estrada Palma Republic, which
General Wood set up, never checked that praise, nor the
fact that his work had to be done over again. As I studied what was done both in Cuba and in Egypt and visited

both countries, it is not improper, perhaps, to quote here from a letter I wrote to President Theodore Roosevelt in July, 1903, protesting against the unearned praise bestowed upon Wood:

> *It is certainly a fact that General Wood left Havana without the regard, and often without the respect, of the Americans and Cubans. Is it not curious that Spaniards were the only ones to lament his going? The distinctive feature of Cromer's administration has been his constructive work which has trebled the national wealth. General Wood never did a single piece of constructive work that I have ever heard of. He carried on what had been begun by Brooke and Ludlow in their spirit, but what policy did he formulate, what agricultural improvement did he bring about? . . . Finally, I do not believe that Cromer was ever unfaithful to his superiors. You yourself have told of General Wood's advice to you in connection with your testimony before the Embalmed Beef Commission.*[1]
>
> *Now to answer your specific questions. General Wood said to me, speaking of the Italian archbishop, Sbarreti, "I told him to buy off his Cuban rival with an office. That is the way to get on with these people." I replied, "General, do you think this policy pays in the long run?" "No," he replied, "I have only done it in a few cases." He then gave me a list of ten or more people whose influence he had purchased by offices or by outright gifts of money. . . . I afterwards tried repeatedly to find out if there was any principle of public morality behind his actions. His own lips convinced me that there was not.*

[1] Colonel Theodore Roosevelt and Brigadier General Wood gave directly contradictory testimony as to the effect upon the soldiers of the embalmed beef. Col. Roosevelt declared that he testified as General Wood told him to.

When General Wood was nominated in 1903 to be Major General, there was a very vigorous fight against his confirmation on the ground of his record in Cuba. He was upheld by Mr. Root and Mr. Roosevelt. Anybody who is interested can peruse the mass of testimony taken at that time and anyone who does so with an open mind will find much therein to make him wonder. But politics and friendship triumphed and he was confirmed. It is, however, a fact that in Executive Document C, confidential, 58th Congress, second session, published January 18, 1907, there will be found 900 pages recording secret hearings held by the Committee on Military Affairs from November 19 to December 16, 1903. Herein will be found charges against General Wood, supported by testimony, witnesses, and documentary evidence, which, as the *Army and Navy Register* puts its, "embraced accusations of disloyalty to and conspiracy against his superior commander, abuses of authority, favouritism, improper acceptance of a valuable gift, broken faith, duplicity, and untruthfulness."

A final word about Bellairs. When he was recalled from the Philippines he had just published a book attacking Governor General William H. Taft, whom he described as "an able lawyer but without the highest grade of executive ability"; as a "politician, not a diplomat." At the very end, there came out just what Bellairs was after: "The difference between Taft and Wood is that the former is a politician and a 'trimmer,' while the latter is a diplomat and a statesman, and it is to be hoped, in American interests, such a man as Leonard

Wood will succeed Taft in the Philippines. . . ." He was at his old tricks. He was, indeed, skilful in imposing upon many people, this ex-convict; years after his exposure in America he was acting as a special correspondent of the London *Times*. Leonard Wood was at first innocently imposed upon like myself and so many others. The curious fact is that there is testimony before the Senate Military Committee in 1903 that General Wood was, after a time, repeatedly warned as to the character of Bellairs, yet continued to defend him. Contrary to Mr. Stone's statement cited above, General Wood did not go to the Philippines until 1903, nearly three years after Bellairs had joined General Chaffee. General Wood was Governor of Moro Province from July, 1903, until April, 1906, during which time the pacification of the islands took place with really Prussian thoroughness. I have an interesting photograph taken at the battle of Mount Dajo showing the bodies of *dead women and children* in the Moro stronghold, killed by American soldiers of General Wood's command who stand by, rifles in hand.

General Wood did not achieve the position of Governor General of the Philippines, which Bellairs was so determined that he should have, until 1921. He held it, as stated, until his death, and there is no doubt that this is the best chapter in his entire record as an administrator. True, he was in frequent conflict with the Filipinos, and he did his best to postpone the day of Philippine independence by declaring privately and officially that the Filipino people were not ready for independence, "either from the standpoint of instructed public opinion, preparation for defence, a common language, or economic resources. . . ." But he died heralded by the press of the country as our greatest Colonial administrator.

HENRY FORD

The Eccentricity of Genius

"I N my opinion he could realize his supreme ambition if he were to follow the example of a good shoemaker and stick to his last, that is, to the human and production problems in industry, and leave national and international and racial problems alone." Thus Dr. Samuel S. Marquis upon the political ambitions of Henry Ford. No one could know Mr. Ford better than the man who was for years his candid friend, his pastor, and his employee. For three years the head of the sociological department of the Ford Motor Company, Dr. Marquis saw the inside of that amazing organization as have few others; and the results of his observation of Henry Ford, the man, the manufacturer, and the employer he has set forth in a volume entitled "Henry Ford, an Interpretation." It is a book remarkable for its extraordinary detachment and its refreshing honesty, so rare in biographies of this type.

"I know of no study more absorbing than the Ford psychology," writes Dr. Marquis. It is beyond question fascinating. No other man outside of political life has so challenged the admiration and the imagination of the American people, for no other man has risen as rapidly from poverty to the point where he either is or is about to be the richest man in the world. No other personality has been so much in the public eye and is yet so little understood and so rarely analysed. "Tell us what manner of man is Henry Ford," is the demand most often flung at those who know him, or at the newspapermen who are supposed to hold a key or two to this complex, paradoxical personality—Dr. Marquis calls him a "puzzling mixture of opposing natures." "There rages in him," this Boswell says, "an endless conflict between ideals, emotions, and impulses as unlike as day and night—a conflict that at times makes one feel that two personalities are striving within him for mastery, with neither able to win a final decision over the other." What wonder that Ford "stuff" is the best kind of newspaper material? It is not only the puzzle of the man himself and his phenomenal rise; ever since the New York newspapers read the Ford Company's balance sheet for 1922, with its amazing entry of "cash in bank $151,-000,000," they have been calling him the richest man on earth. That was enough to endow him at once in this land of Sunday newspapers with extraordinary and quite mythical qualities. He was not only a genius; he became one of the ablest of men. Next came his Senatorial and Presidential ambitions and his attacks on the Jews and they naturally won for the most-advertised man in the world endless additional free advertising.

Those were for a time serious political ambitions and they did not cease when Mrs. Ford stated to a reporter that "if Henry goes to the White House he goes without me." Dr. Marquis felt the menace of that candidacy throughout his study of the man, precisely as he revealed his belief in the unfitness of Ford for high political office. Every detached observer who had studied the career of Henry Ford and knew the requirements of the Presidency at this juncture in the affairs of humanity must have shuddered at the thought of this man being in control of our national destinies. This was not because he was and is an uneducated man and has to sit with a dictionary on his lap when he tries to read Emerson. There are unschooled men who have natural aptitudes and good horse sense, whom one would trust in any position. They have the inborn wisdom and patience of Lincoln; they have achieved an understanding of human nature; they have that divine sympathy which is the key to so many a human problem; and above all they are rooted in firm principles. When such a man, be his name Jackson, or Johnson, or Lincoln, reaches high office we have a triumph of democracy; we have something to make every American a bit prouder, a bit taller, a bit straighter.

But Henry Ford is not one of these, despite his amazing successes. The milk of human kindness is not within him though he may be charitable and philanthropic. He is without the traits to offset the blanks in his scanty education. He is without a quality for which I can find no better word than the old-fashioned "gumption," which has helped so many a man over obstacles otherwise insuperable. He is without that patience which is wisdom and beyond price. He has no philosophy of the universe upon which to build. "He has," records Dr. Marquis, "the not uncommon conviction among mor-

tals that he has a real message for the world, a real service to render mankind." He would like, so Mr. Ford himself has said, "to make the world a little better for having lived in it." Yet with that laudable ambition he has
not learned to control and subordinate himself, or to
think things through, or to order his mind. Dr. Marquis is quite clear on the latter point: "He [Ford] has
in him the makings of a great man, the parts lying about
in more or less disorder. If only Henry Ford were properly assembled! If only he would do in himself that
which he has done in his factory!" There lies the reason
for his intellectual failure and the danger of putting
him in any position in which his mental processes would
be compelled to make far-reaching decisions outside
the realm of automobiles and factories and mass production. It is the reason why it would be possible to
stop at any one of the great factories that line the New
Haven railroad between New York and New Haven and
pick out in each one some foreman earning $50 a week,
with no poorer education than Henry Ford, who would
be a safer choice for the White House than the richest
man in the world.

Inevitably my mind goes back to the day when
Henry Ford announced his peace ship, not merely because I was with him and was the second man to be
asked to go on the *Oscar II* and the first to decline, but
because that episode illustrates so clearly the weakness
of the man's mental processes. I am quite of Dr. Marquis's opinion that the motive behind that venture "was

a laudable one." Rightly handled it could have been made an amazing publicity "stunt" on behalf of that peace which all humanity desired, no one more so than the men in the trenches—that peace which the governments of Europe were too rotten, too crooked, or too incompetent to make at that time. It was I who suggested that the slogan Mr. Ford hit upon for his venture, "We'll get the boys home by Christmas," be toned down or abandoned. "Why?" demanded Mr. Ford with instant suspicion. I pointed out that as the ship would not sail until December 4 and could not arrive in Holland before December 15, the time left before Christmas was too short even to communicate with the belligerents and get their replies before December 25, to say nothing of the impossibility of physically getting the millions back to their home in ten days after his arrival. My efforts produced no other change than the modification of the slogan to "We'll get the boys out of the trenches by Christmas," and that only when I suggested that a Christmas armistice might bring the men out on top of their trenches.

That a man should be willing to hire a great liner and cross the ocean on such a bit of knight-errantry held the imagination even of those who doubted the practicality and common sense of the venture. He complied completely with the American demand that if one stands for an idea, one must "put up" for it; he put up hundreds of thousands. He had conceived a glorious idea, or rather others conceived it for him; yet he did not know how to carry it out. Nothing could have been more naïve or pathetic than that first interview with the news-papermen when the venture was launched. "Well, boys, I have got the ship." "What ship, Mr. Ford?" "Why, the *Oscar II*." "Well, what are you going to do with her?" "We're going to stop the war." "Going to *stop* the war?" "Yes, we're going to get the boys out of the trenches by Christmas." "But how are you going to do it?" "Oh, you'll see." "Well, who is going with you?" "I don't know." "Where are you going?" "I don't know." "What country will you head for?" "I don't know." "But what makes you think that you can put it over?" "Oh, we have had assurances." But he had not had assurances, as the event proved, and when he discovered this, he turned and fled for home.

If reports are true, not until there was almost a mutiny among his guests on the ship as she neared Norway did Mr. Ford trouble to read the letters which he had been assured were invitations from foreign governments—only to find that they were merely the most general, formal, and polite expressions of goodwill, such as would have been forthcoming for any well-meant move for peace. It was the mind of a suspicious and ingenuous child with which we had to deal; a mind without the necessary background of history and human experience to think its way through the first essentials of such a vast human problem. The instinct was sound, the necessary gumption lacking. So he and his guests went to sea in the *Oscar II*, he believing firmly that the war would cease as soon as he got across. He was without sufficient business sense to assure himself that there was a real prospect of success by inquiries in the proper quarters; he did not even know how to obtain the right kind of a ship's company. Just as soon as he discovered how gullible he had been, he displayed both cowardice and selfishness in abandoning the whole venture and returning home almost by stealth. Yet there are multitudes of Americans who have wished to entrust a mind like this with the handling of our foreign affairs!

Curiously enough, there are certain traits in Henry Ford which were the worst traits developed by Woodrow Wilson during his sojourn in the White House. He plays a lone hand. Dr. Marquis even goes so far as to say that if Ford were President we should have a cheap administration because he would dispense with the Cabinet and a good many executives. Just as Mr. Wilson secluded himself more and more, so Henry Ford has said to an employee: "You know me too well; hereafter I am going to see to it that no man comes to know me as intimately as you do." Of Mr. Wilson the same words have been written which Dr. Marquis uses in describing Henry Ford: "The isolation of Henry Ford's mind is about as near perfect as it is possible to make it. For this reason the confidence born in him of success along one line never forsakes him when he enters other spheres of thought and action. Adverse criticism reaches him, of course, but it does not penetrate." Elsewhere this biographer speaks of Ford's "one-way mind"—ominous reminiscence of a "one-track mind" in the White House!

Again, both men have had a perfectly ruthless way of dealing with subordinates who have offended them.

Dr. Marquis deplores and cannot defend the fact that Ford has quarrelled with and discharged all the magnificent group of men who with him built his success. Every one of these men has been forced out of the company. Sometimes the quarrel was open and resulted in litigation; sometimes they were just dropped out. Sometimes subordinates have been thrown out under circumstances that reflect the utmost discredit upon Ford himself and reveal a side to his character that stamps him as at moments dangerously uncontrolled. Dr. Marquis observes that in many cases in which gross injustice was done to employees, Henry Ford, when cognizant of the facts, refused to lift a finger to right the wrong. One instance is worth going into at length—the summary discharge of a man whose task in the company "was a colossal one and greatly complicated by conditions which arose during the war." Dr. Marquis told Henry Ford that his treatment of this man was neither just nor humane, that it robbed him not only of his job, but of his reputation. Mr. Ford professing a desire to reinstate the official, Dr. Marquis went at his request to a certain executive to discuss the case with him. What followed I give in Dr. Marquis's own words:

> *I told this executive that I thought he had acted most unfairly in the discharge of this man. "How do you know I did it?" he shot back. "Maybe you are barking up the wrong tree. How do you know the Chief did not do it?" I answered that I did not believe the Chief would be capable of doing such a thing. While we were in the midst of a heated discussion Mr. Ford came into the*

office. He listened to what we were saying for a few min-
utes and then turning to me said: "I did it. I discharged
that man and what is more he is not coming back." This
within an hour after he had said for the second time that
he would be taken back. "What have you got to say
now?" said the official. "I told you that you were bark-
ing up the wrong tree." "I have to say," I replied, "just
what I have said before. The discharge was not merited,
and the manner in which it was done was neither cour-
teous nor fair." Mr. Ford then said: "Bring the man down
to my office in the morning and we will go over the whole
matter with him." I did as requested. Mr. Ford failed to
keep the appointment. That was the end of the case.

It is not surprising that Dr. Marquis adds: "It is
sufficiently painful and humiliating to be brought face
to face with unemployment and all that follows—loss of
income and of savings, accumulation of debts, eviction
and hunger—without being kicked like a dog into it."
Elsewhere he squarely places upon Mr. Ford's own
shoulders the responsibility for this policy of "treat 'em
rough" which seems to pervade the organization. More
than eighty men in one department went home one evening without any intimation whatever that they were dismissed. "They came to work the next morning to find
their desks and chairs taken from the room in which
they worked. They were left to find out as best they
could that they had been fired. The request to be permitted to tell men in a decent, gentlemanly manner that
the company no longer required their services met with
refusal." More than that, some employees came to work
to find their desks *smashed with an ax*—a kind of sa-

distic vengeance which in no wise suggests the self-control and sense of justice which surely are requisite in anyone who would guide the destinies of 115,000,-000 Americans. More than that, Mr. Ford is the victim of great gusts of passion as "sudden and terrible as those which break over the tropics."

To my mind Labour has gone strangely wrong in its attitude toward Henry Ford. True he gives a $6 a day minimum wage but, as Dr. Marquis says, there was no excuse for a company in such a position not giving the original $5 a day. It is also true that he has a fine social philosophy as to the "down and out" and the ex-convict, that his theory of well-paid work as the salvation for most human shipwrecks is eminently sound. But these things do not offset the absolute despotism of the Ford management, its bitter opposition to all unionism, its refusal to introduce co-operation, and its working human beings at a terrific speed at such monotonous jobs as must inevitably affect the mental and physical health of those who labour for hours at one single, never-varying task. No, the American labouring men may be spellbound by the success of this mechanic who toiled with his hands, but they err, indeed, if they see in him the ideal employer, or an industrial liberator of workingmen. He is an industrial autocrat—nothing else.

None the less, Mr. Ford is a genius in his own field, and his desire to create more work in the world for human beings is altogether to his credit. He conferred an inestimable boon upon the rural and the urban

dweller alike. He made the countryside free for multitudes who could never have dreamed of possessing
a horse and buggy. He supplied a most valuable adjunct
to industry. He has enormously increased the radius
of activity and the sphere of employment of the artisans
of the small town and the country village. And he did
all this and much more besides by the fairest and squar-
est methods, so that he may well be the despair of
socialists. For in building his success he enjoyed no
special privilege whatever; he injured nobody and drove
nobody out of business—at least not directly. He is
guiltless of having profited by rebates and special railroad facilities and he has enjoyed no political favour.
He was simply wise enough to see that to produce a
good, cheap automobile by the thousand and ten thousand, and to stick to one good model year in year out
without attempting changes or the experiments that have
wrecked many established automobile corporations, was
the road to success. Success came to him in a magnitude
unsurpassed in the history of the world. It is impossible
to believe that he foresaw anything of the kind, for
his success was beyond human imagining in 1903.

It has often been averred that to his earlier associates and executives, the Dodges, Couzens, and others,
the lion's share of the credit for Ford's success belongs.
The fact that his companies continued up to 1927 to
do marvellously well and that he is constantly reaching
out and establishing new enterprises is proof enough of
his business ability and his mastery of organization. His
being able to get on without going to the banks for aid

when he was apparently in distress several years ago is another achievement which reflects lustre upon his industrial generalship. He is the only man I know who can do things that would ruin any other capitalist and still "get away with it." There seems to be no limit to his power of industrial achievement; the whole South yearned to have him take over the Muscle Shoals project, believing that with one wave of his fairy wand he would create new and unexampled prosperity for that section. For all the efforts of the older railway men to break the effect of Ford's success in running his railroad by attributing it entirely to the freight traffic which he is able to throw to it himself, there is no doubt that, coming to railroading with a fresh mind and freedom from red tape and the dry-as-dust methods of the older railway corporations, he has blazed the way and put new life and efficiency into what was a dead, or nearly dead, artery of traffic. His capture of the water-power in St. Paul and Minneapolis, which ought to have been reserved for the public, is another instance of the ability of the man to affect the imaginations of his fellow-men. In anybody else this would have been denounced as a "grab" and a "steal" deserving of the utmost public condemnation.

Mr. Ford is beyond question philanthropic—he does give money away. There is a hospital upon which he has lavished millions, and he has doubtless done many private acts of generosity, though he has by no means mastered either the art or the happiness of giving on a large scale. And here, too, his record is sullied.

I am familiar with a case in which he publicly announced that he was going to give $10,000 to a certain cause, and then welshed because he did not like an interview given to the press by a single member of the group of men connected with the undertaking. For this trivial reason he refused to reimburse the organization for expenses incurred after his public promise. There is a Western college which makes a similar charge against him—again proof of his inability to control his feelings. After his flight from Norway he set up an international peace bureau, inducing a number of foreign savants to resign their university positions upon the promise that they would be permanently taken care of. Some years later he discharged them without recourse. In no such case is there evidence that Mr. Ford ever has moments of contrition and repentance. Like Woodrow Wilson he feels that he can do no wrong; he, too, looks with suspicion and positive hatred upon anyone who dares to oppose him or thwart him.

Nor has Mr. Ford ever expressed any regret at his own lack of educational opportunities. The geographical ignorance of Lloyd George and Woodrow Wilson at Paris has been the subject of many a jest and many an anecdote—Lloyd George could not at first distinguish between Silesia and Cilicia—but those men were towers of knowledge when compared with the master of the automobile industry. Ignorance of geography can, of course, be supplied, when those ignorant are willing to surround themselves by others having knowledge, and then to use that knowledge. But when it comes

to the profound, deep-lying economic issues of the day,
one cannot so safely or so easily suck the brains of
others without at least running the risk of being deceived and imposed upon. Take Henry Ford's crusade
against the Jews. I attribute it to nothing else than utter
ignorance. He fell for the long-since exploded and over-
worked Protocols and every old slander—I have no
doubt that if he did not believe in ritualistic murders it
is only because he had not been plausibly told about
them. His retractions and apologies would have hu-
miliated any other man beyond repair. In the matter of
finance, Henry Ford is utterly unsound. He would be
guided by the fiat-money views of his friend Thomas
Edison rather than by the opinion of the most liberal
and detached students of finance and economics.

Yet there can be no doubt as to the popularity of
Henry Ford throughout the country. Wherever he
travels, East, West, North, or South, the observer will
find proof of the amazing appeal of Ford to the popular imagination and profoundest interest in his new car.
The plain people are convinced that he is just one of
them who has broken the bank, who played the luckiest
card ever played by any mortal and carried off the largest sweepstakes from the green-baize table of fate, and
they are betting on him to win again. It was astonishing how many of them believed in 1924 that in some
miraculous way he could make over the government of
the United States into that efficient, up-to-date, smooth-
working business organization it ought to be. The people like him because, being rich, he still hates Wall

Street and refuses to be drawn into it, and they do not mind if he frequently turns a trick for which they would denounce any well-known Wall Street operator. It pleases them that being enormously wealthy he refuses to go in for social ambitions and build a palace at Newport. They admire him because his private life is so exemplary, because he still holds to the wife of his youth, and adores his promising and able son. They don't mind if he makes Fords and drives a Rolls-Royce, and that he lives in a big and particularly ugly house. They are not really interested in politicians though they have a shrewd one in the White House. They want a successful man of themselves to try his hand at the governmental game and bring them some relief. The farmers especially would like to see Mr. Ford take hold of their problems. He gave them their car and their tractor and he promised them remarkably cheap fertilizer when he tried to get the Government to lease Muscle Shoals to him. Who else has done as much for them? What do they care if he does not know who Benedict Arnold was, that he is a pacifist today and tomorrow wants to go to war if necessary to enter the League of Nations—the Covenant of which he has surely never read?

So far fortune has, indeed, smiled upon him. Will it continue to now that the new Ford is "just another" conventional gear-shift car? As one beheld Mr. Ford taking an almost daily plunge into something new— a huge plantation in Georgia, railroading, airplanes, banks and trust companies, in addition to all his vast

automobile, mining, foundry, and wood-working enterprises, one wondered whether fate was perhaps not bent
on killing him with good fortune, or whether it was
merely driving him ahead into greater and greater expansion, in order to make the American people ask
themselves how much money and how much power one
single man could be allowed to amass. Who knows?
He, at least, can have no conception whither he is
drifting.

WILLIAM RANDOLPH HEARST

Failure

A T sixty-five William Randolph Hearst is a failure
as a man, a newspaper magnate, and a politician.
True, he owns more newspapers and magazines than any
other American, and he has piled millions of dollars
upon his patrimony. He has the satisfaction of knowing
that he has created money-making dailies and magazines, that he has acquired magnificent estates in California and on Long Island, besides one of the oldest
castles in England, and that he is one of the greatest
landowners in Mexico. He can also boast that he has
profoundly affected—for the worse—the entire journalism of his day, probably more than any other individual has affected it since the beginning of journalism
in America.

But there his case rests. Once a serious contender
for high public office, even the Presidency, he is now
politically dead. Politicians of lesser degree doubtless
still fawn in his vestibules, but in the approaching Presidential campaign, it is safe to assert, no politician of
any national standing will trouble to inquire where
Hearst stands or whom he will support. Even Tammany Hall no longer cringes before his power since
Governor Smith drove him from the political life of
New York in 1922. The Governor had said three years
previously, standing on the platform of Carnegie Hall,

that Hearst was "a man as low and as mean as I can picture him," one who "has not got a drop of good clean pure red blood in his whole body." The Governor went further; he branded him "a pestilence that walks in the dark." Three years later, thanks to the stupidity of bosses, Charles Murphy decided to nominate Hearst for the governorship a second time and to kick "Al" Smith upstairs by giving him the nomination for the United States senatorship, then to be filled. When Boss Mc-Cooey of Brooklyn came to the Governor, during the convention in Syracuse, with this news, "Al" Smith replied, "Nothing doing. Say, do you think I haven't any self-respect? You can tell Murphy I won't run with Hearst on the ticket, and that goes." Murphy remained adamant; there was a stampede to Hearst, but the Governor uttered six words that finished the political career of the man who for months had pictured him as permitting the poisoning, through bad milk, of the little children of the metropolis. To the reporters he said, "They don't vote until tomorrow night." It was sufficient. Hearst did not dare face the possibility of a repetition upon the floor of the convention of the denunciations of Carnegie Hall. In a panic the publisher withdrew his name. There are still other reasons why Mr. Hearst will never again be nominated for any public office.

In his own chosen field of journalism he is no longer looked up to because of his success, or dreaded as a competitor. The business of newspaper making no longer regards him as a superman. He has been surpassed by others in the art of gathering garbage from the gutters of life. He never mastered the technique of the tabloids; his sale of them is a confession of complete failure. Pre-eminence in this field now belongs to the owners of the New York *Daily News.* In the older-fashioned journalism he has scored as many failures as he has successes. The profession knows that the dullest of his dailies is the one with which he concerns himself most, in which he takes the deepest interest. If it was his hand and brain which gave us the comic strips, the flaring headlines, the overweening emphasis on sex, snobbery, sensation, and sin, his creative period seems happily past.

As was the case with the two Bennetts, Dana, and Pulitzer, this journalistic extremist has steadily modified his yellowness; compared with his latest rivals, he at times seems positively pale. Moreover, his touch is uncertain, as his journalistic aim is less clear. His papers are nothing like the belligerent fighting organs they were twenty years ago. True, his *Mirror* compelled the reopening of the Hall-Mills murder case in New Jersey and again spread abroad the dirt of that case—only to see the objects of its attacks acquitted. True also that he and his eldest son sacrificed one airplane on the Pacific Ocean and one on the Atlantic, with five human beings, in the never-ending effort to build circulations. But when one considers, among many other things, his incredible blunder in publishing recently the forged Mexican documents—contrary, it is said, to the advice

of the best men in his own organization—which led to
denunciation of him the country over, notably by Senator George W. Norris, and his miserable showing on the
witness stand before the Senatorial committee of inquiry, it is obvious that even his hand is losing its cun-
ning. The very verbosity of his unconvincing reply to
Senator Norris—itself a departure from his usual custom of accepting criticism without replying—is proof
that this time the galled jade winced under Mr. Norris's
declaration that Heart's dailies are "the sewer system of
American journalism." The truth is that his journals
suffer from the evils of standardization as they do from
the owner's bad political judgment and the gross inconsistency which has always marked him as an opportunist
utterly devoid of principle.

Hearst is surrounded by a group of executives
whose loyalty to him, with several exceptions, has been
open to doubt but which is now headed by an honest
and able man, David E. Town. If it is true that "his
own people don't give him a square deal," his own
methods are not such to create a loyal and devoted force,
or to train men into becoming great journalists. He is
himself a poor executive by choice, whose interest in
his dailies is spasmodic, but his employees are always
in danger of being discharged on the slightest notice—
"he listens to the last man who talks to him." Often
enough they are victims of the cabals within the organization. Hence the employees who enter his service
determined to protect his interests, and to remedy the

unhappy conditions which render some of his dailies unprofitable, speedily lose heart and ambition and either resign or accept conditions as they are and become part of the system. Hearst is thus a victim of his own organization and is in turn in large measure responsible for its weaknesses. Had he been willing to be the able executive leader he could be, a genuine journalistic teacher, a real leader of men, sincerely and genuinely devoted to the public weal, he could have created a chain of dailies which would have brought him rich returns and been a credit to him and to his country. That he knows the technique of the trade is indisputable; he can himself make up the pages of his dailies, and he has an extraordinary knowledge of the great presses which grind out his papers and of the other machinery used in a great newspaper shop. His own employees and his former employees say that he is "smarter than any man who ever worked for him," and they all insist that he has been the greatest showman of the newspaper business, the P. T. Barnum of journalism. But his lack of character and of stability, and his unwillingness to be on the job of directing his papers all the time, have together made him the failure that he is from every point of view except the financial.

None the less, Hearst continues to buy newspapers. On July 30 last, the city of Pittsburgh rejoiced in five dailies. The next day it woke up to find the number reduced to three, and it appeared that William Randolph Hearst had added one of these to his string; indeed, there is evidence that one which now stands in the name of another man is really Mr. Hearst's property, to be transferred to him by the present dummy owner in due course—a proceeding which has often marked Mr. Hearst's acquisition of his dailies. When that transfer takes place Pittsburgh will obtain all its news from Hearst and the Scripps-Howard daily, the Pittsburgh *Press*—absentee ownership with a vengeance.

At the end of forty-two years of newspaper ownership Hearst now admits the possession in seventeen different cities of twenty-three daily newspapers and three that appear only on Sunday. His chief competitor in group ownership, the Scripps-Howard dailies, comprises twenty-six papers. Today the list of the Hearst properties is as follows, with the circulation claims for each:—

Morning	*Circulation*
Chicago Herald and Examiner	*435,074*
New York American	*227,969*
San Francisco Examiner	*186,372*
Los Angeles Examiner	*199,708*
Seattle Post-Intelligencer	*94,164*
Washington Herald	*54,383*

Evening	*Circulation*
Albany Times-Union	*46, 539*
New York Evening Journal	*680,681*
Chicago American	*532,376*
Boston American	*301,689*
Detroit Times	*326,786*
Washington Times	*75,762*
Wisconsin News (Milwaukee)	*110,340*

Atlanta Georgian	*67,569*
Syracuse Journal-American	*66,917*
Rochester Journal-American	*47,640*
Baltimore News	*145,011*
San Francisco Call	*108,501*
Los Angeles Herald	*206,879*
San Antonio Light	*37,205*

Sunday [1]

Syracuse Sunday American	*88,017*
Atlanta American	*128,583*
Rochester Sunday American	*65,315*

In addition, he and his wife own the following magazines: *Cosmopolitan, Good Housekeeping, Harper's Bazar, Nash's Magazine* (London), *Good Housekeeping* (London), *Motor, Motor Boating, International Studio, Town and Country,* and some trade journals. His California properties are, with the New York *Evening Journal,* undoubtedly the most successful. In 1925 the five California dailies earned a net income of $4,556,-667, less bond interest of $780,000. In 1926 the net was $5,277,229, less bond interest—a handsome revenue, indeed, for debauching the public taste. In addition to these very prosperous properties, the Detroit, Seattle, Chicago, Albany, and Milwaukee papers are earning their way well—the Chicago *American's* net profit is rated at $2,000,000. The newspaper fraternity believes that the New York *American,* Mr. Hearst's particular pet, is at best breaking even; that his Baltimore, Boston, Rochester, Syracuse, San Antonio, Washington,

---

[1] These are really Sunday editions of evening newspapers.

and Atlanta dailies are losing money, notably the Baltimore one—the Baltimore *American* after being a tabloid for two months was killed. It is needless to add that the earnings of the successful journals far offset the losses of the others, precisely as, among his magazines, the enormous profits of his *Cosmopolitan, Good Housekeeping, Motor,* and *Motor Boating* easily take care of the losses of those of the group which are not prospering, with millions to spare. In New York, however, the profits of the *Evening Journal,* once put at $3,000,000 a year, are now estimated to be $1,000,000, and the total result of his operation of the *American,* the *Evening Journal,* and his tabloid, the *Mirror,* in that city was supposed to be a slight loss. Prior to its sale to Alexander P. Moore on March 6, 1928, the *Mirror* had declined in circulation, since 1924, from 327,936 to 307,956, and its advertising had decreased approximately 800,000 lines in two years.

One Baltimore venture is characteristic of his unsuccessful undertakings. He purchased the *American* for $2,500,000, went out on a street, saw a tower building, and ordered it bought. It cost $1,000,000 and proved to be unusable. Thereupon he bought another site for approximately $250,000 and erected a building said to have cost $500,000. In the four years since then his operating losses are estimated to have been $5,000,000, his buildings are heavily mortgaged, and the slowness of his agents in paying small bills is the despair of tradesmen. But, as stated, he changed his *American* into a tabloid, undeterred by the failure of

the New York *Mirror* to become a profitable concern—
it was said to be losing $30,000 a week just before its
sale—only to kill the *American* when he sold his other
two tabloids. His Baltimore *American* investment and
expenditures thus cost him at least $9,500,000, most of
which is lost. Yet there are newspaper men a plenty to
be found who believe that if he had hired an able business manager and freed him from control by the committee of his executives, which attends to the details of
the various enterprises, this Baltimore paper could have
been saved and made to pay.

For many years Mr. Hearst financed himself as
has Henry Ford, without reference to the bankers or
the public, though of course he borrowed and mort-
gaged heavily. That was the correct policy for him to
pursue. In 1923, however, he was compelled to go to
the public for aid, and since then he has sold more
than $60,000,000 of bonds on his newspapers alone,
in addition to a $10,000,000 issue for the benefit of his
magazines and several series of bonds for which some
of his real-estate holdings are collateral. Thus, he placed
$2,000,000 of 6 per cent secured notes for the benefit
of the Chicago *Herald-Examiner* and, in 1925, $12,-
000,000 of first-mortgage collateral trust 6½ per cent
bonds on his California properties. Of the latter, $4,-
600,000 had already been paid off when, in October
1927, he disposed of $20,000,000 of similar bonds bear-
ing 6¼ per cent interest, out of which he retired the
remaining $7,400,000 of the first issue. To serve the
New York *Evening Journal* he disposed of $15,000,000

of 6¼ per cent first-mortgage bonds, while the Chicago *American* profited by the sale of $3,000,000 of 6 per cent sinking-fund notes, and by an issue of $9,000,000 of 6 per cent debentures which, among other things, retired the $3,000,000 of sinking-fund notes. Mr. Hearst has had no trouble whatever in getting bankers to market these securities and individual buyers for them. He has already paid off $3,500,000 of the *Evening Journal's* $15,000,000 indebtedness, paying $1,000,000 on December 1, 1927, and has been steadily reducing the outstanding notes of the Chicago *Herald-Examiner*. At the present time there are still, according to the *Editor and Publisher*, about $40,000,000 of bonds and notes outstanding.

The truth is that much of this indebtedness would never have been incurred if Mr. Hearst personally had been interested in the financing of his properties and if he had not constantly mulcted his papers in order to meet his own enormous personal expenditures. His business managers have lived in daily fear of being ordered to turn over to him large sums on a moment's notice, and their fears have usually been justified. If, as on one occasion, he appeared to demand, after banking hours, $2,500 from one of his dailies, which, heavily in debt and unable to pay small bills, had nothing like that in its till, he none the less insisted on having it borrowed for him and went off with it. The money was never refunded to that daily. A like story of his arrival in Chicago in a private car, en route to California, is well vouched for. He found that there was $30,000

available in his Chicago office, and demanded it. "But,"
said the manager, "Mr. Carvalho [of the New York
American] has ordered me to send him $25,000." Mr.
Hearst was much amused. "What a joke on Carvalho!"
said he, and went off with the money, without a further
thought as to what that might mean to Carvalho's financial plans. Similarly, he has been known to withdraw
from a meeting of his executives, called to deal with a
matter of great moment to him personally as distinct
from his papers, and to say as he went, "I pay you to
take care of things like this for me."

It is agreed that he does not care for money itself, yet he has a mania for spending, a desire to buy
whatever takes his fancy, especially real estate, and he
maintains fabulously costly establishments. His California estate comprises some 400,000 acres. It is nearly
half as large as the State of Rhode Island; it has thirty-
five miles of ocean frontage, and he can drive for fifty-
five miles in a straight line over his own land. In addition to a huge house and guest houses, he has on hand
all the material which was once Tattershall Castle in
Lincolnshire, but he has not yet carried out his plan
to re-erect it in California. From Spain he has brought
both a castle and a church, stone by stone, for re-erec-
tion. His English castle—St. Donat's in Wales, with its
thirteen hundred acres, a famous old Norman structure—was purchased by cable within three hours after
he saw the pictures of it in an English weekly. Once,
when visiting the Grand Canyon of the Colorado, he
bought a hotel because he liked the view from its porch;

it is not recorded that he has ever seen it again. He himself estimates his holdings in mines and ranches in Mexico as being between four and five millions of dollars; in every direction he owns lands—mines, ranches, estates—and possessions beyond the reach of prince or king.

As for art treasures, he now spends a great part of his time at galleries and auction rooms—the most important business must wait if there is an auction on hand. His purchases fill his houses in California and New York, are stacked in boxes on wharves at his estate and piled in storage warehouses in every direction. In one year his storage bill for space in New York was $80,000. He has now built, in the Bronx section of the metropolis, a huge warehouse for his own use. In it are objects which he has not seen in ten years.

Mr. Hearst's collection of armour is the finest in the world; it is surpassed by that of no museum. His silverware has been valued by an international expert as being worth between $5,000,000 and $6,000,000. His collection of lace is one of the very best—and so it goes. What good does it all do him or anybody else, except as an example of the futility of wealth when it has passed beyond a certain stage? But the pride of possession controls him; the means he has drawn from exploiting the gutters of American life. What said Isaiah? "Woe unto the wicked! it shall be ill with him: for the reward of his hands shall be given him."

One chronicler estimates Hearst's annual personal expenditures at fifteen millions of dollars. That may be apocryphal, but there can be no question as to the vastness of his fortune in California alone. Bankers there rate his wealth far higher than is known in the East. But the danger of overexpansion remains, as well as the risk of tying up too large sums in immovables, of borrowing too widely, of having your newspapers managed by a group of men who are constantly at loggerheads, though some are honest, able, and faithful. There is the peril, too, of maintaining a group of papers that lose money and of milking the profitable ones to sustain them. Even very, very rich men have been known to go ahead too fast—as witness Henry Ford. The sale or suspension of four dailies and two magazines in March and April 1928, would seem to prove that Mr. Hearst is realizing this.

Why, then, does Hearst hold on to some of his newspapers that are losing money? Why does he buy more? Why does he allow his general staff to be torn by dissensions? Why does he carry on with his great group of dailies and not run them efficiently? What is the answer to the puzzle of this extraordinary and extraordinarily sinister figure? What is the real passion behind this whole enterprise? Is it power, money, personal ambition, the love of notoriety?

The enigma is profoundly difficult to answer. There are those who have been close to William Randolph Hearst who tell you frankly that, though they have worked with him for years and are personally fond of him, they can neither understand nor explain him.

There is something in his mental processes which baffles them. It is as if there were a connecting rod wanting; the several parts of the engine function brilliantly, but they do not always co-ordinate. The balance wheel appears lacking; there are forces and counter-forces at work—the result is what it is. He refuses to give up dailies that are losing money because his pride is at stake; because he always thinks that somehow he will pull them out; perhaps because his investment is so great that he cannot usually admit defeat; because even the losers absorb some of the overhead which would otherwise have to be carried by the others. There is but one single recorded case in which Hearst let go of a daily that he owned until he sold his tabloids, the *Mirror* in New York and the *Advertiser* in Boston, to Mr. Alexander P. Moore. In Fort Worth, Texas, lives Amon G. Carter. He must be an extraordinary person, for single-handed he went after Hearst, when the latter purchased the Fort Worth *Record,* and knocked him over the ropes. Hearst lost $1,700,000 so quickly that he surrendered and sold to his rival. Amon Carter wears at his belt a scalp that many others have tried for in vain.

To the rest of his losers Hearst holds on because he wants his will and his way, because he cares less about those losses than an ordinary man would, because he loves the power that he thinks each additional daily gives him—it would be truer to say *gave* him. "He must know," writes one who worked for him, "that he is a bigger man with his newspapers than he would be without them, and this is my guess for his willingness to lose millions yearly."

Perhaps that also explains in part why he buys more dailies—except that there is abroad in newspaperdom a trend toward chains of dailies as in the rest of the business world we see chains of banks, or drug and tobacco and ten-cent stores. The lure of the reduced overhead and the additional outlet for editorials, special features, comic strips and supplements, foreign cables, and so forth, is very great. But if personal ambition was once a considerable factor in impelling Hearst on a journalistic course, he must now be, for the reasons already stated, without political hopes and aspirations. He has long since ceased to be a progressive leader; time has made him conservative—time, and the piling up of those millions of his—and conservatism usually makes against new ventures at sixty-five. Social ambition he no longer has—or can have. As for his sons, they are still too young to have demonstrated their fitness for the successorship to their father.

As for the dissensions in his staff, there are times when he is accused of fomenting them as if in the belief that there will be life in the organization if it is fighting within itself. Yet this makes for an inefficiency to which Hearst appears so blind that there are those of experience in his service who seek to explain it on the ground that he does not know what is really going on within his own forces, despite his extraordinary ability to master details. His new interests in art and his fever-

ish passion to buy, buy, and buy are plainly distract-
ing him from that work of supervision and control which
in the last analysis cannot be delegated by the head of
such huge undertakings short of complete retirement.
It is the writer's guess that what keeps him still at the
helm is his love of power and, in lesser degree, his
love of notoriety. It does not hurt his feelings to see
WILLIAM RANDOLPH HEARST in large type at the foot
of his editorials; he is not displeased when he is sum-
moned to Washington to explain why he has perpetrated the most scandalous chicanery in order to embroil the United States with Mexico when a few years
ago (February 7, 1922) he was saying, "Every human
interest that appeals to a nation calls on us to do justice to Mexico—politics, diplomacy, national defence.
. . . Why inflict conspiracy and injuries on a government that is trying to be friendly and from whose friendship we can derive only benefit?"

The truth is that nothing so grips any man as the
combined thrill and power of journalism. None who
have tasted it ever yield it willingly, and this alone
would explain why Hearst holds on and why he seeks
new cities upon which to lay his evil spell. He does not,
of course, realize that the technique, once so effective,
to which he still sticks is entirely outmoded, that the
great financial successes in journalism are now dailies
like the New York *Times,* or like the Detroit *News,* the
Chicago *Daily News,* the Philadelphia *Bulletin*—totally
different types from his own. In the field of sensational-
ism, sex, and crime, others are beating him at his own

game. It is said that he knows he is now a conservative at heart, but he plainly does not realize that his old technique no longer applies as it did during the time when he was getting us into the war with Spain, when he was warring upon the "Plunderbund" by day and by night, and putting Mark Hanna into a suit covered with dollar-marks. He does not realize, either, that while he still has circulation, he has vastly less influence.

Amazing it is that he should ever have had any! Yet it is true that, when he was prating loudly his pretence that he was fighting the battle of the common people, millions of our citizens and many politicians took him seriously. They ignored or excused the vulgarity, the baseness, the filth of his journals because, they said, he was a voice in the wilderness—as if something worth while could come out of such shameless alliances with evil. Clerics fawned on him. Bishop Henry C. Potter gave him benefit of clergy in his matrimonial venture; Dr. Parkhurst has for years been a paid Hearst circulation getter, side by side with the latest husband killer, the most notorious prostitute, or seducer of young girls. "See," his defenders once said, "he opposes monopoly and greed, the exploitation of the poor; the bourgeois, the small tradesman, are the special objects of his benevolence; they will yet rise up to call him blessed." Was he not against graft, against lawless capital? Did he not drape his dailies with American flags and inculcate patriotism? Did he not sponsor Bryan and other champions of the people, and was it not he above all others, as his hireling Brisbane insisted, who cleared the way for Roosevelt, especially in 1912?

Well, where does he stand now? Why, he is for Andrew Mellon for President, with Coolidge as his second choice. Mellon, twenty years ago, he would have pictured in prison stripes as the very head of the "Plunderbund." Forgotten are all his old shibboleths. Forgotten his demands for government ownership of railroads, for the initiative and the referendum, for higher taxes for the rich and lower for the poor. Turn today to his editorial pages. When are the chief planks in his platform as printed in the New York *American?* Improved state and local roads; through continental highways; more schools, better school buildings, better pay for teachers; an all-American ship canal from lakes to ocean; revision of state and local taxation toward equity; and a co-operative compact between English-speaking nations to maintain peace in the world. Hardly anything in that to stir men's hearts and set the populace to marching on Washington! Here are some of the thrilling editorial subjects which were "featured" in the *American*—Mr. Hearst's favourite—in the month of January, 1927:

> *January 10. The need of more and better highways.*
> *January 11. A plea for Congress to pass the Curtis-Reed Bill, establishing a Federal Department of Education with a Secretary of Education in the Cabinet.*
> *January 12. A plea to back up Governor General Wood in the Philippines.*
> *January 13. A plea for Congress to pass the Robinson-*

Rogers Bill forcing banks to lend to war veterans, using their adjusted compensation certificates as collateral.

January 14. Stand by the President in his defence of our rights in Mexico!

January 15. An editorial approving of Governor Smith's plan to have New York State develop its own water power.

January 17. An editorial advocating the extension of movie censorship to the stage.

January 18. A plea for a vote in Congress on Boulder Dam.

January 20. An editorial advocating that New York City compel the five-cent fare for new subways as well as old.

January 21. An editorial in favour of the Foreign Commerce Service Bill.

January 22. A plea for Congress to restore to Governor General Wood the power to appoint and remove governors of the non-Christian provinces in the Philippines.

January 24. An attack on Wayne B. Wheeler for the poisoned alcohol.

These are not exceptional titles; they are the run of crop. Why should any man expect that the masses should come cheering to him when he offers nothing else to warm their hearts?

Mr. Hearst has much to be thankful for. The short-lived memory of the American people has quickly forgotten his sins in helping to bring on the war with Spain; also the bitterness against him for his alleged (but unproved) part in instigating the assassination of McKinley, and for the conduct of his papers during the

World War. But even a cat has only nine lives. There comes a time when so tortuous and twisting and hypocritical a career as this begins to be measured. The masses buy his papers, let it be said again, not for his editorial doctrines, or for any love or reverence for him, but for the merchandise he has to sell—such as it is. How can Hearst expect to be taken seriously today when he solemnly grants to the *Editor and Publisher* a long interview in which he declares that good taste in publishing crime news should be the guide for every daily—he whose dailies have stopped at nothing in retailing the stenographic reports of some of the filthiest of our recent court sensations? But this hypocrisy is nothing new in Hearst. His cynicism, his willingness to advocate one thing one day and another thing the next, have been repeatedly revealed. It was not an exception that the Atlanta *Georgian* took the anti-Frank side in the famous lynching case in that city, whereas his other newspapers urged upon the Governor of Georgia that this man's life be spared.

"The evil that men do lives after them"—it would be hard to guess what journalistic good will be interred with Hearst's bones. Undoubtedly the evil devices which he has grafted upon a large part of the American press are here to stay and will long commemorate his career in journalism. It must be obvious, however, that when the hour comes for him to retire, some of his group of newspapers will be allowed to die if he does not leave behind him a machinery capable of operating honestly and efficiently and putting the money losers into the profit-making class. There will be no more interesting experiment than that which will then prove whether a string of single-ownership dailies can be maintained without the leadership of one able, directing personality. The outcome of this, like the development of the Scripps-Howard newspapers, will be of enormous importance to the future of American journalism.

Today the net result of all of Hearst's efforts is failure. He is himself a picture of melancholy futility and tragedy. He who had the greatest opportunity in American journalism to influence it to better things, and influenced it to its hurt, stands an outcast, beloved by nobody save a few who intimately surround him, and despised by the great majority of his own profession and by thoughtful citizens everywhere. The rewards of his hands have come to him, but also the rewards that invariably come with lack of character. Never has it been more clearly shown that riches avail not when one has lost one's soul. Is it not probable that the very feverishness of that piling up of endless possessions which he can never hope to enjoy is the conscious or unconscious anæsthetizing of Hearst's mind to the totality of his failure? Is it not possible that those castles have been acquired to give fictitious grandeur to one who had spiritual grandeur and the love of fellow-men within his grasp and deliberately cast them aside to play the most unworthy role in American journalism?

HENRY LEE HIGGINSON

Pillar of Massachusetts

HENRY LEE HIGGINSON was long known as the fore-most citizen of Boston and one of Harvard University's chief benefactors. He was a notable financier, the head of one of the greatest banking houses in America, a princely patron of music, a devoted citizen of the commonwealth. His very presence bespoke the sterner qualities of his generation and of New England. Here was a man who had himself rigidly in hand, in every line of whose face was written strength of character. He had much of the Puritan in him, but the outward mask of severity he wore, enhanced by the deep scar inflicted by a Confederate sabre, concealed a warmth of devotion in friendship, a loyalty to those who had won his affection, and a romance and a sentiment rare in men of affairs. No one who knew Civil War history could look upon him and not see in him the exemplar of that brilliant group of young Harvard men many of whose brief careers are recorded in the Harvard Memorial Biographies—Wilder Dwight, Robert Gould Shaw, the immortal Colonel of the Fifty-fourth Massachusetts Infantry, Oliver Wendell Holmes, of the Supreme Court of the United States, William D. Sedgwick, Lucius Sargent, James Savage, the Putnams and Lowells, and a host of others. A number of them gave their lives to free the slave, although they had every-

thing to lose—position, family distinction, means, all
that goes to make life rich, comfortable, and happy.
There were, of course, other similar groups North and
South who made similar sacrifices, but these Harvard
men stand out because of their historic names and because so many were grouped together in the Harvard
regiments, the Second and Twentieth Massachusetts Infantry and the First and Fifth Cavalry.

It was in the First Cavalry, at Aldie, Virginia, in
a brilliant but costly and futile charge, that Henry Higginson received those wounds that for ever marked him
as one who had served Mars. The names of six of his
intimate friends who never returned he inscribed on the
simple and dignified monument which stands on Soldiers' Field, his great gift to the athletes of Harvard
University. Illness finally forced him out of the regiment, and he was quick to turn again to civil life. He
was not one of those to make his military record his
stock in trade, or to exploit the ardent patriotism, the
purity of motive, and the selflessness which took him
and his associates to the front. That chapter was ended
for him at Appomattox, save that he tried his hand at
cotton-growing as a contribution to the reconstruction of
the defeated States, only to fail. He then turned to
other fields where he rose to highest rank. He speedily
became one of the most potent influences in the world of
finance. Under his leadership the firm of Lee, Higginson & Company played a large part in our tremendous
industrial expansion and that opening up of the West

which transformed America from a set of provincial communities into a great, and the richest, World Power. There was practically no phase of that amazing development in which Major Higginson did not share—the railroads, the telegraph, the telephone, the shoe machinery, the street railways, the electric light and power plants, the mills of New England—in all of which he amassed the wealth which he expended so generously.

From generations of men and women of gentle breeding he had inherited the habit of using his means well, and his long business experience added to his knowledge of how best to invest his benefactions. Of these, by far the most important was his gift in 1881 of the first American orchestra to be organized on the European plan. Older ones there are in this country, notably the Philharmonic in New York, but these were at that time on what may be called an amateur basis. Major Higginson wanted an orchestra like the best of the German organizations, composed of a permanent band playing together year in, year out. He brought over such notable conductors as Gericke and Nikisch, who gave two concerts weekly during the winter season, and speedily built up one of the best orchestras in the world. Abroad the state has supplied this need of the public; in America it is the privilege of the well-to-do, and surely no one ever carried on such a princely undertaking in a more self-effacing manner than Major Higginson. It was always "the Boston Symphony" and never "Major Higginson's Orchestra." The huge annual deficits he concealed for many years—they totalled more than a million dollars. Annually he guaranteed contracts with the musicians averaging between $300,000 and $400,000, and often faced the possibility of a deficit as high as $100,000. In the early years this was risking entirely too much in proportion to his means, but he called himself a fool and persevered and the reward came. As President Eliot wrote to him, near the end of his life, on behalf of several thousand signatories to a testimonial of gratitude offered him as a slight recompense for intolerable injustice:

> *Your purpose was to create an orchestra out of the best available material in all the world, competent to render to perfection the best music in the world. In this very difficult undertaking your success has been marvellous. Your plans and policies have been wise and generous toward both your public and the artists whom you employed. . . . You have steadily insisted that the skilled musician's occupation is not a mechanical trade, but an artistic profession. . . . You have enlarged and strengthened the appreciation of sweet and noble music in this community.*

And far beyond that New England community, in the numerous cities which the Boston Orchestra visited in the course of years, many devout lovers of music rose up to call its founder blessed. If one could measure the part of the Boston Symphony in furthering the work of American musical education, it would be found that it had figured in the development of the orchestra in every single American city which now possesses one.

More than that, out of the Boston Symphony came the Kneisel Quartet—the most finished and inspiring interpreters of chamber music that this country has heard; it is doubtful if its standards have ever been surpassed in Europe. It remains today, though long disbanded, with its great leader dead, the literal inspiration of the large group of new chamber-music organizations which has sprung up with no higher aim than to achieve the standards of Franz Kneisel, who came to America in his early twenties as the brilliant young first violin of the Boston Symphony.

As for Major Higginson's relationship to Harvard University, that would require a chapter in itself.[1] He gave to it the loyalty and devotion he gave to his regiment and to the comrades who, as he said, he saw looking into the sun and riding into the Valley of Death never to return. He was to Harvard, as to Massachusetts, a rock of wisdom, an institution. Harvard had no need to look further to find an alumnus to hold up to its students as a model of the devoted citizen and patriot, the acme of personal probity. More than that, he embodied in his own romantic career the whole story of the development of the country from the simplicity and small means of the anti-slavery period to the rich and frenzied civilization of today. Others whose lives were cast in this mould have become wasters, gamblers, exploiters, profiteers, and shameless masters of privilege; their characters were based upon no such principles as

[1] The record may be found in Professor Bliss Perry's "Life and Letters of Major Higginson."

Major Higginson's. Yet it is true that long before his death he was entirely out of step with the social and political tendencies of the twentieth century.

Hence he was to be found passionately defending the great capitalists and big-business men, and rich men as such, among whom he lived, against the assaults of Theodore Roosevelt and other reformers. He had worked and profited with them. He saw them as they were in their first enthusiasms, in the beginning of that wonderful development when they were building railroads through trackless forests, creating cities overnight, and tearing wealth out of the apparently inaccessible bowels of the earth. He could never realize that the pioneers of that day had carried their pioneering and wealth-garnering to such limits that it had become the duty of the state to interfere. He could not understand that perspective, as well as conditions, had changed; that what was justifiable and admirable in the seventies and eighties must needs be bitted and harnessed by the state in the nineteen hundreds. He upheld his associates of great wealth by attributing to them his own Puritan virtues and idealism and seemed unable to comprehend that their wealth had often eaten into them and warped them when it had not corroded them. He was profoundly indignant when President Roosevelt wrote to him that "the present unsatisfactory condition in railroad affairs is due ninety-five per cent to the misconduct, the short-sightedness, and the folly of the railroad men themselves." All of the Roosevelt legislation for the regulation of trusts, and railroads, and public-service corporations he resented, not only as limiting the free development of capital and of individual initiative, but as a reflection upon the character of men like himself.

Against it all he fought and lost, only to feel that the politicians were destroying a world which he had helped to create, which seemed to him extraordinarily fine and dear. He could adjust himself to no new concept as to wealth and privilege. The truth is that not even a Spartan like Major Higginson could wield his great power and carry on his manner of business without being somewhat adversely affected by it, even though he tried to keep an open mind and held his wealth as a public trust—like Carnegie he, too, wished to die poor and did not succeed. There are no entanglements as subtle or as dangerous as those that come with great and lasting business success in America. For one thing it seems to draw class lines and assuredly sets men apart from the aspirations of the bulk of the people. Thus, there appears to be scarcely a line in Major Higginson's printed correspondence to show that he took the slightest interest in labour as such, or that he had the slightest sympathy for its efforts, so often mistaken, to better itself by collective action and group initiative against the capitalists. The labouring classes remained to the end for him, it would seem, like the men of his regiment, to be led by gallant "gentlemen" along the by-ways and on to the fields of battle which their officers deemed best—he rejoiced during the Civil War when he heard that the Massachusetts coloured regiments were

being officered by men of family; they needed "gentlemen" to lead them, he wrote. The ideal of service in
business, rather than profit, he never accepted. Against
the newer trends he stood as rugged and unyielding a
monument as that on Bunker Hill itself.

It is hard enough to see the tides flowing triumphantly past one when one has done one's best to stem
them. It is infinitely worse to find oneself overwhelmed
with abuse and misrepresentation, at the end of such
a career as has here been outlined and charged with
lack of patriotism in the very community in which for
a lifetime one has stood four-square. This was Major
Higginson's bitter fate. He was one of the earliest and
most deplorable victims of our entry into the World
War. Many of the Boston Symphony's musicians were
Germans—though the conductor Dr. Muck asserted his
Swiss citizenship the Washington government ranked
him as an enemy alien. The failure to display an American flag at just one concert, and his refusal, entirely
justified, from a musicianly point of view, to open a
symphony program with the "Star Spangled Banner,"
brought down upon Major Higginson and the orchestra
all the hysteria and the frenzied passion of the war
period. The patrioteers fell upon them like a pack of
ravening wolves. Dr. Muck, whom Major Higginson considered "the most industrious, painstaking, and the
ablest conductor whom we have ever had," was finally
arrested and interned in Atlanta with that unnecessary
brutality which characterizes secret-service men in war

time—only to have it come out that underneath the brilliant orchestra conductor was concealed a despicable personal rascality no one suspected, least of all Major Higginson.

All of this broke down that glorious orchestra and exhausted Major Higginson himself. He became seriously ill. For once his great influence availed him not. He was bewildered, overwhelmed; his mail teemed with abuse, the number of his critics was swelled overnight by legions of faithless friends. Others stood aloof in dire fear. To the subject of these attacks, conscious of his own rectitude and of his devotion to his country which his scarred face attested, the public ingratitude must, indeed, have seemed far, far sharper than a serpent's tooth. On the fourth of May, 1918, he yielded to fate and terminated his connection with the orchestra, leaving to the public-spirited men and women of the community the duty of carrying it on. He ended this tragic episode, so disgraceful to Boston and to the country, with an address of extraordinary dignity and calmness, and was given an ovation by the audience and the musicians. Yet there can be no question that though he received subsequently many proofs of the love and affection in which he was held by those whose regard was worth having, he bore his new, if invisible, scars to the grave.

As for the World War itself, it staggered and bewildered Major Higginson like so many others. It made no appeal to his finer nature. Although he went out to

Cambridge and besought the undergraduates "to keep their shirts on" when the mobilization of the National Guard units on the Mexican border threatened to stampede the students, he none the less threw himself into the preparedness movement. Forgetting the admonition —"Let us have Peace"—of the great commander of the army of the Potomac in which he had served, he demanded in 1916 an army of five hundred thousand men "for service anywhere, whether on land or on the water, and thus let Mexico see we are in earnest." This was in direct contrast to the attitude of the volunteer Major Higginson of 1864 who wanted to fly to the aid of Mexico and expel the French from her soil, and the man who in 1899 had vigorously and publicly opposed our conquest of the Philippines. Naturally, if only because of his business associations, he was among the first to be eager for our war with Germany, and he was quite content with its outcome, visioning not at all the dire results and apparently not looking beyond the collapse of that militarism which he had, as a boy student in Dresden, come to hate. Here again, Major Higginson was characteristic of his type; the survivors of the Civil War, who after Appomattox abominated the thought of a large standing army and were bitterly opposed to the suggestion that we should have a large fleet, yielded after this war, as did President Eliot, to the new-fangled doctrine that we must thenceforth rival Europe itself in the naval and military fields.

None the less, Major Higginson remains a fine and forceful figure, a citizen of courage, of power, and of shining integrity, a patriot of the days when a true patriotism voiced itself not only on the battlefields of the Civil War but in thousands of homes where the flame of liberty burned unceasingly and undimmed.

ANNA HOWARD SHAW

Apostle of Justice

ANNA SHAW was the ideal type of reformer, if unlimited courage, unquenchable determination, and unusual eloquence, plus humour and good nature, count for anything. She was, moreover, one of those reformers favoured by Providence in that after a lifetime of service she lived to see the coming of victory prior to her own passage from the scene. She witnessed the submission to the several States of the Constitutional amendment conferring suffrage upon women; the day she died a third Southern State voted for the change. If she was not spared to take the leading part in the nation-wide rejoicing when the battle was actually won, she never had any doubts as to its outcome. Her serene faith in the ultimate triumph of the cause sustained her at all times. Indeed, nothing daunted her, nothing dampened the ardour of her rare spirit, and nothing could embitter her. She was as certain that women would vote as she was convinced that there is a divine plan for humanity by which it will yet be saved from itself. The very nobility and fineness of her nature rendered her absolutely certain of the justice and wisdom of her cause, and therefore permitted no doubt as to its success.

It is a fact that she believed in miracles from her girlhood. With her father and two brothers at the front in the Civil War she became in her teens the principal

support of her family on their far-off Michigan farm.
Of that period she wrote that they were "years in which
life had degenerated into a mere treadmill whose monot-
ony was broken only by the grim messages from the
front." A rural Cinderella, she walked seven or eight
miles a day to school and back, and then did all the
work of the household afterward. From this never-
ceasing round of drudgery no escape seemed possible.
Yet she was as certain then as she was of anything in
her later life that she would realize two ambitions—go
to college and become a minister. Both miracles took
place. At twenty-three, in the face of the bitter opposition of every member of her family, she began her
preaching and soon won her license, although she was
still in high school. At twenty-five she was a student at
Albion College, and both her dreams had come true. So
it was with the suffrage cause. She knew that her miracle of political freedom for women would be realized
and knew it through every fibre in her body. She would
have died content had her spirit sought the stars years
before it did. Still harder days were before her—she
tried to put herself through a Boston theological semi-
nary by living on crackers alone, and did so until too
weak to climb the two flights of stairs to the classroom
without sitting down a couple of times to rest. Again,
her Scotch family turned away from her for doing the
unpardonable thing, for trying to change herself from
an itinerant, locally licensed preacher, into a thoroughly qualified teacher of theology. It was un-
womanly, immodest, improper for "a female" to as-

pire to stand up in a church and tell men how they should think and act. In those trying experiences her soul, like many another's, was forged. But no hardships could harden her spirit or embitter her; they left her sweet and gentle, unwarped and lovable, with her rare sense of humour and her passionate faith in humanity intact.

The secret of it is that she was always normal and sane, sound and effective, and these were unusual qualities in one who was for ever violating conventions, first as the itinerant girl preacher, next as a full-fledged minister of churches on Cape Cod, then as a graduate physician, and finally as a roving platform preacher for temperance and woman suffrage. She left the pulpit and turned to medicine because she felt that the woman medical missionary to women had greater opportunities for usefulness than the bringer of spiritual tidings. But after a few years of that service it came to her that beyond all else women needed political freedom if they were to achieve social, economic, and moral freedom as well, and so the suffrage cause finally became the dominating influence in her life. As she herself put it, "in my association with the women of the streets, I realized the limitations of my work in the ministry and in medicine. As minister to soul and body one could do little for these women. For such as they, one's efforts must begin at the very foundation of the social structure. Laws for them must be made and enforced, and some of those laws could only be made and enforced by women." So many great avenues of life were opening up to her that her Cape Cod environment seemed to her a prison where she was held "with tender force." So she became preacher extraordinary to the entire American public and minister plenipotentiary to women everywhere. There was never doubt nor question in her mind; she chose the incredibly difficult and exhausting life of the platform lecturer in the seventies and eighties when railroad transportation was undeveloped, hotels of the worst, and private hospitality diverse and often difficult.

The story of these days she has set forth in her reminiscences—tales of winter nights and delayed trains, and sudden sickness, and bitter cold night-drives over the frozen prairies. Once she was pursued by wolves and was saved only by the speed of her horses and the nearness of a town. Human wolves were never far away; once when she was talking on temperance the other crowd set fire to the building in which she was speaking and her auditors barely escaped with their lives. That episode she characteristically turned to account, for the minute that she was out of the burning building she called for another meeting and led the crowd to the Congregational Church. She was at her best then, which fact she concealed afterward in telling the story by saying: "We were able at last to make clear to the people of the town the character of the liquor interests we were fighting, . . . at the following election we carried the town for prohibition by a big majority." The speech she thought her greatest was not delivered in this country, but in the State Church of Swe-

den, after international attention had been drawn to
her by the fact that she had been excluded, merely because of her sex, from the State Church in Norway.
She realized at once the necessity of being worthy of
this extraordinary occasion and what happened she describes in these words:

> *Also, I experienced a sensation such as I had never
> known before, which I can only describe as a seeming
> complete separation of my physical self from my spirit-
> ual self. It was as if my body stood aside and watched
> my soul enter that pulpit. There was no uncertainty, no
> nervousness, though usually I am very nervous when I
> begin to speak; and when I had finished I knew that I
> had done my best.*

These were the high spots. For the rest there were floods,
blizzards, railroad accidents, and endless meetings,
large and small, responsive and unresponsive; a severe
and exhaustive post-graduate course in the United States
of America such as few have ever taken and passed.

Wherever she went Anna Shaw was the despair of
the anti-suffragists. What could you do with a woman
like this if you were an anti? You insisted that for any
woman to leave home meant the loss of her charm, her
modesty, her every womanly attribute, and then along
came Anna Shaw who as a girl had preached in the
roughest Michigan lumber camps, who in her twenties
had mastered a rebellious congregation on Cape Cod.
Preacher, doctor, and itinerant suffragist, there she was,

all rolled into one, and that one a woman distinguished by her sweetness, her womanly charm, her normality, her impressive dignity! You pictured a woman suffragist as a short-haired termagant, an habitual spoiler of the lord of creation's dinner, a trousered, unsexed person who undoubtedly advocated free love and the ruining of the home—that cornerstone of the family and of the nation—and here was a little woman with long silvery hair, whose winning personality gave the lie to every one of those allegations.

Not only in her person did she refute those who were so certain that suffrage meant the destruction of what was best in American life; she met and defeated all such arguments with common sense, facts, figures, good humour, wit, or searing sarcasm. Not that she was without the power to hit hard. She could be rough in debate if deeply aroused, and she was capable of distinct antagonisms in personal relationships. Her eloquence was genuine and moving. It was inborn, not cultivated save by practice; she, too, began by preaching to the trees of her Michigan forest. She rarely used notes. Her points she ticked off in advance on her fingers and checked off as she spoke. Her ability to sway her audiences was remarkable; her power to adjust herself to any situation nothing short of marvellous. No unexpected happening seemed to throw her out of gear. Her quickness of mind and wit made her a most formidable antagonist in debate, especially with that type of male mind which felt sure that any woman's brains

were inferior to the poorest male's. Added to her oratorical powers was the horrid fact that she not only
knew every phase of American life, but that she was
American to the last drop of her blood, though the
foreign-born daughter of a pioneer and a patriot from
Scotland who did not come to this country until Anna
Shaw was four years old.

No wonder that she was a thorn in the side of all
who opposed suffrage, especially editors. If there was
one thing she enjoyed above all else, it was taking some
solemn editorial pronouncements, like those of the New
York *Times* or *Tribune,* and puncturing them with
lightning-like thrusts of her rapier of wit and knowledge.
She was so confoundedly logical and clear that you
could not down her by accusing her of having the unstable mind of a blue-stocking theorist, and all the time
she remained so happy that it was perfectly obvious that
you could never hope to touch her to the quick. Worse
than that, she had a rare gift of making converts under
your eyes. Her years in the narrower pulpit, where she
had so often brought sinners to public repentance in
the good old-fashioned manner of the revivalist, helped
her to win adherents to the suffrage faith. In only one
aspect could she be used as the "horrible example" of
what happens to a woman when she leaves her sheltered
home and dares the disrespect of the emancipated male
—she was shining proof that if you give the disfranchised and disadvantaged an inch they are certain to
take an ell. The question was where would this rebel
woman stop who refused to remain a drudge on a

Michigan farm, to accept domesticity, or to be content
with high-school learning; who had gone from pulpit
and operating-room to the public forum?

Well, naturally, when the great leaders and pioneers in the suffrage cause passed off the stage the
mantle of leadership fell to Anna Shaw. To wear it as
president of the National Woman Suffrage Association
she freely gave everything that she had to give without thought of self. Only the few near her realized
how heavy was the burden, how unceasing the toil. Of
course those who knew her loved her and took the pro-
prietary interest in her that is the surest proof that the
way to the heart has been found. But it was not merely
for her engaging personality, or her unselfishness, or
her devotion to duty that she was loved. She had vision
and true statesmanship besides. Others might lay out
more skilful strategy and were probably better organ-
izers, but none surpassed Anna Shaw in leadership, in
oratory, and in the qualities that make the true reformer
irresistible. In return nature gave her the joy of living,
the love of outdoors, that sparkling optimism and good-
will. Her humour carried her past every obstacle and
nothing pleased her more than a good joke on herself.
She revelled in the story of two nieces aged eight and
six, who became suffragists. Their first day at school
was made so rough that when they returned home the
little one wished to be a suffragette no longer. Her elder
sister took her to task. "How," she said, "can you be
upset by being laughed at for one day? Look at Aunt
Anna, she's been laughed at for hundreds of years,"

All of these qualities enabled her to write about herself these true words: "I have made many friendships; I have looked upon the beauty of many lands; I have the assurance of the respect and affection of thousands of men and women I have never even met. Though I have given all I had, I have received a thousand times more than I have given. Neither the world nor my Cause is indebted to me—but from the depths of a full and very grateful heart I acknowledge my lasting indebtedness to them both." Yet she was wrong. The world and the cause were very much in her debt when she died. If there is such a thing as human gratitude Anna Shaw will remain one of the saints of her time.

ABRAHAM JACOBI

Last of the Forty-eighters

WITH the death of Abraham Jacobi there passed
the last of an extraordinary group of Americans,
the Germans who immigrated to the United States as a
result of the abortive revolutions in Germany in 1848—
revolutions which, had they succeeded, would have
democratized Germany and made impossible the most
terrible chapter in history. No finer or more loyal pa-
triots, no better stock of citizenship ever came to the
United States than these men of Forty-eight. They had
been willing to risk all in the battle for liberty and
nearly every one of those who became leaders in
America, Carl Schurz, Gustav Koerner, Hans Kud-
lich, the Hilgards of Belleville, Illinois, Franz Sigel
and Abraham Jacobi and all the rest, had had the death
sentence passed upon them or had paid for their share
in the revolution by years in prison. Dr. Jacobi was
of the latter; from his twenty-first to his twenty-third
year he was behind prison bars, for months wearing
chains in dark cells.

Prison is often good for the soul when the sentence is imposed upon one whose only offence is battling
for liberty—as Eugene Debs, one of our great Americans, bore witness in his cell at Atlanta. I have often
wondered if Dr. Jacobi would have been the splendid
man he was if he had not had those months of facing

the worst and of the loss of the light of day. I have felt
that it was during this period that he worked out his
whole theory and philosophy of life, that he formulated
the basic principles with which throughout long years
he measured men and events. For he was one of those
fortunate men who never consult expediency, who do
not, as the Germans says, hold a leaf before their
mouths. He never had to puzzle as to what position to
take on any matter and he always took the enlightened
one because he always applied the yardstick of principle. Being a great scientist and searcher after truths,
he could never allow passion or prejudice to cloud his
judgment in matters political or social. Being in the
best sense a man of the world, he could not be a narrow American; being nobly tolerant of the right of
others to their views, he believed not at all in the suppression of opinion, and, being the foe of wrong everywhere, he could not be silent when America yielded to
imperialism.

Being the son of one, I have sat at the feet of
many of these Forty-eighters and I never heard fall from
the lips of any one of them anything but the most ardent love for the old America. They valued their citizenship in this country and its ideals more than any native
American I have ever met. Americans who are born to
their heritage, alas, usually take it as those of us who
are born to wealth and comforts take our good fortune—as something quite a matter of course and our
due, entailing no obligations and no specia'

sibilities. These Forty-eighters had dreamed about America as they dreamed about heaven in the days when they plotted the overthrow of their home governments. It meant to them paradise—liberty, equality, freedom, and humanity, the most exquisite words in any language—as they wore their chains and wondered when the executioner would sever their heads from their bodies. It was America that inspired Carl Schurz as he stood outside of the guardroom of the prison in Spandau with a revolver in each hand, bent on freeing his teacher Kinkel and wondering, as he stood there and heard footsteps approaching, whether it meant freedom for Kinkel or suicide for himself in the event of discovery. To America these men came with a thankfulness and a gratitude which they were quick to reveal in the ardour with which they threw themselves into the fight for liberty for the slaves and the zeal with which they fought on the battlefields of the Civil War. They were to their last breath as devoted to the ideals of America as George Washington, or as the Abraham Lincoln most of them knew and all supported. They were as jealous of its good name and its freedom from the mistakes of the Old World as a lover of his mistress, and I know well the agony of mind which many of them suffered in 1898 when we fought our unjust and unnecessary war against Spain and began our career of overseas intervention, of colonizing, of imperialism, and of faithlessness to the teachings of the fathers, which landed us in the maelstrom of European political en-

tanglements—for a time. Carl Schurz foresaw and protested against our great navy and our imperialism when
both were in their inception.

He and Dr. Jacobi could not bear to see this country putting up the bars against the hapless and perse-
cuted of other nations, because, having developed much
of its resources by the brawn of foreigners and become
rich thereby, it was suddenly so purse-proud as to be
willing to cast off the "Dutchies," "dagoes," "wops,"
Chinese, Irish, and others whom it was once so glad to
welcome to its shores. Mr. Schurz died before we abolished by law the right of political asylum in America
and made it a criminal offence to plot here for a revolution within another country—this in the land which gave
such a royal reception to Kossuth and raised money by
public subscription for revolutions in Greece, Hungary,
Italy, and heaven knows how many other lands. Nothing
could, I believe, more clearly indicate the change that
has come over the spirit of the America that inspired
the Forty-eighters than this sudden alteration of our
national attitude toward those struggling for liberty
abroad—unless it be our attitude toward those who are
so wicked as to believe that there is something wrong
with our own institutions and social system.

Abraham Jacobi held to the end his hatred of
everything that smacked of royalty. When we were planning the unveiling of Karl Bitter's noble statue to
Schurz, Dr. Jacobi protested most earnestly against Ambassador Bernstorff's taking part in the ceremonies, not
because of any personal feeling against the man—it

was before the war—but because he represented an emperor and the monarchies against which Schurz and he in his boyhood had rebelled. When Nicholas Murray Butler and other Simon-pure Americans were busy toadying to Kaiser William at Cassel and Berlin and accepting bauble decorations from him, Jacobi was unwavering in his republican refusal to tolerate anything that looked like an approach to that potentate. Why may not a son of Henry Villard here recall what any other American citizen would surely remember with pride, that when offered by a President the position of American minister to Berlin, Mr. Villard declined it because he had never learned to crook his knee to a king.

The passion for republicanism of these Forty-eighters, I believe, cannot be surpassed today in any group of Americans, yet they would not have been acceptable to the Security League or the American Defense Society. The difference is that their republicanism was bred in the bone and that it was not to be adulterated by foreign admixtures, the adoption of the attributes of monarchies such as universal military service, or K.C.B.'s. More than that, they were neither for America for the Americans, nor for our country "right or wrong." It was Schurz who amended Decatur's declaration to read: "My country when right, when wrong to be set right." He would have deemed it treachery to democracy and American institutions to give any politicians the right to do wrong and then to enslave all the country by demanding blind, patriotic adhesion to their

policies under the alternative of jail. How Schurz would
have exposed the sophistries and hypocrisies of Woodrow Wilson anyone will understand who recalls how
Schurz flayed and, more than any other one man, defeated James G. Blaine in 1884 by a series of overwhelming speeches.

Politics was not of course Dr. Jacobi's specialty.
I hate to call him a "good citizen" because that calls
up the memory of so many men of good intentions who
for years led us in New York City but helped us out of
our political sloughs not at all—perhaps because they
were so completely class-conscious. But Dr. Jacobi was
always ready to serve any movement for betterment. If
they formed a Committee of Seventy or One Hundred
his name was always on it. Yet, he having the modesty
of the truly great, few people realized how steady was
his contribution to reform causes. The City Club, the
Citizens Union, civil-service reform, better housing, the
medical care of the poor, and every movement for com-
bating human disease came to this wise man for his
support. And wise man he was. That magnificent head,
the shaggy brow, those all-comprehending eyes formed
a countenance to awe and impress until one knew the
kindliness and warmth underneath and that he was always as generous to worth as he was tender to the little
children who were his chief concern. Yet he could cas-
tigate with a vigour that spared no one when his feelings
were deeply aroused, as when he heard of some friends
who sought to apologize for the dastardly sinking of the
Lusitania on the ground that the Germans had a legal

excuse for that atrocity. That he never forgave. He saw
in the Germans going to war and their method of conducting it merely the flowering of the Prussian system
of government against which he as a boy had revolted,
the inevitable result of universal military service and
the drugging of the conscience of the people by the
various forms of state benefactions.

Yet he was never revengeful or bitter. He would not
consent to a dissolution of the Germanistic Society of
which he was the head because he wished and hoped for
a new and republican Germany when the old, against
which he was so outspoken from the day the Germans
crossed into Belgium, had perished. He did not lose
faith in the German people nor altogether in their sci-
entists. The latter, by the way often tried to lure him
back to Germany; he could have had his pick of any of
the German universities had he desired to return to his
fatherland, but nothing could tempt him to leave America. But above America with him was humanity, and he
lived this doctrine where others have merely mouthed
it. What he did for the spread of knowledge of and the
treatment of children's diseases can hardly be set forth
by a layman, but for sixty years he led in this field. It
was stated at his funeral by Dr. Sayre that no child
would be born hereafter but would be in debt to Dr.
Jacobi. Not that he was a narrow specialist; that extraordinary thoroughness he acquired on the other side, his
clarity of judgment, his command of principles and his
great reasoning powers, together with his remarkable
learning in all branches of his profession and in many

other fields, made him in great demand as a consultant in all sorts of cases—even surgical.

As a teacher he was of the best because he was one of those instructors who know so much more than they can possibly give out; one felt instinctively that he never had to and never could reveal all the solid deposits of learning he possessed. There were depths that were never plumbed—which makes it all the more tragic that his autobiographical writings and many professional studies of great value were destroyed in the fire which nearly cost him his life in 1918. Dr. Jacobi was also the clearest of teachers as he was a most impressive speaker because of the clarity of his thought and its expression. More than that, he was of the old type of physician who was also counsellor and friend, and he was about as far removed from the modern specialist of a certain fashionable type who helps rich patients to enjoy comfortable and long illnesses as this sphere is from Mars. Indeed, he was always more interested in aiding the children of the poor than those of any other class. The uncollected and uncharged fees of Abraham Jacobi for services rendered would have made a half-dozen physicians well to do. Was it not a perfect ending to this life of unending service that though eighty-nine, he practised to the last? Four days before his death his last prescription restored to health a little babe. How touchingly, how exquisitely fitting! Who can behold this life and not feel that sometimes sheer goodness and profound merit *do* find their reward on earth?

But it is to the man himself and not to the physician that I turn finally—he was so big, so generous, so fine, so noble! To have known him was to receive a quickening of faith in all humanity because that rock of character was so immovable from its base. Why do we not have such characters in our public life, men who will hew to the line as Grover Cleveland used to even when he was told that it would cost him his career? If I thought a soviet form of government would draw men into our public life of this type in place of the professional politician, however oratorical, I should be for it tomorrow—because it is just the lack of such rugged, unchangeable characters in the public life of the world that is responsible for more than half its troubles. I believe that Dr. Jacobi would have withstood temptations in office and the insidious undermining of character by office as did Schurz—twenty years after his service as Secretary of the Interior they were still speaking in Indian affairs of the "halcyon days of Schurz." I am most profoundly not of the belief that the day of giants like these is over. We shall produce them here at home and they will come to us surely from abroad, yes, even from Germany again. But not unless we give them the old America and the old American ideals to inspire them and to bring them to us, in place of the modern, imperialistic, heretic-hunting, truth-suppressing, super-patriotic America, swept from its true moorings by a false press, by skilful propaganda, by disingenuous appeals to that inherent quality of idealism which made America the land of such hope and promise to the Forty-eighters.

KARL BITTER

An American Sculptor

LET us turn to the best known and least known of books; to stories of a thousand days, a thousand nights, in garden and in courtyard, in every clime, under any sun, under every moon. Nowhere do we find within it a tale more stirring or more touching than ours to-night. The theme is old; in ages past genii and fairy adorned it; magic lamps illuminated it; wizards' wands waved over it, yes, the spirit of stark tragedy o'erhung it, and the wings of angels have fluttered through it long, long ere this. The wicked old king, his cruel servant, the handsome gifted youth, incomparable in stature and in form, who breaks intolerable bonds and crosses the seas to distant lands, there to win fame and prosperity—this is the groundwork of our story. Of just such material the minnesinger spun the slight web of his fiction in the very dawn of literature, and the story-teller of the bazaars during long ages conjured the pence out of the pockets of his squatting hearers. Yet surely never were their versions so fair and so unsullied, so compelling, so full of inspiration as ours.

Let us recall it as it was. Karl Bitter [1] inhaled freedom of spirit with adolescence. He was early of those who stand in the market-place and stir their comrades

[1] Karl Bitter was born in Austria, December 6, 1867, and died as the result of a street accident in New York on April 10, 1915.

to thought—out of full, generous hearts. He spoke from
a soul born for beauty, radiant with ideals that demanded permanent expression and would not be denied—until an unnatural law of the military inter-
fered with the law of his nature. The restraint, the
cruelty of the martinet, of the military caste oppressed
him sorely, became intolerable. Soon thereafter, out of
the East, he, a fugitive, stood before the imperial city
of the Western world. Great walls it had and high; how
could he scale them without name or friends or speech
or means? Behold, it needed but the trump of his genius
to lay them low. A short year and a half and his fame
had spread among all who like himself were devoted to
the cult of the beautiful. His genius, transplanted, took
root like some wild plant at the edge of a swamp and
grew straight up toward heaven, never ceasing to flower
with greater and greater charm.

Day by day the spirit within him broadened and
deepened. The very atmosphere of America was tonic
to his nature. No bonds here to constrain, no castes to
fetter, no hidebound traditions in art or life to enslave,
no king to bow before. Here was an Austrian born to
be an American; in him every string was attuned to
democracy; every note responded to our republican
overtones; the more he tasted American liberty the freer
and freer he grew. Indeed, coming from abroad with
fresh eyes that looked beneath the surface he saw and
felt things that were veiled to the multitude born to
Americanism—precisely as did in other fields Jacob
Riis and Carl Schurz before him. So it soon came to

pass that Americans turned to him, this foreigner, this "Dutchman" of the East Side work-shops, to interpret their Americanism, yes, even to celebrate in plastic art the triumph of an American fleet in Asiatic waters.

But far greater than that victory of our arms is the triumph of democracy which Bitter's whole career symbolizes. He was the clearest living proof of the wonder of its ways. One can speak evil of America if one will, and sneer at the melting-pot, too. One can scoff at the multitudes of immigrants who appear to the unthinking only as uncouth burdens, those great masses that stand wonder-eyed within the portals of the land of liberty and know not which way to turn; that crave leadership yet fear to trust; and ever and anon have concealed among them some precious jewel like this, some divine human gift as their recompense to the haven of refuge that bade them come and be welcome, rest, and be free. So to Karl Bitter swung wide the gates, and he who is just must respect and praise the nation that laid its spell upon this man, that raised him up from among the struggling, unloosed his artist powers, bade him work, filled his heart with love for its aims, and inspired him in the twinkling of an eye with the spirit and the majesty of its institutions.

The charm of his personality, the rugged force within him, the skill of his tools carried him through one after another of the open doors of opportunity, and as he passed each door it was ever clearer that America had made this man its own. How abundantly he repaid

this confidence and trust, how warmly he appreciated
the generosity of his welcome, his work attests a hun-
dredfold. He recognized the obligations as well as the
privileges of citizenship; the opportunity for public
service never passed him by unheeded. For if his art
was a jealous mistress, so was his new country, which
he came to adore without forgetting the love for the old.
The immensity of its spaces, the vastness of its problems, the staggering importance to humanity of their
proper solution—these ever impressed themselves upon
his mind.

It was not altogether by accident that he perched
upon his enchanted Weehawken cliffs, nor was it merely
the beauty of the river and the vitality of its ever rest-
less traffic, or the grandeur of the skyline in the evening light that lured him back there at the end of his
life to work in the open, so that when his glance rested
from the figure before him it fell upon one of the wonders of the world. Yet the visions upon which he gazed
were not always those he saw, for his was the inward-
looking eye so often to be noticed in those whom fate
has marked early as its own. Beyond the city he saw
the country, beyond the country mankind. So more and
more it seemed as if his work turned to the interpretation of American life as it appeared to his enthusiasm
and loyalty, reinforced by his deep reading in American
history and the writings of the Fathers. His statues of
Jefferson, Marshall, and Hamilton, the Louisiana Pur-
chase group, his Franz Sigel and Carl Schurz—only an

historian can realize just how much of America's past is herein expressed, but no one can fail to read in them his sincerity, the earnestness of his purpose, the idealism that ruled his gifted chisel, and the knowledge they bespeak.

What wonder that his fellow-sculptors should three times have chosen him their national president? What wonder that three great American expositions should have made this artist chief of the sculpture that was to interpret American progress to their hundreds of thousands of visitors; or that one of the most characteristically American of our universities should have made him the portrayer of the rise of the Middle West and of its noble, democratic aspirations? Or that his genius should lightly have touched upon the Negro problem and yet have illumined it in passing? Or that for him, the lover of his fellow-men, his finest monument of war stood not for the warrior ready for the fray, but for the war-worn citizen soldiers returning, burdened with wounded, with great gaps in their ranks, to their waiting, pathetic women and children, eager to turn again to the paths of peace, to the upbuilding of the beloved republic?

Surely the heavy hand of Destiny was early laid upon him. What seemed an irretrievable boyish misfortune proved the making of the man; his cruel military persecutor became his benefactor; his exile but a translation to unbounded opportunity and to lasting happiness. Then as if it were foreordained that the thread of life should soon be severed, Providence crowded much into this existence. Karl Bitter drank deeply from the cup of success; the plaudits of the multitude long rang in his ears; the praise of the elect spurred him on in fullest measure, without the power, however, to make so earnest and devoted a nature vain or proud. The admiration of his fellow-craftsmen, their generous bestowal of rewards were freely his and so was the joy of serving his fellows, while unconsciously moulding rare monuments to his soul in portraying the lineaments of others. He knew what it was to be a leader of men; his was the stimulating consciousness of having won by sheer merit, without favour or fawning, a place among the foremost of his time. To how very few is as much vouchsafed; how few even at threescore and ten have carved as much out of the quarry of life? And always the true artist was wholly subordinated to his work. His was to give, never to obtain; his genius was not for self-glorification but for the generations to come. Why weep for him? In all his life there was no single thing to depress or to pity, but everything to elate. He quickened our faith in our art, in our life, in our nation.

How fast our little bark slips down the river of life! Surely it was but yesterday that Karl Bitter took his seat in it, so calm, so kind, so brave. How strong the paddle, how vigorous the arm, how keen the sight, how straight he went! See, others are in the rapids, some upon the rocks. *This* pilot knew the way, the truest course, for he took it from the stars.

A NOTE ON THE TYPE
IN WHICH THIS BOOK IS SET

====

*This book is composed in a type called Bodoni,
named after its designer, Giambattista Bodoni
(1740–1813) a celebrated Italian scholar and
printer. He drew his letters with a mechanical reg-
ularity that is readily apparent on comparison with
the less formal old style. Other characteristics
that will be noted are the square serifs without
fillet and the marked contrast between the
light and heavy strokes.*

SET UP, ELECTROTYPED, PRINTED AND BOUND
BY THE VAIL-BALLOU PRESS, BINGHAMTON, N. Y.
PAPER MANUFACTURED BY
S. D. WARREN CO.
BOSTON